Adolescent Sex
and
Love Addicts

Adolescent Sex and Love Addicts

Eric Griffin-Shelley

PRAEGER

Westport, Connecticut
London

Library of Congress Cataloging-in-Publication Data

Griffin-Shelley, Eric.
    Adolescent sex and love addicts / by Eric Griffin-Shelley.
      p.   cm.
    Includes bibliographical references and index.
    ISBN 0–275–94681–9 (alk. paper)
    1. Sex addiction in adolescence. 2. Relationship addiction in
adolescence. 3. Sex addiction in adolescence—Case studies.
  4. Relationship addiction in adolescence—Case studies. I. Title.
RJ506.S47G75   1994
616.85′83′00835—dc20   94–1149

British Library Cataloguing in Publication Data is available.

Library of Congress Catalog Card Number: 94–1149
ISBN: 0–275–94681–9

First published in 1994

Praeger Publishers, 88 Post Road West, Westport, CT 06881
An imprint of Greenwood Publishing Group, Inc.

Printed in the United States of America

∞™

The paper used in this book complies with the
Permanent Paper Standard issued by the National
Information Standards Organization (Z39.48–1984).

10 9 8 7 6 5 4 3 2 1

Copyright Acknowledgment

The author gratefully acknowledges permission to reprint the following material:

Carnes, Patrick, *Out of the Shadows: Understanding Sexual Addiction* (Minneapolis, MN:
CompCare Publications, 1983), p. 15, "The Addictive System." Reprinted with permission.

Contents

Acknowledgments

I am deeply grateful to my Higher Power who has led me on this challenging and exciting journey. I find the inspiration comes from a grace that I experience on a daily basis in my work and my writing. My earthly support comes from the two most precious people in my life: my wife, Helen, and my son, Griff. Their love and caring is a constant source of joy. The teenagers with whom I have worked over the past five years have also taught me a lot and I owe them a great deal for their gifts to me. My hope is that, through this work, suffering will be diminished—both theirs and the suffering of so many other adolescent sex and love addicts.

Adolescent Sex
and
Love Addicts

1

Introduction

Three adolescents who could be diagnosed sex and love addicts came to my attention today. Three in one day. It is time that such a diagnosis for adolescents be recognized by the therapeutic community, so that these three and so many others may be treated appropriately and directed toward recovery. As I begin this book on adolescent sex and love addiction, I am reminded of my own early skepticism about adolescent chemical dependency. My experience with substance abuse and drug and alcohol addictions began in 1970. At that time, I worked at Eagleville Hospital and Rehabilitation Center in Eagleville, Pennsylvania. The hospital was engaged in an exciting new venture funded by a large grant from the National Institute of Mental Health (NIMH). Eagleville was treating drug addicts and alcoholics in the same treatment program. This combining of chemical abusers in one program was rare in those days, and the approach had many opponents. However, in the years since then, almost all substance abuse programs have been opened to people who are addicted to any drug, including alcohol. The approach that was considered an experiment twenty years ago has become almost universal.

Our understanding of and approach to adolescent chemical dependency has shown a similar growth. Twenty years ago, there were no programs that treated addicted teenagers. Young people could only get treatment by becoming part of a program designed for adults. Fortunately, treatment professionals recognized that adolescents have special needs and respond better in a program designed just for them. In fact, most chemical dependency programs now have at least a special track for teenagers, and some institutions treat only adolescents.

My own realization that adolescents could indeed be addicted to drugs and alcohol developed once I began working with young people in the mid-1980s. When I was first hired to work with the teenage addicts and alcoholics on the adolescent unit of an inpatient psychiatric hospital, I did not think that teenagers could really be addicted. Unlike the adults with whom I had been working for years, young people simply could not, in my mind, have had enough time to develop a full-blown addiction to chemicals. I thought that it took years to become truly hooked, and that these youngsters were simply too young. Was I wrong!

I learned, for one thing, that these adolescents had often been using drugs and alcohol since they were eleven or twelve. If they came into treatment at age seventeen or eighteen, they may have been using and abusing drugs and alcohol for seven or eight years. This was almost half of their young life. I now know that some children start abusing alcohol (the cheapest and easiest drug to get) at around age eight or nine. In fact, some have been exposed to alcohol and drugs *in utero* because their parents were users or addicts; some are introduced to alcohol as infants when parents or caretakers use it to soothe the child, such as by rubbing alcohol on the child's gums when he or she is teething; and some begin their abuse of drugs and alcohol as small children when they are given sips of booze or tokes of marijuana because an adult finds it amusing to see the effects. By junior high school, many young people are abusing alcohol and other drugs on a regular basis, especially on weekends. By high school, adolescents who are chemically dependent often have a reputation among their peers as being a drug abuser, a "burnout," a "pot head," or some other such derogatory and degrading term.

In determining whether someone is an addict, it is often helpful to distinguish among use, abuse, and addiction. In fact, there appears to be a continuum of chemical abuse, starting from abstinence on the one hand and extending to addiction on the other hand. Typically, a person progresses from abstinence, to use, to abuse, and finally to addiction. As the person becomes increasingly dependent, it becomes harder and harder to stop using and abusing. Addicted people have less and less freedom to choose not to use the addictive chemical. Finally they are enslaved to the substance; they "have a monkey on their back." The teenage burnouts were not addicts when they first used drugs or alcohol. For most, the progression was relatively gradual; in other words, it took months or years to move from abusing alcohol to abusing marijuana, and longer still until they found cocaine or heroin.

Dependence usually creeps up on a person. In some ways, the addict is the last to realize how dependent on drugs and alcohol he or she has become. In our treatment program, finding the level of the adolescent's dependency was usually the first order of business. We asked the adolescent's parents about their child's drug and alcohol abuse and most often found that the parents had been worrying, nagging, confronting, and begging the teenager to stop for a long time. Peers were also important as sources of information about the intensity of the adolescent's dependence. As for the addicts themselves, we found that, in a group therapy meeting with other chemically dependent teenagers—and with a counselor who is also recovering from chemical dependency—many teenagers do finally feel safe enough to tell the truth about the extent, amount, and damage caused by their own use and abuse of chemicals. Bibliotherapy—that is, reading stories about people who have recovered from chemical dependency, as well as written work on the Twelve Step program developed by Alcoholics Anonymous (AA)—can also bring a young addict back into contact with reality.

Addictions have a profound effect on a person, especially on a person who has not yet completed his or her development into adulthood. Addictions affect the whole person. The damage done to teenage addicts and alcoholics can be seen in their health, in their family and peer relations, in their schoolwork and other responsibilities, and in their spiritual lives. Chemically dependent teenagers on our unit had been using and abusing drugs for an average of almost four years (Griffin-Shelley, Sandler, and Lees, 1992). They had usually stopped any sort of regular exercise, such as sports activities, and were regularly risking unforeseen physical damage to their bodies by ingesting drugs bought on the street without any form of quality control or assurance of purity. Their relationships with their families were so strained that they often fought with family members or else rarely went home. Their peer group tended to be other adolescents who were as troubled as themselves. Academically, they were two years behind, on average (Griffin-Shelley, 1991). In short, their lives were a mess. Unfortunately, their defenses—denial, for example—and their drugs combined to numb them from the pain in their existence and was a form of self-medication.

Addictions are characterized by tolerance, dependence, cravings, withdrawal, obsession, compulsion, secrecy, and personality change (see Chapter 2). Chemically dependent adolescents have all of these symptoms to varying degrees. Clearly, then, adolescents *can* become addicted to drugs and alcohol, and dependence on chemicals has a profound effect on any person's life—especially a young person who is in such a dynamic phase of development. However, the fact that teenagers can be addicted to chemicals does not necessarily mean that adolescents can be addicted to sex and love. Or does it?

MULTIPLE ADDICTIONS

One area of recent concern in addiction treatment is the possibility of "switching addictions." Twenty-five years ago, at Eagleville Hospital and Rehabilitation Center, the staff and patients together, used to celebrate the successful completion of heroin addiction treatment by throwing a party that included alcohol. It was soon discovered, however, that a significant number of the program's graduates went on to become alcoholics, so the practice of drinking at graduation ceased and total abstinence from "mood-altering" chemicals became the standard recommendation for anyone who was in recovery from any sort of alcohol or drug addiction. Similarly, cigarette smokers are often worried that they will gain weight (and about a third do) when they quit smoking; in other words, they are afraid that nicotine dependence will be followed by overeating, or food addiction. Some people who are obsessed with sex will experience a religious conversion and become religious fanatics: a sex addiction has been transformed into a religious addiction (Booth, 1991). Harvey Milkman and Stanley Sunderwirth (1987) have suggested there may exist common neurochemical pathways that underlie all addictions.

In order to investigate the possibility that many of our chemically dependent teenagers might exhibit patterns of multiple addictions, a pilot study was conducted to survey their identification with symptoms of addictive/compulsive behaviors in the area of illicit drugs, alcohol, prescription drugs, sex, relationships, food, gambling, and nicotine (Griffin-Shelley, Sandler, and Lees, 1992). In addition to identifying with alcohol, drug, and nicotine dependence, the dually diagnosed, inpatient adolescents in our study saw themselves as having a large number of the symptoms of sex addiction and relationship dependency. In fact, 86.8 percent (66 out of 76) of these teenagers related to symptoms of love addiction, and 73.7 percent (56 of 76) connected with symptoms of sexual dependency. In comparison, 60.5 percent identified with food addiction signs, and 18.4 percent reported symptoms of compulsive gambling.

In fact, in our work with these adolescents, their problems with relationships were quite apparent. In recovery from chemical dependency, one of the common recommendations is "no new relationships in the first year." In our hospital treatment program, we had a similar, strong rule: "no relationships," which included no physical contact (touching, fondling, and kissing) and no note passing, love letters, or any other form of communication between two patients that would foster a special, intimate relationship. We constantly struggled with our clients over this issue. Many of them formed "love relationships" or "rehab romances" despite our best efforts to discourage this sort of unhealthy attachment. When we confronted them, some of these clients could eventually see that, during their withdrawal from drugs and alcohol, they were medicating their pain, soothing their loneliness, and "getting high" from romantic and sexual intrigues and contacts on the unit. Most of the clients clearly saw that this preoccupation distracted them from their primary task, which was to begin a recovery process from chemical dependency and to engage in a therapy process that would start to heal their emotional wounds.

The work of therapy and recovery from addictions is difficult and painful. Most of us want to distract ourselves from this sort of pain if we do not think that we can cope with it, if we do not feel that we can survive the trauma of change and letting go of the past. People who have learned to cope with pain through some ritualized, trance-inducing, mind-altering compulsion like drug and alcohol abuse and addiction will look for some other activity that provides similar relief. Sex and love have great potential for distraction, soothing, consolation, preoccupation, and elation (Griffin-Shelley, 1993). It is no wonder that these troubled, suffering teenagers look to relationships and sexuality to escape the hard work of treatment and recovery.

In our study, more than 80 percent (4 out of 5) of the young addicts could identify with symptoms of relationship dependency from the fifteen-item questionnaire in Robin Norwood's (1985) book *Women Who Love Too Much*. Some of these yes/no questions are listed below:

2. Having received little real nurturing yourself, you try to fill this unmet need vicariously by becoming a caregiver, especially to people who appear, in some way, needy.

4. Terrified of abandonment, you will do anything to keep a relationship from dissolving.

5. Almost nothing is too much trouble, takes too much time, or is too expensive if it will "help" the person you are involved with.

10. In a relationship, you are much more in touch with your dream of how it could be than with the reality of your situation.

13. By being drawn to people with problems that need fixing or by being enmeshed in situations that are chaotic, uncertain, and emotionally painful, you avoid focusing on your responsibility to yourself.

15. You are not attracted to people who are kind, stable, reliable, and interested in you. You find such "nice" people boring.

Both male and female adolescents related to these questions, which are signs of relationship addiction.

Some might argue that obsession and compulsion are what love is all about, especially for teenagers who are first experiencing the intoxication of love and the power of relationships to become the total focus of personal existence. However, a "crush" or adolescent romance is not immune to reality; one of the ways to distinguish between a healthy relationship and an unhealthy, addictive one is to consider whether the relationship causes and/or tolerates pain. When people are in love, they are also capable of functioning in the world—for example, at work or in school. In our treatment program, we were asking these adolescents to set aside their romantic interests in order to concentrate on saving their own lives from the real threat of damage and death due to drug addiction and alcoholism. Most of them could, even though they would have preferred to focus on the excitement of a new relationship. When they could not get the relationship off of their minds long enough to be able to benefit from treatment, we began to work with them on their relationship addiction issues, which *they* called "male dependency" and "female dependency."

Adolescent sexual addiction is harder to spot than love addiction—which is generally true for adults as well. Even though we live in a culture that fosters sexual preoccupation—after all, this is the basis for a great deal of our advertising—it is difficult to get accurate information from people about sexual behavior; as individuals, we tend to be quite secretive about our sexuality. People with sexual shame (such as the embarrassment induced by being out of control of one's sexuality, or sexually addicted) tend to cover up their thoughts, feelings, and behaviors related to sexuality. Adolescents who are sexually compulsive/addicted have a double reason to hide: their developmental issues that relate to feeling comfortable with sexuality, and their sense that they are not really normal and have behaviors that are extreme.

In our survey, we asked hospitalized adolescents to respond to the Sexaholics Anonymous series of twenty questions that describe typical symptoms of sexual addiction. These questions included the following:

1. Have you ever thought you needed help for your sexual thinking or behavior?

5. Do you resort to sex to escape, relieve anxiety, or because you can't cope?

10. Does an irresistible impulse arise when the other party makes the overtures or sex is offered?

14. Does pursuit of sex make you careless for yourself or the welfare of your family or others?

18. Do you want to get away from the sex partner as soon as possible after the act?

Almost three-quarters (73.7%) of the adolescents identified with at least three of these questions, suggesting problems with their sexual behaviors. The sexual thoughts, feelings, and behaviors of the adolescents both in and prior to chemical dependency treatment suggest that relationships and sexuality are quite difficult areas for these troubled teenagers. Their survey responses suggest that sex and love addiction needs to be considered as a possible explanation for the problems they experience with sex and love.

CAN TEENAGERS BE SEX AND LOVE ADDICTS?

I hope at this point that the comparison between chemical dependency and sex and love addiction and the results of our inpatient survey, have opened at least some reader's minds to the possibility that young people can be addicted to sex and love. The adult sex and love addicts whom I treat tell me that their addictions started in their teen years or even younger. Often, adults in their thirties, forties, and fifties will say to me that they wish someone had noticed their problems when they were teenagers, so they could have gotten help as an adolescent and would not have had to suffer so long and so much.

Teenagers are suffering every day with sexual behaviors and relationship dependencies that they cannot control. These addictions drive them into increasingly insane and dangerous situations and can lead to death through suicide, homicide, and sexually transmitted diseases. Consider the three adolescents whom I mentioned at the beginning of this chapter. The first was referred into treatment involuntarily because she had attacked her mother after her mother accused her of "being a whore." The sixteen year old in question dresses seductively, stays out overnight at her twenty-one-year-old boyfriend's house, and has had treatment for a sexually transmitted disease. While she denies having any problems, her neck bears a scar from the time her boyfriend smashed her head through a car windshield in a fit of jealous rage and "macho" domination. Her family relations are in total turmoil; her school performance has dived from As and Bs to failure; her church attendance has ended; and she is so preoccupied with the activities and whereabouts of her boyfriend that she cannot concentrate on treatment.

The second adolescent I encountered today calls herself "male dependent," although this seems to be done more to please the treatment staff than to describe her own understanding of her problems. This fourteen year old cannot live without a boyfriend. She has had a series of destructive relationships with drug-addicted boys who were physically and emotionally abusive to her. She comes from a family that has poor boundaries and has seen a series of disasters in the development of the children: suicide, drug dependence, prostitution, and jail. She is desperate to find love. She feels abandoned by her father and tortured by a love/hate connection with her mother. She sees a relationship with the opposite sex as the solution to all of her problems. During one of her hospitalizations, she fell madly in love with one of the sickest, most damaged boys on the unit and managed to keep the relationship going after both of them were discharged—despite warnings from the staff, demands from her parents, and physical distance separating the two. (It sounds like Romeo and Juliet, doesn't it?)

She too has ended up being involuntarily committed as dangerous to herself and others after a wild escapade with her lover. She stole her parents' car, credit cards, and cash while they were out of town, and went off to start a new life with her eighteen-year-old boyfriend. She was abusing drugs and acting out sexually without taking precautions to protect herself from pregnancy or disease. When her parents located her, she and her mother physically attacked each other. Fortunately, police were close at hand and no serious damage was done. However, she became suicidal when the guilt from her behaviors began to sink into her well-defended psyche.

Her lover—the third adolescent to claim my attention today—has been severely abused by his father, physically and emotionally, to the point where the state intervened and the young man was removed from his father's home. Also, he was sexually molested by his high school teacher and subsequently developed a fascination with inappropriate sex. This adolescent is preoccupied and obsessed with sex and experiences a great deal of sexual shame and anxiety, compulsively acting out heterosexually as if to prove to himself and the rest of the world that his abuse has not turned him into a homosexual. He seeks sexual excitement in pornography, exhibitionism, and voyeurism, including the making of his own home movies of some of his sexual acting out. He cannot go to school or work, nor function in his family or with his peer group. He is overly aggressive, threatening, and intimidating to male peers. With female peers, he is overly solicitous, seductive, and endearing. He abuses drugs and alcohol to medicate the pain from the many forms of abuse that he has suffered in his short life. He is afraid of therapy and recovery and wants to keep running from his problems in the company of a young woman with whom he can act out sexually.

Each of these three young people has some signs and symptoms of sex and love addiction. Their behaviors are compulsive and out of control. They are saying to those of us who are listening that they have been hurt a great deal and need to learn healthy ways to cope with pain. They have found that sex and relationships can be powerful distractors from the stressful effects of childhood trauma. Most of the adults in their lives—even the ones who are trained to help them—do not see or conceptualize their problems as possible sex and love addictions. They may not get the help that they need and deserve because we are blind to their compulsions and have a need to see all adolescent sex and love behaviors as somehow "normal" for teens.

MORALISTIC AND LEGALISTIC RESPONSES TO SEX AND LOVE ADDICTIONS

Because we did not have a comprehensive view of the clients' addictions on our adolescent unit, we treated only their chemical dependency with objectivity, compassion, and understanding. We did not expect teenagers to recover from drug and alcohol problems without cravings, ambivalence, and turmoil. But we did not extend to the teenage sex and love addicts among them the same degree of sympathy and support for a trying disorder that is difficult for even the most motivated people to overcome. Our approach was moralistic and legalistic, rather than therapeutic and nonjudgmental.

An example of this was our approach to any physical contact and romantic involvement of the clients with their peers in treatment. We had rules against both. If two patients interacted in these ways and got caught, they received consequences; namely, they lost some of their privileges and free time. If they persisted, they were "restricted" from each other—which meant that they were not to sit together, talk, or otherwise communicate, including using an intermediary such as another peer. Most of the sex and love addicts could not follow these rules. Rather than coming up with a more intensive therapeutic response, we reacted with increasingly legalistic, punitive, and frustration-driven measures to the offending teenagers' "lack of self-control." In other words, we turned the offending behavior into a problem of willpower. That is, we saw the difficulty as the person's unwillingness to cooperate, rather than as an inability to cooperate due to a real (and treatable) disorder: sex and love addiction.

The legalistic/moral/willpower approach to chemical dependency is old hat. It clearly does not work. Professionals in several fields and the public at large agree that alcoholism and drug addictions are illnesses requiring treatment, rather than legal or moral problems requiring punishment, more willpower, or better morality. Chemically dependent individuals are viewed as "sick" and in need of care, rather than "low-life bums," and "lazy degenerates." Unfortunately, when it comes to compulsive sexuality and driven relationship dependency, this same enlightened view does not yet exist for adults, let alone for adolescents.

I spoke with a seventeen-year-old drug addict who identified herself as "male dependent." She told me a story about her outpatient addictions counselor, who was becoming increasingly frustrated with her inability to stay sober from chemicals. He discovered one day that she had a fairly large amount of cash with her, and he confiscated it. His intention was to prevent her from using the money to buy drugs—which she was indeed planning to do after their session. She became enraged and threatened to harm him. The counselor called the police and charged her with "terroristic threats." He failed to see that her pattern of relapses was intimately tied to her abusive relationship with a boyfriend. This young woman was an incest survivor who looked to chemicals and relationships to ease her pain. Recovery from drug and alcohol abuse only brought on more pain, and she tried to soothe it in relationships. Rather than treating her other addiction (to sex and love) as he was attempting to treat her chemical dependency, the counselor has fallen into the trap of seeking a legalistic solution to a therapeutic problem.

This seventeen-year-old addict had been in various types of treatment since she was twelve years old. She brought to mind the "borderline personality" diagnosis to most staff and had been diagnosed "manic-depressive" just prior to my encounter with her. At the core, she wanted to be in control of herself; she dreamed of living a "happy life" and of making her mother proud. Somehow, though, she could never live up to the expectations of others, and she believed deeply that it was her fault she was not successful. She knew her chemical dependency had a genetic/biological component because of extensive alcoholism on her father's side of the family, but she blamed herself for her problems with relationships and her apparent inability to "get it right" despite extensive effort. She could stay sober for days at a time, but then would binge and go out of control. Most of these incidents were triggered by painful encounters with her mother, her boyfriend, or her past (in which there had been sexual abuse). No one ever affirmed her efforts to change and her desire to be better. Instead, her mother and counselors blamed *her* for *their* failure to provide the support and understanding she needed to be successful. This was primarily due to their moralistic attitude toward her sex and love addiction. They wanted her to cure herself with an act of willpower. They knew she needed therapy and support groups for her chemical dependency, but they did not think to provide her with the same sort of help for her "male dependency."

ROMEO AND JULIET

When two sex and love addicts find each other, a spark ignites. In fact, in recovery, most sex and love addicts come to say things like, "When I walked into a room, I was mysteriously drawn to the other sex and love addicts in the room." Of course, early in the recovery process, sexual intrigue, nonverbal cues like dress, and "cruising" for partners are examined as behaviors driven by the addiction; and the mystery fades away. It is not at all unusual for two sex and love addicts to get involved with each other, dreaming that the relationship will magically dispel all of their problems. One sex and love addict I treated was repeatedly trying to establish this miraculously healing relationship with partners he met at adult (read: pornographic) bookstores. Another found a partner in a gym and gave up recovery for almost a year before she admitted it would not work. A third met his addictive lover at a Sex and Love Addicts Anonymous meeting.

The seventeen-year-old woman described in the preceding section tried to make "friends" with another recovering alcohol and drug addict on her therapy team. In her "innocent" effort to be friendly, she bragged about not being prejudiced and having a number of black friends. The young man she was opening up to saw her as "cracking" on him, or coming on to him. He responded with an offer to be her boyfriend and lover after treatment. He took the liberty of making clear his love/lust with a sensual caress of her rear end. She reacted with shock and terror. Fortunately, the young woman was in a safe place with a lot of sophisticated help; the two were able to talk out their misunderstanding in the presence of staff.

Interestingly, our young woman had managed to choose as her "friend" another sex and love addict. The young man in question had been accused of sexually harassing female staff members at a youth detention facility. He reported having sex daily—and more often "if I could get it." He knew a number of women (and he preferred "older" women in their twenties) with whom he could be sexual, so he did not have to worry much about finding a "fix." His father apparently was hypersexual and had sixteen children by five different women. Both father and son bragged about how they were "a lot alike," especially in terms of their sexual appetites. The young man did not believe in masturbation and told me that it would "make you stupid." Consequently, he was sexually preoccupied during his inpatient stay.

For some reason—probably their sex and love addictions—these two young people were drawn together within days of their arrival on the unit. In any case, their compulsive sexuality was no secret to the staff. Responding to an inventory taken from *What Everyone Needs to Know about Sex Addiction* (Anonymous, 1989), the Juliet of this classic pair spoke about an earlier boyfriend, and gave life to the pain of her addiction in comments like these:

I drink to deal with the way I feel with and without him.

I was always with him to escape from myself.

He always told me what I wanted to hear.

Towards the end, I felt like I was just a piece of ass. There was not more love, but I didn't want to be alone.

If I did not give in to his demands for sex, he would belittle me and make accusations of me, like I must be sleeping with other people.

We would agree to cut down on sex [from a level of 2–5 times a day] and, then, he would say that sex is "enjoyable" and I should want to do it because it feels so good.

He would treat me like shit. I would want every thing to be ok, so I would have sex with him.

I did not want to be alone. After we broke up, I slit my wrists to try to prove I loved him.

In other words, her sex and love addiction put her life in jeopardy. The above comments were made about a relationship she had prior to admission and the encounter with the peer in treatment. This previous lover had been "a virgin" when she met him, but their relationship progressed into a full-blown sex addiction in a short amount of time. She had a knack for finding relationships like this, much like a moth drawn to the flame.

LIFE OR DEATH

Addictions have a profound effect on the physical, social, emotional, financial, and spiritual lives of those who suffer under their spell. Sex and love addictions can be life threatening, as indicated above. There are a variety of ways that sex and love addictions can kill. Sexually transmitted diseases cause pain and suffering, and HIV/AIDS brings death. Sex and love addicts suffer severe and suicidal depressions. Some experience aggressive and violent impulses, such as jealous rages that can lead to homicides.

A recent article in the major Philadelphia newspaper was captioned "Teen Fatal Attraction" and the headline screamed, "OBSESSIVE JEALOUSY FUELED LANCASTER COUNTY MURDER." The story went on to say,

"At her trial, M. looked like a teenager coming out of Sunday school. But M. was a coldhearted, empty person. You could look at her and think—there's a person with no soul." Those are the words of H.S., whose 16-year-old daughter, L.S., was one of the teenagers at C.V. High School in Lancaster County who underestimated M. In the summer of 1991, L. briefly dated M.'s boyfriend and unwittingly became the target of M.'s jealousy—an obsession so intense that it turned to rage and terrified L. for six months—until December 29, 1991, when it took her life. (*Philadelphia Inquirer*, October 18, 1992, A1, 16)

Nowhere in the story about this deadly triangle did anyone speculate that "M." may have been suffering from sex and love addiction. There was a great deal of shock, anguish, confusion, disbelief, and disgust. But there was little in the way of constructive speculation as to the underlying cause of this tragedy.

In my work with adolescents, I have noticed a tendency on the part of parents, professionals, and other adults to see problems with sexuality and love relationships as simply a part of growing up. While this is true for the vast majority of teenagers, it is not true for all of them. Our blindness to the pain of those whose sexuality is out of control may result in consigning them to years of torment.

Adolescent sex and love addicts can hurt themselves physically in a number of different ways. They can cause harm to their genital areas with unusual or dangerous activities that are intended to improve their sexual high. They can create sores, cuts, and tears on their genitals through compulsive masturbation. The use of foreign objects can cause harm—such as the insertion of a bottle into the vagina. Teenage sex and love addicts can easily contract sexually transmitted diseases (STDs). Most of the young people I speak with tell me that no one who treated them for STDs ever suggested they may be engaged in addictive/compulsive behavior that could require professional help. Usually, the adults who know about their problems react with moralistic and shaming advice and putdowns—for example, "slut" or "whore," or saying they don't know how to control their appetites.

Pregnancy is another major problem for sex and love addicted adolescents. The girls may have multiple pregnancies, multiple abortions, as well as miscarriages. The boys may have pregnant girlfriends or acquaintances, and have children by many partners. It is usually quite difficult to get these young people to focus on the underlying dynamics, especially if they have parents with similar behaviors or if they feel there is some cultural sanction for their situation.

The social effects of sex and love addiction are profound. For the adolescent, these focus around their relationships with their families and with their peers. Generally, there is great alienation from both. The families of young sex and love addicts tend to be horrified by the adolescents' behavior. The parents or caretakers might be overly rigid or perhaps overly chaotic in their expectations—such as about following rules—and their emotional style might be detached or—conversely—enmeshed. Most of them are "dysfunctional" in that they have not been able to provide adequate nurturing, unconditional love, healthy boundaries and support, and education about relationships and sexuality. They often have numerous problems of their own—such as addictions, depression, and anxiety disorders.

When they find out that their teenager has molested another child or has been otherwise compulsively sexual (including compulsive masturbation), they either overreact or underreact. In essence, they do not know how to respond. However the families react, though, the adolescent sex and love addicts usually feel terribly alone and misunderstood. They are children who do not understand their own feelings and behaviors. They need adults who can see what is going on and can help them. Instead, their families sometimes make these young addicts feel like they think the child is doing something to hurt them. And, in fact, they usually think that the adolescent could control the behavior "if he or she only tried."

Similarly, the addicts' relationships with peers are quite difficult and painful. Other teenagers may have a sense that the adolescent sex and love addict is overdoing things. They may see the "male/female dependency," or they may think that the person is "oversexed." However, most teenagers are not clear enough about their own development and what is "normal" and what is healthy to provide much support or structure for the adolescent sex and love addict. Sometimes, peers are terribly cruel to teenage sex and love addicts, judging them without mercy. Most of the adolescent girls I work with think that being seen as "a whore" is the worst thing that can happen. Teen sex and love addicts might be regarded as prostitutes or nymphomaniacs and often have "terrible reputations." They might be shunned by other adolescents and their families.

In our society, adolescent boys are usually admired for being sexually active, so they may not experience the same sort of shame around (specifically) heterosexual acting out. But they do experience a great deal of embarrassment about compulsive masturbation, pornography, and prostitution. Peers may seem to admire the "macho" acting out of multiple relationships and partners, but they often separate themselves from these hypersexual peers, leaving them feeling alone, isolated, and even more driven to find comfort in their addiction.

On the mental and emotional levels, all addictions have a profound impact, most of which will be reviewed in Chapter 2. It is important to note here that sex and love addiction in a teenager affects how he or she thinks and feels. The most common result is the sexualization of the person's thought processes. That is, the young person reads into normal interactions the presence of a sexual message. For example, one young man thought that a waitress was coming on to him and wanted to have sex with him simply because she smiled at him. Similarly, relationship addicts can read innocent comments or eye contact as saying that the person is attempting to establish a romantic relationship. Typically, adolescent sex and love addicts are entirely preoccupied with sexuality or relationships—even more so than their peers—and because of it they cannot function normally in other areas of their lives, such as at school or a job.

On an emotional level, the teenage sex and love addict can be either hyperaroused or numb. The ritualized, repetitive aspects of the compulsive behaviors tend to create a trancelike state that soothes and disconnects the addict from painful emotions. On the other hand, the overly stimulated state can come from childhood trauma (especially sexual trauma) that is unresolved; the sexual or relational acting out may be an attempt to master the trauma. What typically results is a repetition compulsion or addictive disorder that actually continues to reinjure the person, rather than providing the corrective resolution of the past trauma. Since the past cannot be fixed and the present is becoming more and more insane, the sex and love addict needs to become more lost in his or her addiction in order to survive. The result is a disconnection from the real self and the creation of a false self—that is, the addictive self—who can present an image to the world of pseudomaturity. The hurting child is hidden behind a facade of competence and phony integration. In other words, the real emotional life of the teenage addict is well hidden from the rest of the world, and possibly even from the addict.

On a financial level, addiction has an impact even for adolescent sex and love addicts. The addicts must "feed" their addiction; so they will spend too much money on a lover whom they are not really close to, or they will spend money on expensive pornography or sex "toys." Hiding the amount of money involved and how the money is used can take a fair amount of effort and a good deal of manipulation.

Finally, on a spiritual level is where the sex and love addiction probably has the profoundest effect of all. Sex and love addicts are disconnected from their spiritual selves. They have lost any sense of worth or reverence for their being. They have become alienated and outcast at home and with peers, so they do not have any sense that some "Higher Power" or God could care about them or love them in any way. They see themselves as "bad" and worthless and hold themselves to account mercilessly for not being in better control of themselves. They feel "evil" and "possessed" by some sort of devil or demon that they do not understand but feel compelled to follow. They have given up hope for change or salvation. They do not see themselves as worthy of being rescued, cared about, and loved. Their prayers are the prayers of desperation: "Lord, get me out of this one and I will change." Their eyes are lowered in shame and humiliation and they have no concept of healthy devotion or humility. It seems that their spiritual health is the first to go and the last to come back in the recovery process.

Adolescent sex and love addiction exists. The remainder of this book is devoted to describing the symptoms, clinical vignettes, and treatment issues. I encounter teenage sex and love addicts almost every day. My original blindness has been replaced with seeing eyes, as will hopefully happen to others who read this book. These teenage sex and love addicts need our understanding and support. They need us to see that teenagers can be addicted to other things besides chemicals. They need us to see that theirs is not a moral or legal problem, but rather a progressive and potentially fatal disease that is beyond their initial control. They need us to see that they are suffering physically, socially, emotionally, financially, and spiritually despite our prejudices about what is normal in terms of adolescent sex and love behavior. They need our care and our love.

2

Definition of Sex and Love Addiction

Defining sex and love addiction can be rather simplistic on the one hand, and rather complex on the other (Griffin-Shelley, 1991). Unfortunately, at the time of this writing, there is not a generally agreed upon diagnostic criterion, nor a universal definition for sex and love addiction. In fact, there continues to be controversy over the reality or existence of sex and love addiction. The experts in the field each seem to have their own definitions. The Twelve Step programs have differing names, for example, Sex and Love Addicts Anonymous (SLAA), Sexaholics Anonymous (SA), Sex Addicts Anonymous (SAA) and Sexual Compulsives Anonymous (SCA). Most do not combine sex and love. Love addicts are variously known as relationship addicts, romance addicts, and codependents.

The prestigious *Diagnostic and Statistical Manual*, or *DSM-III-R*, of the American Psychiatric Association (1987) does not list either sex addiction or love addiction as a primary diagnostic category. After listing the paraphilias (exhibitionism, fetishism, frotteurism, pedophilia, sexual masochism, sexual sadism, transvestitic fetishism, and voyeurism) and sexual dysfunctions, there is a listing of "other sexual disorders." This classification is for "sexual disorder not otherwise specified." The second example (of three) of this disorder reads as follows: "distress about a pattern of repeated sexual conquests or other forms of nonparaphilic sexual addiction, involving a succession of people who exist only to be used" (p. 169). Obviously, this vague reference is quite limited as well as being rather unclear. There are no references to love addiction in this manual. By way of comparison, substance abuse and dependence has a whole host of classifications with numerous subtypes and great specificity in diagnostic categories. Sex and love addiction has a long way to go in order to be fully accepted and integrated into our common categories of mental disorders.

CONTINUUM OF BEHAVIORS

Most behaviors can be placed on a continuum from one extreme to the other. For example, an extremely addicted alcoholic will keep a bottle of booze by the bed because he or she will not be able to go for six or eight hours without a drink, due to the onset of uncomfortable withdrawal symptoms. At the opposite or polar extreme, a teetotaler could go an entire lifetime without ever allowing alcohol to cross his or her lips. Likewise, sex and love behaviors can be placed on a continuum from avoidance or phobia to addictive and compulsive behaviors. The sexually anorexic person is repulsed by sex and wants to have nothing to do with it. The sexually addicted person is obsessed with sex and rarely has it out of his or her conscious mind.

The distribution of the population along this continuum probably falls under the bell-shaped curve illustrated in Figure 1. Most adolescents' sex and love behaviors are in the middle of the curve and are what we regard as "normal." Roughly two-thirds fall into this center category. On either side, there are probably 15 percent who tend toward avoiding sex and relationship issues and another 15 percent who are abusive with sex and love but have not reached the point of addiction. Finally, there are two extreme groups on either end: those teenagers who fear and abhor sex and/or love relationships to the point of being sexually or relationally anorexic or phobic (estimated to be about 5–10%) at the one end, and those adolescents who are obsessional and compulsive about their sexuality and/or romantic attachments to the point of being addicted (5–10%) at the opposite pole.

Figure 1
Behavioral Distribution of the Population

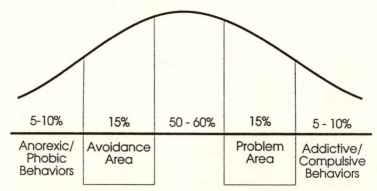

5-10%	15%	50 - 60%	15%	5 - 10%
Anorexic/ Phobic Behaviors	Avoidance Area		Problem Area	Addictive/ Compulsive Behaviors

Source: Eric Griffin-Shelley, Observations on healthy sexuality. *The Priest* (January 1993), 29.

Because adolescents are just learning to deal with their sexuality and to be in primary relationships, almost all of what goes on with teenagers is seen as "normal." Most adults remember the intensity of this developmental phase and are not alert for problems in the extremes. Generally, the adolescents who are on the avoidant/anorexic end of the continuum get support and sympathy because adults can recall their own painful struggles with understanding and coping with love, romance, intimacy, and sexuality. Often, however, these teenagers are not seen for what they are: likely victims of serious childhood trauma, which is at the root of their fears. Their pain is not recognized when we say, "They will grow out of it"—and otherwise minimize their difficulties. These children are in great pain and need to be seen, affirmed, supported, and helped.

Similarly, the adolescents who are acting out with compulsive sexuality and/or relationship dependency are not seen as having problems and are usually expected simply to mature with time. Only the extreme adolescent sex offenders have any type of specialized treatment—and they are so stigmatized and rejected by normal society that they have a secondary level of shame and trauma to work through, besides the original trauma that led to their compulsive behaviors. Sex offenders' programs are segregated from other treatment programs for teenagers, and the care that they receive is limited by their "separate but equal" status. More often than not, parents, teachers, therapists, and other adults do not want to believe that adolescents could be out of control of their sexual or relational lives. We want to believe that their extreme behavior and obsessions are simply a "phase that they are going through," rather than a serious mental disorder. The teenagers who will be described in Chapter 3 of this book are not simply going through a "stage" of their development. These young people are in great pain, and their hurt is being communicated through their painful behavior.

SHORT DEFINITION

The short definition of an addiction is this: a pathological relationship with an experience that is dangerous to one's self and/or others. There are three important elements in this definition. First, the relationship is *pathological*. Second, it is with an *experience*. And third, it is *dangerous*. In order to more fully understand the meaning of this definition, the elements need to be examined in more detail.

First, pathology means the study of disease. The root word is *pathos*, which is Greek for suffering and disease. So, a pathological relationship is a sick connection, an unhealthy attachment, an imbalance in the homeostasis, and a state of disease and suffering. Addictions such as alcoholism and gambling are well known for their sickness, their lack of balance, and their damage to the addict and all those around him or her. A pathological relationship is not one characterized by joy, experimentation, excitement, or enhancement. Adolescent sexuality and romance is usually classified with the latter terms, not the former. Adolescent sex and love addicts, then, have a pathological relationship with their sexuality or relational lives; this implies that they are suffering from a disease. They are out of balance. They are sick and need to be restored to a state of health.

Second, addicts have a sick attachment to an experience. Here, we have expanded the view that an addiction can only be to an exogenous chemical substance. While we have learned much of what we know about addictions from our experiences with chemical dependency (and many of their terms useful to that understanding will be examined in detail later in this chapter), most addictionologists now believe that it is possible to develop an unhealthy attachment—a sick relationship—with experiences. We have observed that people appear to be hooked on or addicted to activities like running, exercise, prayer, work, shopping, spending, gambling, sex, and relationships. We are becoming clearer that nicotine dependence is not simply a "bad habit," but is a real addiction. We are learning that people can be addicted to food and that this addiction may involve certain chemicals like refined sugar or processed flour. Food addiction is more complex than a simple chemical equation, however, and includes psychological as well as physical dependence. In short, we can get "high" from our experiences; and when we can get high, we can get hooked.

Third, the last element—danger—is crucial to the definition of addiction. All of us have probably had pathological experiences with food, but most of us are not food addicts. Similarly, many of us have had unhealthy experiences with alcohol, but most of us are not alcoholics. These "bad" experiences would fall under the abuse or problem area of the continuum (i.e., the 15% that comes before addiction). On the other hand, many of us have probably had experiences with food or alcohol where we were avoiding or tending toward the anorexic or phobic end of the continuum. Abuse or avoidance is not anorexia or addiction. Abusive or avoiding experiences usually teach us something so that we can modify our behaviors, attitudes, and thinking to become more balanced and more in the middle. Typically, addicts and anorexics do not learn from their experiences. They tend to distort their painful experiences and blame something other than the real cause of the difficulty. These cognitive distortions place the addict and anorexic in potential danger. The more compulsive the person becomes, the more danger that he or she and others are in.

Adolescent sex and love addicts have unhealthy attachments to their sexual and/or relational experiences to the point where they and others are being hurt. Two examples come to mind. The teenage boy whose sexual activities become obsessive can easily fail to use protection and then exposes himself to sexually transmitted diseases (STDs). Or, the adolescent girl who needs to engage in anonymous sex will also be careless and fail to protect herself, and likewise becomes vulnerable to catching and passing on STDs. Sex and love addictions are dangerous in more ways, however, than simply the transmission of STDs. Such relationships and sexual activity can become violent and physically dangerous. Often, the violence or threat of violence adds to the sexual high or to the intensity of the relationship. Since sex and love addicts do not know real intimacy, they often confuse intensity with intimacy. Danger, then, becomes an attractive element in the experience, rather than a warning sign that something is really wrong with the relationship. Adolescents usually do not have enough experience to distinguish between intensity and intimacy, so they are more vulnerable to getting entangled in this dangerous activity.

Addictive sexuality and/or relationships include all of the parts of the short definition of addiction, that is, a pathological relationship, an experience, and danger to self and others. For teenagers who have not had a great deal of life experience and who perhaps do not trust adults to guide them, sex/love is a powerful drug. I have suggested elsewhere that sex and love have the addictive potential of cocaine (Griffin-Shelley, 1993). Sex and love addiction among teenagers does not seem to have the same epidemic spread as "crack" cocaine. But this could be a reflection of our inability to see the disease, to acknowledge the sickness in our adolescents. Teenagers laugh when adults wonder whether they are sexually active. Perhaps more is going on than we have allowed ourselves to see. When I educate professionals about sex and love addiction, I find that they discover more sex and love addicts among their clientele than they previously expected. When professionals have a new vision, a different cognitive set, and some tools with which to be helped people, they often have the experience of finding more people to be helped with these tools. Possibly, the same blindness exists for sex and love addicted teens.

LONG DEFINITION

A more comprehensive definition of sex and love addiction would include more than pathology, attachment, and danger. Using concepts developed to describe chemical dependency in more detail, I have elsewhere proposed a definition that includes nine characteristics of addiction: the "high," tolerance, dependence, craving, withdrawal, obsession, compulsion, secrecy, and personality change (Griffin-Shelley, 1991). These key elements continue to categorize sex and love addiction, and the last on the list has been expanded to include dissociation. A sex and love addicted person, then, is someone who gets high with sex and love, shows signs of increasing tolerance, exhibits both physical and psychological dependence, experiences cravings, goes into withdrawal during a period of abstinence or cessation, thinks obsessively about sex and/or love objects, feels driven or compelled to act out sexual desires and/or romantic fantasies, develops a veil of secrecy around sexual and/or relational thoughts and behaviors, and is able to continue to lead a "double life" through a process of dissociation that appears to others to be like "Dr. Jekyll and Mr. Hyde" in terms of the apparent personality change. This latter definition is quite a mouthful and will be elaborated in greater depth in the following subsections. A sex and love addict does not need to have each of these characteristics in order to meet the criteria for being defined as a sex and love addict. The more elements that are present and the stronger each one is, the more severe the sex and love addiction is. In other words, the more symptoms the person exhibits, the farther along the continuum the person is in terms of the severity of his or her disease.

The High

I once treated a twenty-nine-year-old truck driver who was hospitalized for depression related to his obsessive dependency on his wife and his need to have her act out scenes he saw in pornographic videos. He told me, "sex is my drug." The patient's father was an alcoholic and physically abusive; the patient's siblings had become addicted to drugs. But he himself had managed to escape chemical dependency. He did this in part because he found a "better drug" in sex when he was ten years old. Compulsive masturbation as a preteen led him into using pornography (magazines) and overly sexualized and dependent relationships as an adolescent. He found a better way to distract himself from the pain of abuse and abandonment in his family of origin: he found sex and love. His addiction was in full swing by the time he was sixteen.

Did anyone notice that he was acting out sexually and obsessed with love as a teenager? No. His family openly bragged at the dinner table about sexual conquests, sexual activities, and sexual needs; so he grew up thinking that he was "normal." When he found partners who were not as sexualized as he was, he encouraged them to become more sexual as his family had encouraged him, and he augmented his relational sexual activity with masturbation. His behavior was like that of the alcoholics who drink before and after going to a party because they do not want others to see their excessive need for alcohol. The young adolescent had already learned to conceal his excessive need for sex. His "drug of choice" was sex and he had become so dependent by early adolescence that he hid his craving for another "fix," another high.

Sex and love addicts learn to "get high" by manipulating their own brain chemistry. They learn there are many creative and exciting ways to get high, to get aroused, to create a "good feeling fix." The high resembles a stimulant high, and patterns of use and abuse are similar to those found with cocaine (Griffin-Shelley, 1993). Sex addicts can get high—can create a "rush" or flood of euphoric chemicals in their brains—by fantasizing, by viewing visual stimuli like partially nude bodies at the beach or hardcore pornographic videos, by touching either with permission or by deception, or by engaging in sexual activities with or without partners. Similarly, love addicts can produce the desired high by thinking about love, romance, or relationships, by reading about or watching soft- or hard-core movies or television, or by actual contact with an object of their romantic, relational, and/or sexual desires.

Teenagers often feel or believe that others think they *should* be obsessed with sex (on the part of the boys) or love (on the part of the girls), and are therefore driven to act out their sexual appetite or their need for a primary relationship. While it is true that discovering, exploring, and learning about sex and love are important developmental tasks for adolescents, normal adolescents are capable of having other things on their minds and setting other priorities when necessary. Adolescent sex and love addicts have lost the capacity to put sex and love in the background. Whether they show it to others or not, for them the compulsion to get high—the need to be intoxicated with sex and/or love—is stuck in their mental foreground and they no longer have the ability to shift their focus when appropriate. Getting high with sex and/or love is what life is all about. For them, nothing else can generate the same level of intensity, excitement, and vitality.

On our inpatient adolescent unit, dealing with sexuality and relationships was always an issue—as it should have been, since this is an important adolescent task. However, what separated the sexually or relationally dependent teenager from his or her peers was the peers' ability to set sex and/or love aside when it began to interfere with their therapy. Adolescent sex and love addicts needed to get high more than they needed to get treatment. They had lost their confidence that other people could make them feel better. People are unpredictable sources of good feelings. Sex/love, when objectified through the addictive process, was something that they could depend on to help them cope with their pain, to give them the good feelings they needed in order to be able to go on with life. Without sex and/or love as a "fix," they felt they would die. Normal teenagers can prioritize and put things ahead of their sexual or relational needs; but sexually addicted adolescents—like their adult counterparts—cannot say no to the impulse to indulge their desires.

Tolerance

The concept of tolerance comes from chemical dependency. All of us have differing levels of tolerance for chemicals. Some people, for instance, react quite strongly to caffeine and cannot drink caffeinated drinks in the evening because they will not be able to sleep. Others can have a cup of coffee right before bed and not be in the least bothered by the caffeine. For some drugs, we need to develop a tolerance in order to use them without getting sick. Alcohol usually has a toxic effect when first tasted or ingested. We need to "learn to drink," which means that we need to develop a tolerance for the bad taste so that we can eventually benefit from the intoxicating effect of the drug. Similarly, "pot" smokers learn to hold in the smoke, because the natural reaction is to cough and gag.

Once the original tolerance has been established, drug users find that their initial dose is not having the same effect. They can tolerate a certain amount without feeling the desired effect. Consequently, in order to produce the high that they are seeking, they need to use more. Eventually, they are using more and more simply to obtain the initial effect.

Sex and love addicts find that they, too, develop a tolerance and therefore need more and more in order to get the desire result. An example would be a young girl who gets high by simply looking at a love object. She feels thrilled with excitement that lasts for a long time. Usually, then, she learns that she can continue to experience the good feeling by fantasizing about what she has seen. She may not even need to speak to the target of her attraction in order to get the rush that sends her "into orbit." Over time, however, looking and imagining begin to wear off and do not create the same level of intensity or excitement. At this point, some sort of contact with the person usually triggers another intense response. Again, after a bit, she needs more. Talking, dating, and physical contact will produce the needed high now. For an addict, however, even this is not enough. She may get a commitment of fidelity, but she becomes possessive, jealous, and paranoid. She begins to pick fights, to imagine rivals, and to make accusations. All of this intensifies the relationship and drives it into a wild roller-coaster ride of "true love" and horrible fights.

Often, at this point, her lover will begin to feel controlled, compelled, smothered, and clung to with ever increasing dependency. The person starts to feel repelled, disgusted, and angry at the sex and love addict's insane behavior. They pull or push away in an effort to get some distance and some balance back into the relationship. The more the lover pushes the addict away, the more intense the sex and love addict's desire to connect. It is not unusual for these relationships to include physical violence, threats, and abuse by both partners. There is a dangerous level of intensity that is being driven by the addict's ever increasing tolerance and inability ever to be satisfied with what is.

Adolescent sex addicts have a pattern of increasing tolerance to sexual stimuli and acting out that parallels the love addiction just described. The sex addicts' ability to be aroused may begin with simply staring at underwear advertisements in the Sunday paper. After a while, this is not enough and the addicts progress to more explicit pictures in magazines like *Playboy*. In time, the visual excitement is augmented by the sexy stories in the letters to the editor. Again, these cues are not stirring enough and more overt and detailed pictures and books are necessary. Then, the addicts may introduce videos and movies. They may need to go to adult bookstores to find something exciting enough to get them aroused, because their tolerance is now so high. They can progress to acting out with other people the things and acts that they have seen and read about. When this is not enough, they begin to make their own pornographic movies or they may write their own fantasy stories, hoping that they will find partners to enact them. They discover phone sex, advertisements in sex magazines, and clubs devoted to fulfilling excessive sexual needs. Nothing is ever enough to fill the hole they feel deep within their souls. Ever increasing tolerance leads them to take greater and greater risks and to seek more and more demeaning and humiliating activities in pursuit of a sexual high.

One adolescent sex and love addict was discovered in our inpatient chemical-dependency program because he had drilled a peephole between his room and a room where girls slept. When asked about his sexual needs and practices, he proudly bragged that he often made pornographic videos as part of his many forms of seeking sexual highs. Another sex and love addicted teenager attempted suicide and tried to kill her lover when he could no longer tolerate her following him, checking on his whereabouts, accusing him of infidelities that he did not commit, and physically attacking him with curling irons, knives, and a telephone. Both of these teenage sex and love addicts had extremely high levels of tolerance that drove their activities progressively toward a life-threatening extreme.

Dependence

The concept of dependence comes directly from chemical dependency tenets. In fact, at one time it was the defining characteristic of drug dependency; in other words, for a person to be considered truly addicted, he or she needed to have a physiologic dependence on the drug. A physical dependence means that, when drug ingestion is ceased, the person's body craves it because the body needs the drug. The body has gradually become adapted to the drug use to the point where bad things happen when the drug supply is ended. The body goes into withdrawal and becomes sick; the person will then have either mild symptoms like the sweats, irritability, or agitation or severe symptoms like seizures and even death. The most physically addicting drugs are alcohol, opiates (like heroin), barbiturates, sedatives, and nicotine. Stimulant drugs such as amphetamines or cocaine and hallucinogenic drugs like LSD or marijuana do not produce a physiologic dependence. Since people have become addicted to these latter classes of drugs, it has become obvious that drug dependence can be both physical and/or psychological. In fact, the physiological treatment of drug and alcohol dependency is relatively easy and can be accomplished in three to five days. Most hospital detoxification units only keep patients for this length of time and then refer them to additional treatment for their psychological dependency on chemicals. Successful recovery from the psychological dependence on drugs can take a long time indeed and is typified by many ups and downs, false starts and relapses, and much agony and trial and error.

At this stage, there is no clear evidence that anyone becomes physically dependent on sex or love. There *is* a distinct withdrawal syndrome, which will be covered in a later subsection, and experiences of cravings, which again is covered in a bit; but there is no ingestion of external chemicals that the body becomes dependent upon. Sex and love addiction is more like the stimulant addictions or the fantasy arousal states found with hallucinogenics.

Sex and love addicts do tend to need a state of hyperarousal, which may then be followed by the relaxing and releasing rush of orgasm. Since most sex addicts have been traumatized as children (Carnes, 1991), they probably experience various forms of post-traumatic stress disorder (PTSD). PTSD patients frequently present with hyperarousal coupled with a persistent need to detach and disconnect from these painful memories. Sex and love can be the perfect drugs because they have both arousing and calming properties.

The tendency toward some type of physical dependence is most clear when sex and love addicts use their "fix" like they would use a drug. For example, some sex and love addicts have reacted with fear and horror to the suggestion that they not masturbate for a period of time, because they are terrified they will not be able to fall asleep without their daily "tranquilizer." Masturbation is so much a part of their nightly ritual that they cannot imagine being able to relax enough on their own to be able to sleep. Others seem to be physically dependent on the arousing characteristics of sexual fantasies or romantic reveries. They need this stimulation to pull themselves out of a chronic depressive state or a feeling of emptiness or boredom. Still others use sex and love to help them simply to feel something. Usually, these people are highly detached and intellectualized or numb; they need a strong "hit" in order to experience any feeling at all.

Adolescent sex and love addicts are familiar with the physiological benefits of sex and love. They use sex to go to sleep, to reduce stress and tension, to relax, to soothe themselves, and to feel something. They can also use relationships, romance, and love to distract them from their pain, to feel alive and worthy of living, to connect with excitement and joy. Rather than having love and sex grow out of a sharing intimacy with a partner, sex and love are for them drugs to be used for arousal, satiation, or whatever "fix" is needed.

Obviously, the division between physical and psychological dependence is not as clear as one might want it to be. From the above account, it should be evident that the physiological uses of sex and love correspond and are related to psychological needs that are being met. Thoughts, feelings, and behaviors are the means we have of getting our needs met; however, when any of these become excessive, repetitive, fixated, and ritualized, they become addictive and express psychological dependence. Usually, the psychological dependence is the most hidden, difficult to treat, and resistant part of addiction. The body can learn to live without physiological dependencies. The mind has a much more difficult time letting go of its "crutches."

Adolescent sex and love addicts look at me like I am crazy when I suggest to them that they attempt to abstain from sex or relationships for a period of time. In reality, it is they who are crazy, but the twisted thinking of an addict makes them project their craziness onto others. One young man asked to leave the hospital for a few hours on a "therapeutic pass." He had previously bragged to me that he had any number of women who would come over or make themselves available for sex whenever he called. I indicated to him that the purpose of the pass was for him to evaluate his discharge plans, not to "get laid" (as he would put it). He seemed a bit surprised that I would have this expectation, but realized that he would have to make me happy if he were to get the pass approved. So, he assured me that there would be no sexual activity while he was out of the hospital. When he returned, he reassured me that he had been "a good boy" and had only spent time with his grandmother. However, he underestimated the excitement that his day's activities would have on the adolescent gossip line and told a few of his peers about some sexual contact. Eventually, the word came back to me and he sheepishly admitted that he "had" to have sex while he was out. This was because he would "never" consider masturbating to meet his sexual needs.

A love addicted teenager had a similar story on her pass. She had told me about a boyfriend who was physically abusive to her and whom she knew she should give up because her life was literally in danger. She swore to me that she had not been having any contact with him and that she *would* not, during a visit home. Again, though, she was so "high" from her forbidden encounter with this lover that she could not keep it from her peers. Their concern for her well-being made him the topic of her next group therapy session. They begged her to let him go, but she could not imagine life without him. She was sure that he would change; she said, in fact, he had told her so when she saw him on her pass. Somewhat shockingly, her mother had apparently colluded with her to keep the encounter secret from the staff because her mother thought this new boy was "good for her" compared with the last boyfriend, who had been a drug dealer.

Recent thinking in the sex and love addiction field suggests that the two scenarios described above are examples of "traumatic reenactment." The driving force behind the obsession and compulsive behaviors, and behind the psychological dependency they suggest, is some unresolved childhood trauma that is being repeated in an unconscious effort to find resolution. The sex and love addict is attempting to place themselves in the power position, rather than remaining the victim as they were in childhood. Unfortunately, the reenactment does not succeed in undoing the past, and the person ends up feeling revictimized. The two teenagers mentioned above felt like victims when we gave them some consequences for having acted against our therapeutic advice while on their passes. Despite having been forewarned not to act out sexually or relationally, they "could not help themselves" and felt unable to choose not to act on their strong dependency needs.

Psychological dependency, then, has strong, deep, and powerful roots in the addicted adolescent's childhood. Needs for love, attention, nurturing, and soothing have been sexualized and/or romanticized. Physical, sexual, and emotional abuse have likewise been entangled in the sex and love arena so that these wounds get acted out in an effort to find closure or resolution to past trauma. Certainly, love and sex pose major challenges to the normal adolescent. But when sex and love are being used to meet all kinds of misplaced needs, they become overly determined and overwhelmingly addictive. The teen's psyche depends on sex and/or love too much for too many things.

Craving

A craving is an intense desire, a strong urge, an irresistible temptation, and an undeniable impulse. The idea and role of cravings come, again, from chemical dependency experiences. Alcoholics and drug addicts find that there are times when they do not desire to drink or use drugs. There are also times when the desire to indulge is extremely intense. These cravings do not happen all of the time, so resisting them is somewhat problematic since they are not always present and their occurrence is not always predictable. In fact, Alcoholics Anonymous (AA) has coined the phrase "cunning, baffling, and powerful" to describe alcoholism—in part, because of cravings. A recovering alcoholic might feel quite strong in his or her resolve not to drink and then suddenly, apparently out of nowhere, an overwhelming urge or craving will overcome the person and he or she succumbs to this temptation. Craving, then, is the *sine qua non* of relapse; it is the ultimate cause of failure. If craving had not reared its ugly head, our recovering alcoholic might have continued to maintain his or her sobriety.

Cravings are not well understood. However, their existence is well known to anyone who has ever been addicted to anything. I used to smoke cigarettes. My nicotine addiction slowly progressed in my thirties until I was smoking a pack of cigarettes a day. I quit smoking a few years ago and still can clearly remember the intense cravings that I experienced during my physical (the first week) and psychological (about 4–6 weeks) withdrawal. Recently—about four years after I became a nonsmoker—I experienced an intense desire to smoke. I was standing next to a lit cigarette in an ashtray and there was no one else around. I was tempted to pick it up and smoke. After all, no one would know! Moments later, I recoiled in horror at the strength of my craving for a cigarette. I can remember minutes, hours, and days when I was plagued with this irrational impulse to do something self-destructive, in other words, inhale nicotine via a cigarette. However, it has been a long time since that was a problem and I tolerate being around others who smoke without ever (well, almost never) having a craving to return to smoking. But one day, out of the blue, there it was: I was faced with an irresistible urge, an overwhelming craving "just to have one toke of that cigarette." Fortunately, I weathered the storm and did not pick up the cigarette. But I was shaken by the strength of the desire, the intensity of the craving, to return to my nicotine addiction.

Why is this? Where do cravings come from? Why do people experience them? We do not have very clear answers to these questions. It would appear that our brains develop "ruts," habit formations, neurological pathways that can be triggered even after long periods of quiescence and lack of use. It seems sort of like learning to ride a bicycle. This information is stored somewhere in the brain and is not too difficult to retrieve under the right circumstances. Similarly, ritualized, obsessive/compulsive, repetitive, chronic patterns of behavior can be triggered somehow and come to our consciousness as cravings. These cravings are usually triggered by some sort of pain. Because sex and love addicts are not sensitive to their "triggers," the urge to self-medicate, to numb feelings, to distract the mind from pain, to dissociate from trauma seems to "come out of nowhere." As sex and love addict begins to recover, they become sensitized to their triggers and can forestall cravings or, at least, are better able to deal with the cravings when they come.

Adolescents appear to be craving sex and love all of the time. At least, this is what some adults project onto them. Actually, while teenagers are learning to cope with powerful interpersonal attractions and strong hormonal drives, they usually are rather respectful of these important aspects of their development. But they *want* to learn about sex and love, so they cannot follow the adult advice that directs them to put off these experiences until they are "older" or married. They need to experiment, to try out relationships, love, and loving sensuality— much as they need to try out the chemicals (alcohol, nicotine, drugs, caffeine) that adults find so important in their lives. Adolescents' curiosity, growth, and experimentation should not be confused with the intense cravings of an addict needing a fix. The drive of the adolescent sex and love addict is far beyond the norm of adolescent sexuality and loving.

One adolescent sex and love addict had such an intense craving that he had to masturbate in the bathroom in the public area of our hospital unit. Somehow, his peers realized what he was up to and he felt profoundly ashamed and humiliated, but he was still tempted to act out again when he felt the urge. And a female sex and love addict had such an intense desire to connect with the object of her obsession that she wrote him explicit sexual notes despite having been caught once. Not surprisingly, she was discovered again. Her cravings for his attention were so intense that she threw caution and restraint to the winds and challenged the staff to try to stop her from being in touch with him both in and outside the hospital.

Cravings are connected to the withdrawal syndrome. Cravings can happen long after addictive acting out has ceased, but they are most intense and most frequent when the sex and love addict is in withdrawal.

Withdrawal

During withdrawal from sex and love addiction, addicts are typically either agitated or numb. For some, their sex and love addiction has been so stimulating that they are "wired" and their system has been on "over-drive." Others have used their acting out to soothe, numb out, and distract them from their pain; they are disconnected from their feeling selves. Consequently, sex and love addicts experience withdrawal from their active addiction in one of two ways: either they are like a "raw nerve," or they are like an iceberg that is slowly melting.

On a physical level, this means that some addicts in withdrawal feel like sleeping all of the time and others cannot sleep. Some have ravenous appetites, while others cannot eat. Some are able to lose themselves in projects or activities, and others cannot think straight or concentrate. Some sex and love addicts have no energy and feel lethargic and slowed down, while others are anxious, agitated, and hyperactive.

On a cognitive level, sex and love addicts in withdrawal can have distorted thinking that may induce depression, anxiety, or panic attacks. They then tend to have thoughts that are negative, hopeless, and pessimistic. Some in withdrawal, however, are overly positive, grandiose, and unrealistic. Their self-talk can be filled with helplessness and victimization or it can be overly confident and super-controlled. Their thinking reflects their internal struggles with self-esteem. Usually they feel quite worthless, shameful, and humiliated. They may have an intense desire to cover these painful feelings with a narcissistic facade of power and self-assurance. Paranoid thinking may also be a part of the withdrawal syndrome, since sex and love addicts see themselves as being hurt or humiliated by the process of coming to terms with the reality of their addiction. Typically, they have been rather out of contact with reality and may project blame onto those who are trying to help.

On an emotional level, the withdrawing sex and love addict is often flooded with a variety of feeling states. He or she usually experiences a great deal of fear and anxiety. This may even include panic attacks. Sadness, grief, and depression are also common feelings that sex and love addicts go through as they give up their "best friend" and source of pseudo-comfort. They may be angry, irritable, sarcastic, critical, and demanding or they may seem not caring, passive, avoidant, and unwilling to be responsible or active.

In the case of adults, drug addicts and alcoholics usually go to a medical detoxification unit before going into active treatment. In the case of adolescents, since they might resist treatment after detoxification, they most often are placed in treatment programs and go through withdrawal while in active treatment. To date, there are no detoxification units for sex and love addicts, or even medical protocols for withdrawal—for adults, let alone adolescents. Sex and love addicts must go through this difficult and challenging time on their own, as individuals, unless they happen to have the support of other recovering sex and love addicts or treatment personnel who are sensitive to this stage of recovery.

One young male sex and love addict was angry, agitated, hostile, and irritable. He complained of having difficulty sleeping and he overate in the dining room.

He was defensive and verbally attacked his peers and the staff. And he could be quite provocative. He felt hopeless and blamed himself. He was filled with guilt, shame, and remorse for his out-of-control behaviors. He saw himself as fulfilling so many people's negative predictions for him, but as being powerless to change. He could not let go of sex as his drug even though he was forced into temporary withdrawal by his confinement in the hospital. He planned to "make up for lost time" when he was released.

A female adolescent sex and love addict was depressed, lovesick, and tearful when staff confronted her "male dependency" and asked her not to continue a destructive relationship. She whined, complained, and pleaded for mercy from this cruel form of torture. She was sad, lonely, and could not imagine that life would go on without her special love object. She was intensely confused, dependent, and impatient for her "sentence" to end. She became fearful, demanding, and dysphoric as she struggled with her withdrawal from active sex and love addiction.

To many readers, these two cases may sound like a description of normal adolescents. After all, are not lovesickness and the exquisite torture of sexual desire the cause of much of the turmoil in adolescence? Sex and love are key elements in the normal development of teenagers; but the pursuit of a sexual and/or romantic high that leads to tolerance, dependence, and cravings and ends in withdrawal is not what normal development is made of. There are teenagers who have gone to the extreme in these areas and can experience a withdrawal syndrome that is as life threatening as a drug or alcohol detoxification.

Obsession

A mental obsession is a thought that just will not go away. An obsessive thought intrudes when it is not wanted, occurs when it is not expected, comes to mind at inappropriate times, and does not take no for an answer. People who are obsessed feel as if they have lost control of their own minds. They think thoughts they do not want to think. They cannot get themselves to stop thinking about someone or something, even when they know that continuing the obsession is dangerous to themselves and to others. They feel powerless to change their thinking patterns and often give up trying.

A classic example of an intrusive, obsessive thought is the dictum, DO NOT THINK OF A WHITE BEAR! For most people, the thought of a white bear immediately pops into their minds. And often, the harder they try to get their mind off the image of the white bear, the more persistent is the picture in their minds. Only when the pressure is off does the mental image fade into the background.

Some people develop obsessive/compulsive disorder, or OCD, which is characterized by repetitive, ritualized behaviors that are driven by obsessive thoughts. OCD patients typically present as "washers" or "checkers." The washers may wash their hands fifty times a day, to the point where they cannot function in other areas of life and their hands are painfully raw. Still they persist in their repetitive, driven behaviors. The checkers, similarly, constantly check on things, such as locking a door or turning off the stove. Both types of OCD have anxiety as the underlying cause of the behaviors. Somehow, for them, the relief that most of us find in such recurring behaviors is so short lived that their mind returns to the fears almost immediately after the ritual is ended.

Sex and love addicts use obsessive thinking to soothe themselves, to distract themselves from pain, to become aroused, and to dissociate from difficulties in the past or in the present. A sex and love addict recently found himself folding dirty clothing because he had committed not to obsess about sex. He was feeling anxious and needed a "fix," so he came up with another ritualized behavior that would distract him from feeling lonely, alone, and possibly reconnecting with the painful feeling of being left alone at a day care center where he had been sexually abused. Obsessive sexual thoughts had kept that memory repressed for more than twenty-five years.

Fantasy, preoccupation, and obsessive thinking create an altered state of consciousness much like a trance state. People can learn to manipulate their own neurochemistry in order to alter mood. If they are feeling down and want a lift, if they are feeling bored and want a rush, if they are feeling good and want a better high, they can learn through frequent repetition how to create a chemical change in their brain that results in an alteration of mood. They do not need a drink or a drug to "get high," although external chemicals can be added to the mix to enhance the high even more.

Romantic and sexual fantasies are frequent in adolescence; this is a part of normal development. Mental rehearsals can improve confidence, reduce anxiety, and enhance performance. Obsessions with love and sex are often seen as normative for teenagers, and adolescents who are not obsessed may feel somehow inadequate or odd. Our culture seems to promote the myth that obsession is love and that intensity equals intimacy. Much of the music that adolescents listen to is based on themes of undying love and overwhelming passion. Commercials have noted this desire for peak experiences, and one product is even called "Obsession for Men." While learning to use one's abilities to imagine, fantasize, and obsess about an object of one's passion may be productive, there is a point beyond which such thinking patterns become destructive and dangerous.

A seventeen-year-old male was reported about in a local television news magazine because he had hired a "hitman" to kill the boyfriend of a girl with whom he was obsessed. The seventeen year old had become so preoccupied with possessing this young woman that he had lost all sense of reality. He had not sought to win her "fair and square" by competing with her current boyfriend, but was so "hooked" that he went to the extreme of trying to hire a professional killer.

The media often present accounts of people who are obsessed with others—sometimes others whom they do not even know. Presidents and entertainers have been known to have "fans" who became fanatically obsessed with them to the point where the object of the obsession was in danger and unable to live a normal life. Recently, "stalker laws" have begun to be passed in order to have some legal recourse when someone is being victimized by an obsessive attachment. And to cite a specific instance of obsession's danger: at the time of this writing, a law student is on trial for the of murder of her lover after he told her that he was returning to his wife. If the state's charge is correct, the student apparently could not tolerate losing the target of her obsession, lost control, and shot him before he could abandon her.

Not all obsessives are as extreme in their behavior as this law student, but the dangerousness of obsessive thinking is often underestimated. Most people do not know how to assist a friend or family member whom they think is obsessed. The most common advice is to "forget it." When the person cannot let go of the thought, fantasy, or preoccupation, he or she usually tries to hide this inability to control his or her own mind. In fact, the obsessive thinking is usually obvious to others, but the sex and love addict continues to rationalize the thinking patterns because he or she is afraid to let go and has no other means of coping with anxiety and fear other than obsessive thinking.

Compulsion

Compulsive behaviors go with obsessive thoughts like hand and glove. The driven, ritualized, repetitive patterns of behavior that addicts engage in are what we mean by "compulsion." There is a saying in Twelve Step programs that goes "Addicts keep trying the same behaviors while expecting different results." A particular sex addict, may for instance, compulsively masturbate, expecting that this will somehow relieve his anxiety when, in fact, his guilt and shame is driving him to repeat the same behavior over and over again in order to find some relief. Most of us learn from our mistakes. When we try something and it does not work, we try something else. The addicted person is stuck trying the same thing over and over again, hoping and praying that something different will result. The more they fail, the more they seem to try again. The repetition of obviously dysfunctional behaviors drives everyone else crazy, but the addict seems oblivious to the concern and pain of others. He or she desperately wants to find a way to make their compulsive behaviors work.

Compulsive behavior is a form of self-medication. The preoccupation and ritual create an altered state of consciousness and a change in the neurochemistry of the brain. The result is an alteration in mood. Sexual and/or romantic fantasies and behaviors can soothe anxiety, alleviate depression, eliminate boredom, and fill emptiness. These compulsive behaviors will create a false sense of power, enhance one's feelings of adequacy, and make a man out of a mouse or a woman out of a wallflower. Sex and love are potent "drugs" that can alleviate pain and enhance normal activities.

Compulsive behavior is a form of reenactment of trauma. In order to cope with, assimilate, and have power over events that are overwhelming in their pain, the human mind needs to revisit the trauma repeatedly. In this repetitive recreation in our minds and dreams, our conversations and actions, and our thoughts and feelings, we validate our experience and learn to have some sort of power over something that made us feel entirely powerless, vulnerable, and harmed. Sexual and relational fantasy and acting out recreate the traumas of childhood in an effort to cope with the trauma and to undo the damage that was done. For example, a three-year-old boy was dressed as a girl and forced by his father to submit to oral sex. As an adult, he has a compulsion to dress in women's clothes and engage in oral sex with men. He is repeating his trauma, but now he is in control: he has the power position and is less vulnerable. Unfortunately, he also retraumatizes himself with this behavior, and has created additional feelings of shame, guilt, and worthlessness that have recently driven him to the point of suicide.

Compulsive behaviors distract the person from his or her current experience. Some sex and love addicts get flooded or overwhelmed with feelings or memories that they cannot process. They cannot tolerate the tension that this creates within them, so they act out to short-circuit their present state. For instance, one sex and love addict was worried about his finances and could not find a way to cover his expenses. As his tension and anxiety built, he wanted to escape the situation. He began fantasizing about engaging in some type of anonymous sexual encounter and immediately disconnected from his money woes.

Do adolescents self-medicate, reenact trauma, and escape from reality? The answer should be obvious: of course they do. They often live with parents and siblings who have modeled these coping strategies for them; and they may, in fact, see these as normal responses to the demands of living. Adolescents usually learn these coping mechanisms before they are teenagers, but the advent of adolescence provides them with the challenges and the opportunities to function more independently and less under the watchful eyes of adults. Consequently, these behaviors flourish in the adolescent environment of experimentation, growth, discovery, risk taking, identity development, and independence, especially in the areas of sex and love.

Children can exhibit compulsive, repetitive, ritualized behaviors. These are usually in the context of game playing. When I spoke with a class of fifth-graders recently, they were familiar with the "Nintendo addicts" among their peers. They understood the idea that some of their friends repeatedly engaged in activities that were repetitious, ritualized, and tended to isolate the person from others. They knew people could get lost in fantasy worlds and could exhibit behaviors that seemed driven and unstoppable.

As these young addicts get older and have more access to other addictive activities—like chemicals, money, and sex and love—their addictions can take off. A fifteen year old bragged to me that he had sex with a different girl every day; he thought of himself as a "stud" and was completely out of touch with his compulsivity. A mother contacted me because her son had charged thousands of dollars' worth of telephone sex calls to their phone in the space of a few weeks; he had a hundred-dollar-a-day "habit," much like the drug habits of heroin "junkies." A seventeen year old who saw herself as quite independent and grown up because she had been in a serious relationship with a woman in her twenties was confronted about making sexual overtures to one of her peers in treatment. She quickly copped to being "bad" and promised to be "good." Meanwhile, she was writing sexually explicit notes to another girl to whom she felt an attraction. She was blind to her dependency and to the driven nature of her behaviors.

While dating and sexual exploration are healthy parts of adolescent development, there are teenagers who cannot live without a relationship. They usually have one intense relationship, but also a number of "rain checks" or dangling relationships that could be picked up on short notice. They panic at the thought of being alone. Having sexual relations outside of their main relationship may not bother them, because they have such a strong desire to be needed. They try to appear to others as if they are in control and know what they are doing, but they too are victims of their addictions. They cannot live without love/sex, and life does not have any meaning outside of the context of sex or romance.

Secrecy

The need to keep a sex and love addiction secret becomes more intense as the addiction progresses. In fact, the opposite of secrecy—that is, honesty—is often called the "key to sobriety." When an addict finally makes the decision to be completely honest with himself or herself and others, the recovery process begins. Until this point, as they say in Twelve Step groups, "secrets keep you sick." The extent of the secrecy is usually a good indication of the extent of the pathology. Conversely, the degree of honesty usually corresponds to the success of the recovery. For example, a recovering sex and love addict came to me one day and said that he was becoming increasingly disturbed by his dishonesty at work. He was making a great effort to be honest in his personal life; but at work he went along with what he perceived as the "company norm," which included lying about expenses and time on the job. He had always felt like a fraud because of his compulsive cheating on his wife. As he was getting better, he began to feel phoney because he was stealing at work.

Many sex and love addicts come from families where there are multiple addictions. The dance between the codependent spouse and the addict promotes a family atmosphere of secrecy. Children are told implicitly or explicitly that they are not to share the workings of the family with the "outside world." Many experts on chemically dependent families have indicated that these families follow the "don't talk, don't trust, don't feel" rule and are highly defensive about exposure to others. These families live with a legacy of shame that appears to be passed from generation to generation. It is no wonder that the children learn the family value of secrecy at a young age. In order to preserve the family's reputation, the reality of family life must be kept secret from those outside the blood lines.

Keeping secrets is powerful stuff. The power of family secrets may be learned early in life. Indeed, children learn that keeping secrets is powerful even if they do not have family secrets to keep. As school-age children, we all learn that the ability to keep a secret is an indication of our trustworthiness and our reliability. A best friend is someone who will keep a secret. In this context, a secret is a confidence. It is a personal and intimate sharing between two people, and the ability to keep the secret speaks to the strength of the bond between the two people. Addicts do not keep these kind of secrets. The secrets that sex and love addicts keep are painful, shameful things that they feel unable to share with anyone else. Their secrets, in their minds, validate their worthlessness, their low self-esteem, and their lack of self-confidence. If known, their secrets would make everyone else reject and abandon them as they were rejected and abandoned by people earlier in their lives.

In keeping secrets, sex and love addicts act out their issues of control and power. Secrecy is a source of power for them. For one thing, they know something that others do not know. For another thing, knowing secrets about someone can give others power because that someone will fear the revelation of the secrets. Thus, at the same time that they give power, secrets also make people vulnerable and powerless. If others know your secrets, they can manipulate you. Even if no one knows your secrets, the possibility that someone might find out places you in the position of a potential victim. Typically, secrets beget secrets. And as addiction progresses addicts tend to have more secrets to hide and more need for secrecy to protect themselves from manipulation and even to fool themselves that they are appearing to be in control when they are in reality out of control.

A seventeen year old who was severely neglected and abused had been given hallucinogenic drugs as payment for his participation in pornographic movies. He was aware that these experiences were profoundly damaging to him, but he felt a need to hold onto his sexual addiction despite its potential for harm. And he could reveal the identity of the barber in an avant-garde section of town who had been sexually active with him. Even when we spoke about the need to protect other young people who might be abused by this man, the adolescent was not able to overcome his need to keep the secret. He was loyal to the "trauma bond" between himself and his abuser; he was keeping a sexual "stash," in other words, a reserve supply, the same way a drug addict will hide a small amount of drugs for an emergency; and he was maintaining a position of power with me as well as with his mother, who was pressuring him to "tell the truth" about this person whom she suspected was an abuser.

Another seventeen-year-old sex and love addict kept the secret of her love addiction to another patient on our unit until a relapse with drugs brought her back into inpatient care. She had lost her mother when her mother's boyfriend shot the mother after losing a custody battle over their son. She tried to be a "good girl" for her aunt who took her in, but she could not quell her intense desire to attach herself to a boy. Her hypersexuality made her aunt furious. The adolescent was so out of control that she could not hide the sexual escapades she had while her aunt was out of the house. Still, while she was in residential treatment, she appeared uninterested in the male patients and seemed to keep her distance from them. Actually, she was really sneaky and secretive and carried on an active romance with another patient behind the backs of staff. She could not tolerate the sense of worthlessness that she felt without a boyfriend; she felt powerful in being so accomplished at keeping this secret; and she had an intense need to bond with another human being because she had lost her parents so suddenly. Secrecy seemed necessary for her, but it also kept her from getting the help that she really needed.

Personality Change/Dissociation

The last teenager described above fits the "Dr. Jekyll/Mr. Hyde" split personality that so many addicts seem to have. When families are questioned about the addicts that they care about, the most common response they give is a reference to the two-sidedness of the addicts' personalities. Some family members go so far as to say that their loved one has "two personalities." Others simply say that he or she can be "so nice" sometimes and "horrible" other times. In either case, outsiders do not understand what goes on in the mind of the addicted person.

In his description of the "addiction cycle," Patrick Carnes (1983) suggested that negative core beliefs such as "I am a worthless person" lead to cognitive distortions in the addict—for example, "Since I am worthless, I cannot get the love that I need." This "stinking thinking" (as it is called in AA) leads to a preoccupation with sex and love. This phase of preoccupation triggers the active cycle of the addiction. An acting-out ritual, such as cruising for a sex partner, follows the fantasy stage. Then comes the actual-acting out behavior. This is followed by feelings of despair that require continued self-medication through more addictive acting out. The addiction cycle—illustrated in Figure 2—leads to unmanageability in one's life and confirms the negative core beliefs. On top of this addiction cycle is a layer of childhood trauma—the source of the damaged core beliefs of the addict. See Figure 3.

Figure 2
The Addiction Cycle

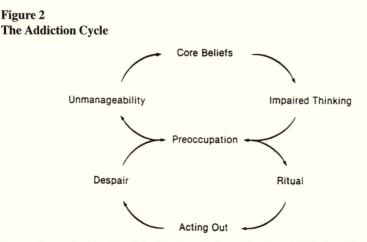

Source: Carnes, Patrick, *Out of the Shadows: Understanding Sexual Addiction* (Minneapolis, MN: CompCare Publications, 1983), p. 15, "The Addictive System." Reprinted with permission.

Figure 3
Childhood Trauma and the Addiction Cycle

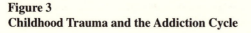

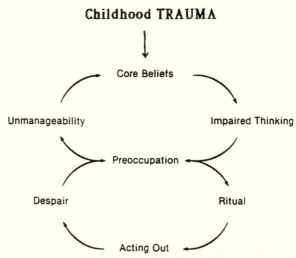

Source: Carnes, Patrick, *Out of the Shadows: Understanding Sexual Addiction* (Minneapolis, MN: CompCare Publications, 1983), p. 15, "The Addictive System." Reprinted with permission.

All of us have the capacity to dissociate. Dissociating is the opposite of associating. So, associating is making connections; dissociation is breaking connections. When the mind dissociates, it splits itself in two. It disconnects. In this disconnected stage, the mind is capable of operating in two areas at the same time. A simple example would be driving to work and thinking about something else at the same time. Because driving has become a routine, repetitive task that does not require higher-level cognitions, we can drive safely while another part of our mind is preoccupied with something unrelated to driving, such as the work that lies ahead when we get there. Sometimes, we can be so engrossed in our thoughts that we do not function so well at our driving and may have a "close call" or even an accident. Sex addicts often get into traffic accidents because they are so focused on looking at a sexy body that they lose their concentration on the road. At other times—hopefully before an accident— we may reconnect with the demands of driving and "snap back" into reality. The process involves switching back and forth between our integrated consciousness and our divided mind.

Dissociation is not only a useful capacity to have while driving, but it can be an essential, life-saving defense mechanism in response to overwhelming trauma. This is what happens when children, who do not have sophisticated defenses to begin with, are placed in dangerous situations that are frightening, harmful, and traumatic. These children learn how to dissociate. For example, when an abusive parent beats a child, the child will learn to tolerate the pain by dissociating or disconnecting from his or her body. The child does not feel the physical pain because he or she has split inside and is no longer connected. Likewise, when a parent becomes enraged over a child's crying (and threatens to "give him or her something to cry about"), the child learns to cut off, to "stuff," to dissociate from the hurt and sadness.

Adolescents in inpatient treatment for chemical dependency tend to come from homes where one or more parent is chemically dependent (Griffin-Shelley, Sandler, and Lees, 1990). The sex and love addicted teenagers described in this book are a subset of this group. Being raised in a family where there is a major illness like chemical dependency is traumatic. The trauma may come from overt violence, abandonment, or sexual or emotional abuse. Or the pain may be more covert, less obvious, but just as traumatic through having to pretend that things are all right when they are not, having to become parentified and a caretaker to the non-chemically dependent spouse, or being physically, socially, spiritually, and emotionally neglected. In either case, the child needs to cope with the pain and trauma of his or her dysfunctional family, and an obvious way is through dissociation.

In a shame-filled, traumatized, and traumatizing family, the children learn to put on a public face and to hide their real feelings and pain. The family cannot tolerate any more pain. The parents are already in too much pain themselves to be able to help their children with their pain. Consequently, the children learn to have a public self and a private self. This inner split is the foundation for the "Dr. Jekyll/Mr. Hyde" personality of the addict that comes to fruition in adolescence. The outer self is the "con" of the addicted person. In other words, this is the image the addicted person cultivates for presentation to the outside world so that he or she will be accepted and allowed to continue to function independently. The inner self is the "addict" part of the person. The addict's job is to cope with pain. Since this part has not had good models for coping with pain and may have had parents who were dissociative, the adolescent's "addict" is out for the "quick fix." The addict part needs to stop the hurt, to squelch the pain, to distract the person from his or her past, and to transform suffering into excitement. The quickest way to accomplish this goal is through addictive acting out. Sex and romance offer great promise for addictive highs.

An example of the personality change or dissociative process in an adolescent sex and love addict can be seen in the two sides of a fifteen year old who was initially referred to us for chemical dependency treatment. This young man was handsome, athletic, and intelligent. He came from a successful upper-middle-class family and had "everything going for him." He kept his drug dependency fairly well hidden until he was hospitalized after a rage-filled attack on his older brother that required police intervention. His mother described him as a "wonderful, caring, sensitive boy" who could also suddenly switch into a "gorilla." In this aggressive personality, he was violent, verbally abusive, threatening, and capable of intense rage that often led to property damage or even physical harm to others. His alternate personality was popular among peers and adults, polite and cooperative, thoughtful and kind—almost like an ideal Boy Scout. A parent could not hope for a better teenager, until the monster side showed up to terrorize everyone in his home.

The young man kept his sex and love addiction much better hidden than his drug problem. He acted out while in the hospital by developing relationships with female peers against the rules and advice of staff. He was hypersexual at home, including regular intercourse with his fourteen-year-old girlfriend, masturbation, and use of pornography. When a condom accidently fell out of his pocket at his girlfriend's home in front of her father, he was able to "play it off" and convinced her parents that there was nothing sexual going on between the two young people. This was far from the truth; they had sexual contact every day. His father had been hypersexual and was involved with transvestitism, bestiality, and affairs outside the marriage. He was also an executive, who provided his son with a model of dissociative behavior in his maintenance of a double life. The boy's mother, in a typically codependent way, tried to over compensate for her angry, abusive husband and became overprotective and solicitous of this middle child. He learned to manipulate both parents to get what he wanted from them; he got money from his father and encouragement and "pep talks" from his mother. He became a "con man," drug addict, and sex addict in his mid-teens.

Similarly, another mother referred her sixteen-year-old daughter to us for treatment because the girl had a "split personality." This young person could be a warm, vivacious, responsible, hardworking student and daughter who would have dinner ready when her mother came home and who did well in school. Suddenly, she would transform into a "bitch" who was impossible to live with and wanted to do whatever she wanted whenever she wanted. She was verbally abusive, defiant, challenging, hostile, and threatening for no apparent reason. She had a drug dependency as well as a male dependency. She found it easier to live without drugs for four weeks than to live without her boyfriend. She was obsessed with contacting him and could not wait to move up the levels of the privilege system to the point where she would earn a "social call." In fact, she snuck phone calls to him—but did not count on her mother "ratting" to the staff. Her mother came to us because she wondered about the appropriateness of the phone calls; she inquired whether her daughter was allowed to be contacting someone with whom she had done drugs. We confronted the daughter, and she declared war on the staff and her mother over whether she could have contact with her boyfriend other than through the mail (which was "legal"). Consequently, we were able to experience the two sides of this young woman's personality. Before this, we had only heard about it from her mother.

Dissociation and splitting are important defensive strategies for abuse victims and are found in addicted clients more commonly than was thought a short time ago. Addicts have always dissociated, but clinicians have not applied this schema to the addicted population until fairly recently. Again, the personality changes of adolescent sex and love addicts are more extreme than the more normal shifts in ego states and identity that is a healthy part of normal adolescent self-discovery, identity formation, and development. For the addicted person, the process of hiding his or her inner self as a protective measure began in childhood and was a functional and possibly life-saving mechanism for coping. As the young people move away from their family during adolescence, however, they should be more and more able to be "real," authentic, and open with others as a means of developing their own support system independent of the family system. Unfortunately, traumatized children are not able to do this, because their damage is interpersonal. They do not trust people to care for them, to meet their needs, or to love them unconditionally. They have found other objects like sex, love, money, drugs, exercise, or achievement that offer a more predictable "fix." They have hidden their discovery behind the cloak of a "Dr. Jekyll/Mr. Hyde" personality that employs dissociation as a primary defensive, self-protective strategy.

So, the long version of the definition of a sex and love addict is indeed long. To summarize: a sex and love addict is a person who uses sex and/or love to "get high," has exhibited increasing tolerance, has become physically and/or psychologically dependent, has cravings and withdrawal symptoms (especially in a period of abstinence), obsesses, has compulsive and out-of-control behaviors, is secretive about these thoughts and behaviors, and shows a personality change or dissociative phenomena. While a sex and love addict does not have to present all of these criteria, the more criteria that are present and the more severe the symptomatology, the more severe the sex and love addiction. To

repeat the short version of this definition: a sex and love addict has a pathological relationship to sexual and/or love relationships that is dangerous to himself
or herself and/or others. Teenagers can fit this definition even though the length
of their addiction may not approach that of an adult. When sex and love are
taken to addictive extremes, they can be dangerous to an adolescent's health,
well-being, and life itself.

3

Case Examples

Since I myself had found it difficult to believe that adolescents could be chemically dependent—let alone sex and love addicted—until I had met some drug and alcohol addicted teenagers, I decided the best way to convince others that sex and love addicted adolescents do exist would be to tell the stories of some of these adolescents with whom I have had the privilege to work. I have taken precautions to disguise the identity of these young people in order to protect their anonymity. Some of the factual details have been changed or rearranged, though the stories remain true accounts of the adolescents' addictive experiences. I have chosen the most obvious cases in order to illustrate in more detail the dimensions of the addiction outlined in Chapter 2.

THE BOYS NEXT DOOR

Case 1: Tom

Tom was as handsome as they come—blond, muscular, tan—and had a winning smile when I first met him just before his eighteenth birthday. He was charming and obviously enjoyed the attention of many girls, who reacted as soon as they noticed him. He seemed intelligent, well mannered, and a cinch to be a football player or a surfer. He grew up in a small community near the Atlantic Ocean, quiet in the winter and rocking in the summer. He appeared to have the world at his command and to feel cool and calm at the helm. I could easily picture him as the "big man on campus." He dressed in a preppy style and had an easygoing demeanor.

There was a dark side, however, to this mild-mannered Adonis. He had been arrested more than a dozen times for breaking and entering. He had a drug problem that included alcohol, marijuana, PCP, "various pills," and "huffing" glue. He had not been to school for "two or three years" because he "hated it." He was depressed, suicidal, and self-mutilative; for example, he carved "Fuck You" in his arm. He punched walls and was taken to court in restraints.

Interestingly, Tom had only limited contact with any mental health treatment before I met him. At age eleven, he gone for treatment for about six months; and two years before, he had seen a mental health professional twice. He reported that he had moved "ten to fifteen times," or almost once a year. As a child he had asthma. He identified himself as a Christian. He was forced to have sexual contact with his sister at age five and was, then, sexually active with girls his age at five and six. At age ten, he was sexually molested by a teacher. He could not identify any emotional or addictive problems in his parents, who were separated; but he himself was addicted to chemicals, sex, and money. He lived with his mother and was protective of her.

Tom's initial treatment was difficult because he did not trust anyone—especially adults. He was superficial, cooperative, and kept a low profile. He was secretive and able to control his rage and despair by presenting a public personality that was pleasant and impenetrable. Gradually, we were able to get him to open up. His response to a sexual addiction inventory was almost overwhelming.

He regarded sex to be love and was obsessed with sex. He saw himself as having special needs and at times would act out the role of "hurt little boy" in order to seduce women. He needed to be sexual in order to feel good about himself. He felt compelled to follow through once he had "hooked" someone with his flirtatious rituals. He had periods of denial and tried to control himself by suppressing his sexual activities and urges. He acknowledged compulsive masturbation, using pornography, and making sexually explicit videos and photographs. He participated in phone sex, multiple relationships, and one-night stands. He had anonymous sex, group sex, and cruised parks, baths, and beaches for partners. He was exhibitionistic and voyeuristic. He talked inappropriately and intrusively about sex. He found that receiving physical harm enhanced his enjoyment of sexual activity.

Tom experienced a great relief sharing his secrets. His treatment began to improve when he was able to let down his guard about his hypersexuality. He had developed a facade of self-control that quickly crumbled into anger and rage when he was confronted for being "phony" and distant. Underneath his smooth outer shell, he was lonely, confused, and terrified. He had had some modest support after that abuse by his teacher was uncovered, but he essentially lived with his pain all alone. His acting-out behaviors were the only voice that he could put to the agony that his soul was in as he tried to cope with overwhelming abuse and neglect. He blamed himself and felt terribly ashamed of his sexual acting out and his inability ever to get really close to anyone.

Case 2: Bill

Bill was another strikingly handsome, reasonably intelligent, sensitive young man whom any mother would want as a date for her daughter. He was happy, engaging, and seemed sophisticated beyond his sixteen years. He was somewhat slow in school, a bit overweight, and charmingly insecure. He was lovable and made you want to cuddle him, much like a teddy bear. He had had a history of bronchitis as a child and seemed like a boy who needed caring for, but also one who could be caring and warm in return.

He came into treatment depressed, suicidal, and drug and alcohol dependent. He had gained twenty pounds recently, had trouble sleeping, was unable to concentrate, and was preoccupied with his girlfriend. He had stolen some marijuana from his mother and had tried to overdose on alcohol the day before his admission to the hospital. He had been hospitalized in a general hospital before he was transferred to our private psychiatric facility.

Bill reported that both of his parents and his maternal grandmother suffered from alcoholism. His parents were divorced, and his mother had remarried three years before I met him. His mother had been treated for chemical dependency in the adult dual-diagnosis unit of the same hospital. Bill had a conflictual relationship with his stepfather and an overly close relationship with his mother. He smoked pot daily and frequently drank. His brother reportedly had a drug and alcohol problem as well.

In addition to his depression, anxiety, and substance abuse disorders, Bill was love addicted. He had an overly dependent, obsessive relationship with his girlfriend, who had "used" and rejected him. He could not tolerate the separation from her and was enraged with himself and her. He wanted to hurt someone to get back at the pain that he found himself in, and thought of hurting himself and his girlfriend. He felt "out of control" and could not predict what he would actually do.

Unfortunately, his treatment experience was not a positive one. He felt angry and wanted to run after he got over the initial panic and dysphoria that had pushed him into the medical hospital. He became more rigid, defensive, and hostile as we sought to get him to open up and share himself with us. He minimized and denied the potential he possessed for harming to himself and/or his girlfriend. He rationalized his impulsiveness and dependency. And he was supported in his distorted view of himself by his mother, who was overly protective and smothering. They seemed to have a symbiotic relationship in which she could not tolerate seeing him in any pain or struggle. She could not set appropriate limits with him and could not see his manipulations and avoidance behaviors. She colluded with him against professional input and agreed to take him out of treatment before his real issues could be addressed.

ABUSED BOYS

Case 3: Al

Al was tall, lanky, and had a haunting look in his eyes. He was friendly in a distant and aloof manner. He smiled but seemed anxious and uncomfortable with the intimacy of our individual therapy. He had a good sense of humor, though he had been exposed to a great deal of living in his first sixteen years. At the time that he came into treatment, he was depressed, suicidal, and drug addicted. He acknowledged being sexually abused by a female babysitter. His story was a long and painful one that took time to unravel.

Al came to the hospital in an ambulance, in four-point restraints. He had a history of throwing things when he was angry. Four years before, he had set three fires. He had attempted suicide five times—three times by jumping from a high place. He shattered his elbow when he jumped from a second-story window. He reported that both of his parents suffered from depression and chemical dependency. He was a "blue baby" at birth. His parents divorced; and his father, who allegedly had physically abused his mother, kidnapped him for a year. He had been in therapy "since first grade." He had once undergone day treatment for six months and had been involuntarily hospitalized twice in the two years prior to our encounter.

Obviously, trust was a major issue for Al. While he was superficially engaging, he was used to keeping his private life private. He used aggressive and passive defenses that made it possible for him to control the level of intimacy he experienced, especially with adults. He seemed in great pain and sorrow most of the time, but he had a sense of humor and a laugh that expressed both hope and longing.

He began to open up when the anniversary of his girlfriend's suicide drew near. He needed support to allow himself to grieve without self-blame and guilt. As he shared his pain, he also began to tell us about being actively involved in child pornography. He was first introduced to pornographic moviemaking by his mother's friend who was caring for him at the time. At this very young age, about six or seven, he was rewarded with attention, money, and small gifts for his participation in movies and pictures. Later, he was given drugs in exchange for his performance in the movie and photography sessions. His mother discovered these activities when she recognized his picture in a pornographic magazine. Al told of his misfortunate adventures with an overwhelming feeling of pain and shame. His desire to die was often triggered by memories of these horrible and degrading experiences of sexual abuse and exploitation. He could not live with himself for having been an active participant in this ugly business. Indeed, he became suicidal while telling us about his role in child pornography.

After he had opened up about his past sexual activities, he began to say more about his current state of sexual obsession. He found himself drawn to pornography and compulsive masturbation. He was sexually hyperactive with his girlfriends. When his mother questioned him about his need to see a certain suspicious barber and about his frequent visits to this barber's shop, Al revealed an ongoing engagement in prostitution. The barber in question would pay cash or drugs in exchange for oral sex, and Al was a regular customer. He tried to play this off as simply being a necessary behavior in order to get drug money, but he clearly was addicted to the sex as well as the drugs. When I tried to get him to tell me the identity of the man who was abusing him so that I could report the abuse to the authorities, Al acted like a drug addict who is trying desperately to protect his "stash." He needed the availability of that sexual fix in order to feel all right, even though rationally he knew that other teenagers were also probably being abused by this person.

Case 4: Jim

Jim came into treatment with a similar history of childhood trauma and adolescent acting out. His early life was chaotic. In fact, we were hard put to get a clear picture of it, especially at first. His parents were drug and alcohol dependent; they neglected and abused him to the point where he was placed in foster care. He reported that he was sexually abused by both male and female babysitters when his mother would leave him with them at around the ages of three and four. When he was in foster care, he had numerous placements, allegedly due to his hyperactivity and aggression. He said he was physically and sexually abused by his foster parents as well. He was adopted at age ten by a Protestant minister who may have had some unrealistic ideas about Jim's ability to adapt to a "normal family."

When Jim was referred for treatment, he was depressed, suicidal, drug addicted, and out of control. He punched walls and cursed teachers. He ran away from home. He threatened to hurt himself and his family. He stole money from home and had been caught shoplifting. He was hyperactive and suffered an attention deficit disorder (ADD). He was in special education classes because he could not cope with attending regular high school. His self-esteem was terribly low. He was abusing alcohol, marijuana, and cocaine. He had been in residential treatment two years before, and in brief outpatient therapy, but was noncompliant. He had had trials of Lithium and Ritalin without apparent benefit. His adoptive parents were at their wits' end; he had created numerous problems for them in their family, in their church, in his school, and in the community. They were desperate for help. He was angry and ashamed of his lack of self-control. His adoptive father was a recovering alcoholic who had some ideas about how to stay sober from chemicals. It was obvious to him that his son had a drug problem at the very least, but he was frustrated by his inability to "get through to Jim" at least around the issue of not using drugs.

Initially, Jim was quiet, insecure, withdrawn, and made an effort to please adults in order not to be punished. He lacked trust, sincerity, and impulse control. His sex and love addiction was well hidden. He was discovered passing notes to girls, and one of these notes went like this:

Yo whats up? Ha I like you *a lot* and you got a good ass and you make me feel special! I've been thinking about you all the time. Well here is my home address . . . call please or I will call you and I would like your address and phone number to ok. I would have like *sex* with but I want to take care of something else first before I get into that ok. Well see ya tomorrow.

We began to explore the possibility that he was sex addicted.

He indicated that he was obsessed with sex; in his own words, "I have massive thoughts about sex and I would have dreams about it." He felt that he had a desperate and destructive need for sex that was overwhelming and shaming to him. He spent most of his time centered around thinking, pursuing, and acting sexual. He equated sex with love and thought that he needed to be sexual to feel good about himself. He got tense and uptight when he could not act out sexually. He was heavily involved with pornography—including magazines, videotapes, adult bookstores, strip joints and peep shows—and with sexualizing people on television, in malls, in catalogues, or in advertisements. He engaged in telephone sex, exhibitionism, voyeurism, multiple partners, one-night-stands, and touching people inappropriately. He talked explicitly about sex, used sexualized humor, and behaved seductively when he thought that he could get away with it. His sexual addiction was a well-kept secret, however, and it only came to light in our treatment environment where we could observe him closely and be sensitive to issues of sex and love addiction. With our support he was able to start getting honest with himself and others about this important set of behaviors that was so wildly out of control and clearly related to the severe abuse experienced in his childhood.

In a letter to his father, Jim wrote,

Well, I have to tell you the things I haven't told you yet so here they are. The first is my sex and love addiction. I've been having some problems with that certain topic and its part of my addictions. I also have to tell you about my gambling and Satanism. Well, I've had alot of problems with gambling. I would make money and loose money and with Satanism I've learned somethings from school and I know a few things about that and that's how I got into it. I also have to tell about my relationships. Most of my relationships were very dirty. I basically had sex with them. I have to tell you about my stash of needles I had when we move to . . . when I first came to live with you. I use to steal needles from the stores and used them when I shot up with them. I have to tell you the rest of my addiction, I haven't told you about everything like my sex addiction. I never told you before. I haven't told you about taking too many lithium pills, when I came home high and you weren't home I took too many pills and I threw it up. I have to tell you that I was molested by my babysitter when I was 3 years old, when I was 3 my mom left me with a male babysitter and he molested me. I have to tell you about my lying to you, for when I told you I would go to my sister's, I wouldn't be there. I would be out getting high. I have to tell you about my girlfriend. Well, I would have sex and now she is 6 month pregnant. I haven't told you that I care and love you, I never thought of saying this to but it's true. I do care and love you. I have not told you about the pot plants, well we planted pot plants in 3 different places in the woods, behind the fire house, and in the cornfields. I also have to tell you that I used to sell my body. I sold my body to other women for my drugs. That's all I have to tell you. Love Jim.

Jim covered a lot of territory in his brief, articulate, and pain-filled letter—from prostitution to pregnancy, from intravenous drug use to gambling, from sex addiction to sexual abuse. His willingness to begin the journey of recovery with the essential step of honesty indicates hope for his troubled path. He identified compulsivity with sex, drugs, and money. He wanted to hurt himself and obviously hurt ones whom he loved. His spirit has survived, but the damage is immense and the road to health slow and tedious. He went to long-term treatment after two months of intensive psychiatric care.

THE HOOKERS

Case 5: Bonnie

At fifteen, Bonnie already had a wild record. She was the daughter of a city employee. Her parents were divorced and both remarried. She had participated sporadically in outpatient counseling prior to her referral for inpatient care. She was depressed, angry, explosive, and violent. She fought with her teachers at Catholic school, ran away often, abused a variety of drugs, and was caught shoplifting. According to Bonnie, both of her parent abused her physically. She started drinking at age nine, used LSD "over a hundred times," smoked marijuana daily, and tried PCP and amphetamines. She was smart, funny, good looking, and a "good con."

After a month in our hospital, she was referred to long-term residential care. She lasted there less than a month and returned to our doorstep shortly thereafter. She was sent to another long-term program all the way across the state and ran from there after a month. She returned to us for a third time via a court order, with charges of prostitution facing her.

While in treatment, Bonnie did some written work that described her sex and love addiction. In response to an assignment addressing her sexual preoccupation and sexualized interactions with peers, she wrote,

For me concentrating on sexual things and sexual joking takes the focus off of my treatment and back on the streets. Talking about sexual things gives me a reason to focus on one of my dependencies and one of my dependencies is sex and by focusing on sexual things, e.g., a guy tells me something good about my body then that builds my self esteem to where I can get good feelings off of it. I use any type of sexual behavior as a drug.

Her painful story continues:

I always went out with guys who drank or did drugs. They were always at least three or four years older. None of them went to my school, they always lived away from my town. I never introduced them to any of my friends. I really never had them "over" and only one of them met my dad. They mostly only wanted me for one thing. If I gave into all the people I went out with. Well lets say I couldn't count that high. I only had one long term relationship (nine months). Most others lasted two to six weeks and they were all "bad guys" not "nice guys." I wasn't interested in them.

About her relationships, Bonnie went on to say,

My relationships interfered in every aspect of my life. I had no life. Of course not in the beginning. Everything seems ok. But as time went by, he became very controlling. I wasn't allowed to have any friends, no phone calls and I had to wait at home for him. Believe it or not, I didn't really mind It was just that I wanted someone to go places with, to fill the time. I depended on him for everything. My life revolved around him. I was skipping school, neglecting my family, and my alcoholism was progressing. I knew he was an ass hole, but what would I do with all my time? I have no friends, no one else could love me. My drinking with him is a direct result of my being here. I knew our relationship was sick, so I drank and drank just to deal with being with him. And then not being with him. I felt like shit. He controlled my mind and my body. I had no me.

She concluded,

I was manipulated, controlled and although I did everything he said he still wanted more. I hated him. I hated myself. But I didn't want to be alone. He would tell me "if you don't have sex with me you're having sex with someone else." And we were having sex seven days a week sometimes two or three times a day. I know he was wrong and I am not any of the things he said. He hit me well actually choked me and pushed me down a flight of steps but guess what!? I blamed myself. And I said he pushed me down the steps because he was on drugs I gave him. When he broke up with me, I still ran to him.

Obviously, Bonnie's tolerance of abuse was extremely high due to her intense dependency needs. She could not attach to a "nice guy" and sought out those interactions that made her feel "high" like a drug. She progressed rapidly in her sex and love addiction to the point where prostitution was not only possible, but a compulsion. She was completely out of control and in extreme danger. Her pain was intense, but she could not trust adults to help her or to support her own efforts at healing. She could articulate the hurt clearly in writing; but learning to live with pain, to suffer through it, and to emerge a survivor on the other side was a lesson she was not yet open to because of her immense childhood trauma.

Case 6: Sue

Sue was a similarly angry, depressed, seductive, highly sexualized sixteen year old who came from a slightly more middle class and sophisticated environment. She too had brains, physical attractiveness, and charm. She could put on a convincing show of competence and control until you got to know her better. She ran away from home, verbally abused her mother, lied, skipped school, and fought with peers in school. She was a chronic underachiever who had low self-esteem and often felt bored, anhedonic, and without meaning or direction in her life. She abused alcohol and marijuana.

Her father was a recovering alcoholic with about a year and a half of sobriety. She had been in inpatient care the previous year and had only sporadically attended any outpatient aftercare. She exhibited a strong male dependency within minutes of coming onto the inpatient unit and was quickly told that she needed to focus on herself, not on finding a boyfriend. We encouraged her not to place an emphasis on her external appearance, but instead to try to discover her inner beauty. She rebelled and fought the rules and restrictions with typical narcissistic, addictive fury. She was arrogant, acted entitled to special treatment, and was demanding of the staff—much like "Her Majesty the Baby," as the Twelve Step saying goes. She was enraged with limitations and had poor boundaries with staff, peers, and her family.

For an educated, urbane teenager, Sue seemed to be heading in the worst possible direction. She had become entangled with the law because she was in a stolen car—a situation that helped to push her into treatment. She had chaotic family relationships and went from hating her mother, to hating her father, back to hating her mother again. Much of her behavior was overly dramatic histrionics designed to get her parents' attention. She identified with fourteen of Robin Norwood's fifteen characteristics of relationship addictions (*Women Who Love Too Much*, 1985, pp. 10–11). She saw herself as having come from a dysfunctional home where her needs were not met. She got little nurturing and sought to get it by caring for others—especially men whom she saw as needy. She longed for love from men who were not able to be loving, much like her parents who were not available to her. She feared abandonment. She would go to any lengths "for her man." She willingly waited for love since she was not used to receiving it and felt overly responsible and guilty in relationships. She thought she did not deserve to be happy and must earn this privilege. She was insecure and had low self-esteem that drove her need to control men. She fantasized a lot about what could be, rather than what was. She was drawn to chaos, dependency, pain, and addictions. She was depressed and addicted to men.

Her rage and antisocial behaviors fueled her addiction and led to prostitution. Sue rationalized her behavior at times as being necessary to "keep her in drugs," but really she was hooked on the traumatic reenactment of her lack of worth and importance to her parents. Her selfish, self-centered, tough image covered great pain and longing for love. She had no sense of her innate beauty, giftedness, and special value as a person. Money made her feel worthwhile; men made her feel worthwhile; sex made her feel worthwhile.

Case 7: Carol

Carol had a sad story that reached the heart of everyone who heard it. She had a winning smile and a kind way about her that endeared her to others. She was stocky, with brownish hair and blue eyes. She had a soulful look that made you wonder what those deep eyes had seen in her fifteen years. She acted older than her years and had trouble relating to her peers—especially the younger ones. She could be a caretaker, but she could not be an equal. She seemed to soak up the attention of adults, although she was never demanding or intrusive. Her presence seemed to draw the eye of whatever staff members were on duty. They usually found time to give her some special attention.

Carol grew up with drug and alcohol addicted parents. She often lived with her grandmother, although the grandmother and Carol's mother shared apartments from time to time. Carol had sporadic contact with her father and often turned to him when things were not going well with her mother. Essentially, though, Carol raised herself and was quite involved with raising her younger sister. And Carol lived on the streets during times when she ran away from home. She had many places to stay and was not above living in an abandoned house if she had worn out her welcome elsewhere. She minimized the profound neglect that she had grown to think was normal. Her parents were verbally abusive and she tended to hook up with men who treated her similarly.

Her first hospitalization came when she was thirteen. Nine months after discharge, she was back in the hospital again. At this point, her treatment was focused on her drug and alcohol abuse. She managed to stay clean for about five months, but relapsed over the summer and was admitted to the hospital for a third time just before Thanksgiving. At that time, she was depressed, anxious, confused, suicidal, and chemically dependent. She was abusing alcohol, marijuana, "crack," and powdered cocaine. She was truant from school and refused to go back. She ran away from home and was gone for weeks at a time. She had few friends other than her "street buddies" and drug contacts. She was bored, anhedonic, sarcastic, pessimistic, and hopeless. She had dramatic mood swings, weight gain, loss of concentration, preoccupation, and feelings of guilt and worthlessness. Her relationship dependency had progressed to prostitution and she had bench warrants out for her arrest.

Carol felt as if there was nowhere to turn. She had a profound sense of shame, especially around her sexual acting out. She had been in a series of abusive relationships prior to engaging in prostitution. This now felt like the "end of the line" for her. She became extremely withdrawn, isolated, and obsessed about her guilt and embarrassment. Finally, she shared with us the fact that her mother was also engaged in prostitution. Carol saw herself as following the same path despite efforts to detour. Her mother visited often, but Carol and her mother managed artfully to avoid all efforts to engage her mother in family therapy. Carol was preoccupied with helping her mother recover from *her* addictions and seemed to feel that she could not get well if her mother was still sick.

When she was around her mother, Carol was a little child. She desperately needed to hold onto the fantasy that her mother was being there for her, since the reality of the situation was so painful. She defended her mother against what she perceived as being attacks on our part. She sacrificed her own needs to attend to the needs of her mother. She felt safe, nurtured, and cared for in our treatment environment, but she could not allow herself to separate enough from her mother to let herself enter a long-term treatment program. Acknowledging her own multiple addictions—sex, food, chemicals—would lead her to examine her mother's same behaviors. And acknowledging this reality touched too closely on the abandonment that she had been suffering so much, most of her life.

DON JUANS

Case 8: Bob

Bob was a "ladies' man" at age sixteen. He was preppy, came from money, belonged to a country club, and saw himself as a "Casanova." He was proud of his ability to attract the opposite sex and came across as sincere and caring. He was sophisticated and suave. He enjoyed being charming and engaging although superficial. He put all of his energy into his relationships and little else. He was comfortable in the fast, active social life of a well-off, suburban teenager. He had a car and money to go places. He had a lot of friends and places to go. He never was without a girlfriend and often had two or three waiting in the wings.

Behind this happy facade was a great deal of personal pain. Bob was adopted at birth. He had asthma. He suffered from a mild learning disability in the area of mathematics. He had been diagnosed with an attention deficit disorder (ADD) five years before, and in seventh grade a trial of Ritalin seemed to help, albeit briefly. Bob's parents worried about him and tended to be overly protective. At the time of his admittance to our hospital program, they were confused and overwhelmed with the extent of his problems.

As a tenth-grader, Bob was out of control. He stayed out late at night and ran away from home. He stole money from his parents. He had severe conflicts with authority figures, especially at school. His school performance had deteriorated greatly. He was truant and had been suspended from school three times. He reported difficulty sleeping, nightmares, poor concentration, weight loss, loss of appetite, anhedonia, lethargy, boredom, and mood swings. He was depressed, angry, and irritable. He was abusing alcohol, marijuana daily, and LSD. He experienced flashbacks from the LSD. He had tried cocaine once and was on the verge of "graduating" to this more potent drug. He had been in residential drug treatment two years before, and in outpatient treatment for four months prior to our program. His parents were becoming more and more angry and frustrated with his obvious lack of progress or change.

He fought our treatment tooth and nail. He was defensive, angry, passive/aggressive, withholding, and manipulative. Bob's psychological testing indicated that his IQ was in the low-average range and that he would regress under stress. His coping style was childlike and impulsive. He played the innocent victim with his parents and made them feel as if they were not taking care of him. With staff, he minimized rationalized, and denied his problems, and projected blame onto his parents. With his parents, he blamed staff. He tried to be superficially compliant and people pleasing and, when he was confronted about his avoidant behaviors, he wanted to run. When his drugs were taken away by virtue of his being in the hospital, his relationship dependency went into full bloom.

Quickly and secretly, Bob attached himself to an insecure female peer who needed attention as badly as he did. They became enmeshed and high on their forbidden love. Like Romeo and Juliet, they were star-crossed lovers who were being pulled apart by cruel and evil adults who had lost touch completely with love and romance. Bob was totally preoccupied with his flame and managed to avoid treatment issues completely. The more his relationship dependency was confronted, the more he felt compelled to continue despite adverse consequences. He saw his efforts to maintain their love affair against all odds as being heroic and romantic. So did she. Eventually, his love addiction pulled him out of treatment completely: his parents withdrew him against medical advice. They could no longer tolerate what he presented to them as being the program's inappropriate restrictions and consequences for "normal" adolescent relationships. He managed to "normalize" his behaviors in their eyes and distorted their perception of our concerns about his dual addiction.

Case 9: Carl

Carl's tall, lanky build, dark eyes and hair, and confident swagger made him a magnet to the female adolescents with whom he came in contact. He had lived overseas with his parents and moved rather frequently, so he had an air of sophistication that added to his charisma. He was intelligent, verbal, and talkative. He appeared at ease with both adults and peers. He made a "good impression" on the parents of his friends.

As an initial assignment in our treatment program, Carl wrote a brief life history. His story was frightening in terms of the anger and detachment that it showed.

The first time that I got high [on drugs] was when I lived in Georgia. I was 13 years old. I didn't like it and didn't use again for about half a year. After living in Georgia I moved overseas with my family. My dad is in the military and got a job over there. This is where my life took a dangerous turn. Overseas, they sell beer in machines on the street. This is where I developed my alcohol problem. After about a year I started drinking every day. Worse came to worse and I got involved in a sexual relationship with a girl. My drinking increased until finally I was told that I had to go to a rehab. I had to come back to the U.S. to go to one. The girl I talked about had to go on emergency leave to the U.S. because one of her relatives died. She would be gone for three weeks. During this three weeks I was to go to the U.S. to this rehab and never return. I did not want to do this. So, I ran away and did alot of bad stuff for three weeks until I got caught. The government caught me and said that I had to go to a rehab and I was never to return ever. So I was sent to rehab. I was in for six weeks and bullshitted the whole program. I even got high in the program and ran from it once. After I got out I moved to another state. I did not know anyone but I knew I wanted to drink. I met alot of people that got high so I started to hang out with them. I got high off and on overseas, but mostly drank. After a while, I met this girl and asked her out. For the next year I got high at least once a day sometimes up to three. On me and my girl's year anniversary, she broke up with me and said it was because of my addiction. She got a new boyfriend the next day. I told her I would stay straight if she would take me back. She said ok. So I went to NA [Narcotics Anonymous] meetings every night and after a month I asked her if she would take me back. She said no and started going out with my worst enemy. I lost my mind and threatened to kill them both. After a week, I left to live with my granddad. I tried to enroll in school down there but did not have enough credits to graduate. So I had to come back. I got back and went to a party and talked about having my friends kill my ex-girlfriend and her boyfriend. The next day I had a long talk with my parents and we decided that I needed help.

Carl was addicted to alcohol and to his girlfriend. He could not live life separated from either of them. His psychological testing shed some light on the dynamics of his personality: "The personality test data suggest that the patient is a very lonely individual who feels wounded, confused and anxious. His severe depression appears related to his feeling that everything is wrong and that his behavior is to blame for many difficulties that occur. He sees himself as very ineffectual, indecisive, and disobedient." Could this be the same suave character who appeared on the unit? The report when on to indicate problems with schoolwork and peers: "He feels quite different from his age peers and sees himself as shy and inferior. He tends to withdraw when he is laughed at, but will sometimes fight back and he feels that his anger frightens his friends. Intimidation of other people seems to be his way of protecting himself from them." His family problems were reported to include a "strict" mother and a distant father and "he does not see authority figures as being concerned about him or providing nurturance." Finally, "the patient appears to have a great deal of anger that he finds very difficult to control, and he sees himself as being too emotional. He worries about losing his temper and hurting someone but, on the other hand, he reported that he was planning to hurt someone else. His anger is aroused when he does not get what he wants, when other children 'bug me,' when he feels picked on, and when he is told what to do. While he sees anger as a major problem, he also reported that he thinks about sex too often." Sex and anger were a volatile combination for Carl, especially whenever he was abusing chemicals.

And Carl's denial concerning the strength of these destructive impulses makes this Don Juan a potentially dangerous character. His ambivalence was articulately presented in an essay he wrote for us on the book *Is It Love or Is It Addiction?* (Schaeffer, 1987).

Alot of what is in this book sounds like me, but alot of things do not sound like me. I was obsessive in my relationships. I wouldn't want my girlfriend to do anything without letting me know and having my permission. I felt rejected when my girlfriend would do stuff on her own will. This obsessive behavior is what I can relate to in the book. I can also relate to the feeling of total loneliness when they leave you. You feel like there is nothing worth living for. The things that I couldn't relate to were the very violent acts done by some people mentioned in this book. I did make violent threats but never took action on them. I probably would, but I'm in here. Another thing that I forgot that I could relate to, was that I always tried to change my girlfriend so that she would say and do exactly what I wanted her to do. It says in the book that this is very addictive behavior. I'm not sure if this book applies totally to me or not. I should read more on this subject. I'd say three-fourths of this book is me.

That is a scary thought for a seventeen year old. Carl's ability to disconnect from his own violence and anger are typical for sex and love addicts. His inability to see himself as others see him is also commonplace for addicted people. Sex and love addicted teens dissociate or disconnect from their feelings, so they are not able to be realistic or rational about potential danger. They use sex and relationships as drugs that fill their emptiness, occupy their boredom, and soothe their pain. People are objectified and useful only in terms of their ability to fix the sex and love addict. Carl's rage at the abandonment by his girlfriend is connected with a deeper anger at abandonment by his primary caretakers. His and their need to avoid this deeper level of pain makes this a highly explosive and unpredictable situation.

Case 10: Sam

Athletic, attractive, intellectually gifted—Sam "had it all." He grew up with both privilege and abuse, however. He came from an upper-middle-class family; but his abusive, alcoholic father destroyed the marriage and divided his family in two. Sam was a "special" child to his mother. He listened to her, comforted her, and cared about her when her husband and other two sons could not be there for her. She rewarded his loyalty and support by never saying no to his demands. When she did try to set limits with him occasionally, he became "like his father," that is, violent, destructive of property, and out of control.

Sam's explosive temper had landed him in four psychiatric hospitals by the time he was sixteen. He never attended aftercare for more than a few weeks. He did not see himself as having any problems. His parents had problems—but he did not. He felt victimized by them and justified in his thinking. He had been hurt, rejected, and harshly criticized by his father and had been smothered, pulled too close, and overly depended on by his mother. Sam was furious that he had lost his childhood and himself in this process. Unfortunately, he was not aware of this dynamic and had an intense need to blame others and avoid any responsibility for his out-of-control and self-destructive behaviors.

He abused alcohol, smoked marijuana frequently, and snorted cocaine. Despite his substance abuse, Sam managed to get average grades (although his teachers knew that he was underachieving), and he played on the high school baseball team. He had lots of friends—especially girlfriends. His chemical and sexual dependencies were well hidden behind an All American facade that had most of his peers and the adults in his life completely fooled. He only showed his addict side to a select group of chemically abusing peers and to girls whom he was "in love with." He had learned early on that adults would use you for their own needs if you let them. He saw adults as people to be placated and manipulated so that you could get your needs met elsewhere.

When Sam was confronted with hospitalization and needed some sort of problem to account for the rages that required police intervention, he chose to focus on his substance abuse. He would give up drugs and everything would be normal. However, in the process of treatment, he seemed extremely superficial, avoidant, and bent on running away from any of his underlying issues. He engaged in power struggles with staff that were quite intellectualized and devoid of feelings. Behind our backs, he was actively flirting, fantasizing, and "talking dirty" with his female peers. When confronted with his inappropriate sexual preoccupation and behavior, he was hyperreactive and defensive. He quickly regressed into narcissistic, grandiose, and unrealistic attitudes to cover his feelings of fear and vulnerability. He threatened his peers with physical harm if they told staff about his intriguing and sexualizing. Slowly—and especially after he left—the extent of his sexual acting out became clear. Unable to use drugs to cope with his pain, Sam used sex to numb his hurt, to control his anger, and to disconnect him from his childhood abuse. His peers only began to open up about his intimidation and sexual obsession when they felt that he would not be able to retaliate. They waited until he was no longer on the scene. Then they shared with us his constant bragging about his sexual activity and prowess. He told them that he and his girlfriend where having sex at least once a day and often more. His sexual appetite seemed insatiable and a bit frightening.

Later, through an accidental slip of the tongue, the girlfriend's father got a hint that the two young people were having sex. When he confronted Sam, the teenager was glibly able to lie his way out of the embarrassing jam he found himself in, and even placated the girl's father to the point that he was again a welcome guest in their house. His girlfriend, of course, colluded with him to protect her image of innocence and purity with her parents. How could such a handsome couple be involved in such sordid activities? From his own family's efforts to hide his father's abuse and alcoholism, Sam had learned well how to cover things up.

Case 11: George

George was referred to us by family court. He was an unemployed, African American seventeen year old who had dropped out of school a year before, stole money from his mother, and tested positive for cocaine. Unlike his sisters who were all in college, George was the family failure and, as such, carried a great deal of shame and terribly low self-esteem. He had refused to get help until forced to by the legal system. He lived "on the streets" and "loved the ladies."

During his treatment, he was sullen with staff and flirtatious with female peers. He was angry, depressed, and felt imprisoned. Sex and romance were his drugs. He was hostile, avoidant, and explosive when he felt cornered. He held tightly to his "macho" image and to his ability to attract females. He engaged in multiple relationships and was unable to follow our expectation that he focus on himself, not on love or lust. Underneath his tough facade, it was obvious that he felt insecure, needy, anxious, and inadequate, but he was totally unable to acknowledge any of these feelings. He had a great deal of difficulty with the rules and with authority figures, and would engage in childlike temper tantrums when he could not get his way. In order to feel some power and control, he threatened peers whom he felt he could push around. He indicated that he was the victim of physical abuse at the hands of his parents. Now, he was passing on this lesson of abusive control to others.

George appeared to be suffering from a combination of neglect and abuse that left him fearful, alone, and needy. His physical abuse had taught him that the way to get what you want is through threats and intimidation. His neglect taught him that he was unworthy of love and attention and that he had to demand it or manipulate for it in order to feel any sense of worth or nurturing. He mainly focused his efforts on female peers to get the love that he was missing.

His psychological testing indicated that his overall intellectual capacity was borderline mentally retarded. This meant that George lacked the cognitive ability to understand fully the effects of his environment on him. His thinking was limited, concrete, simplistic, and childlike. Once we approached his treatment with this in mind, his immature, impulsive, and concrete coping style became more understandable. For example, George fully expected his parents to attend family therapy sessions and was devastated when they did not come in, allegedly because they had to be "at work." He was protective of them and minimized his own neglect, rationalizing his painful situation as being because his parents "have to work." Their need to work overshadowed any feelings of abandonment, worthlessness, and hopelessness that he might be having about their inability to be present for him in a time of great need such as his hospitalization.

George's limited intellectual abilities and resulting inadequate reading and writing skills had a profound effect on him. He was never a success in school (as his sisters were) and he never would be. He had to find other arenas to establish his identity and self-worth. He found the streets and there found drugs and women. He was extremely vulnerable to his peers because he did not have the wherewithal to defend himself successfully. Consequently, he had to prove himself to get their acceptance. George's bravado and risk taking led to drug dependence, relationship dependence, and ever increasing feelings of failure, worthlessness, and shame. His parents were so preoccupied with their own needs, problems, and shame that they were not able to support him or engage in his treatment in any meaningful way. He was on his own and he knew it. He tried desperately to be like his peers and became more of a caricature than a real character. His dependency needs were never met, had become overwhelming, and resulted in addictions to sex, love, chemicals, and money—all of which mean status, on the street.

NYMPHOMANIACS

Case 12: Jane

Jane was only fourteen when I first met her. I was struck by her smile, childlike innocence, and soft manner. She was spunky, "cute," and energetic, with a sense of humor and a delight in the outrageous. She was likeable, slightly seductive, and mannerly. Her pleasing outside hid the intense pain she struggled with just below the surface. Jane could manage to appear "together" for short periods of time; but as you grew to know her, her impulsivity and brokenness became more and more obvious.

She was first hospitalized for psychiatric treatment at age twelve. She was suicidally depressed. When she came to us, she was again depressed and suicidal; she had tried to cut her wrists. She was not going to school, had stopped eating, and was running away from home. She was recently raped while she was a runaway. She reported that her mother had left her and her siblings when she was eight years old. Her father was alleged to be physically abusive; he used a horse whip to discipline the children. She indicated that she slept in her father's bed after her mother left, but did not have any memories of sexual abuse. Her mother had remarried and was separated from the second husband. Jane was now living with her mother. Neither she nor her mother had pursued aftercare therapy after Jane's first inpatient treatment, despite recommendations from staff that she get professional help.

In our program, Jane's initially pleasing presentation quickly disappeared when she had to follow rules. She regressed into an infantile, demanding, narcissistic, hostile child who needed to have her own way. She became verbally abusive of staff when they attempted to redirect her or to give her counseling about her out-of-control behavior. She was labile, hyperreactive, and angry. Her intense power struggle with staff served to help her avoid having to deal with any of her therapeutic issues. In a war with us, she could not allow herself to trust, to let go, to be open, or to expose her vulnerability.

Gradually responding to consistent treatment and loving attention, she slowly began to share with us her many dependencies. Her drug and alcohol dependency was revealed first, then came her relationship dependency. Her written assignments (given once a week) indicate some of this process:

Week 1: Daily one-to-one contacts with staff called "staff assignment," Complete a Step One Workbook on chemical dependency, Write a "daily secret" to your psychologist, Complete a collage "describing your Self," and List the things you are angry with your parents about.

Week 2: Continue staff assignment, Restriction from males (except in therapeutic activities), Restriction from a particular female peer [who was passing notes to boys for her and thereby encouraging her acting out], Continue daily secrets, Write an essay on "Why I need to fight with staff?," List the consequences of your drug and alcohol use, and List the consequences of your seductive behaviors.

Week 3: Continue staff assignment, male restriction, restriction from a particular female peer and daily secrets to your doctor; Write a list of the pro's and con's of long term treatment; Make a collage on female role models and present it to peers in Friday's morning meeting; and Write an essay on "Why I have trouble trusting?"

Week 4: Continue of Special Precautions Level I (for suicidal thoughts); Continue staff assignment, male restriction, particular female restriction, and daily secrets to your psychologist; Hair and Make Up Restriction [given to help the teenager no longer hide behind these outward appearances and feel accepted as herself]; Complete a Step Two Workbook on chemical dependency; List reasons why and reasons why you are not an addict; and List the qualities that you look for in a friend.

Week 5: Discontinue daily secrets and hair and make up restrictions, Continue male restriction, Write an essay on "How can I get rid of my guilt feelings about my past?," Write an essay on "Why I decided that I am an addict?," and List the things that you need from your mother.

Week 6: Discontinue male restriction, Write a letter to your father and give it to your psychologist, List your positive qualities and present these to your peers in Friday's morning meeting, and Write an essay on "How I hope to change as a result of treatment?"

Week 7: Restriction from giving feedback [some adolescents in treatment are not allowed to give feedback to peers since they do not follow their own advice but give it freely to others], Write an essay on "Why I am afraid to hear what people tell me?," and Write an essay on "How I will cope with my fears in the future?"

Week 8: Restart male restriction, Continue feedback restriction, Write an essay on "How I will take responsibility for my recovery?," and Complete a Step Three Workbook on chemical dependency.

Week 9: Continue male restriction and discontinue feedback restriction, Hand in Step Three Workbook, List the things that you have forgiven yourself for, Write an essay on "How my male dependency issues affect me?," and Write an essay on "How the book *Women Who Love Too Much* applies to me?"

Week 10: Write goodbye letters to staff, Write an essay on "How I can fill my 'emptiness' with my recovery program?," and Write a letter to your mother that you hand in.

The story of how Jane's sex and love addiction interfered with her treatment is evident in the frequency of her male restrictions, the appearance of her related suicidal impulses, and the need to focus more and more specifically on these issues in the therapy process until the next-to-last week, when they were the primary topics. Her obsession with sex and relationships so dominated her consciousness that nothing else could get through. She was using sex and love as a drug on the unit in order to suppress and numb any other feelings or memories that might emerge and remind her of the traumatic pain of her maternal abandonment and paternal abuse.

In a brief but heartbreaking response to my question "What do you want?" Jane wrote,

big green eyes
longer eye lashes

flawless skin

cute nose

long brown hair

more muscular legs

more muscular arms

smoother skin

bigger chest

This was from a girl who was strikingly beautiful and needed no assistance with her physical presence. In a haunting way, Jane's inability to go beyond the surface in answering my question reflects her need to hide her emotional pain, to cover up the horror she feels about herself, and to wish there were some external "fix" that would make her loveable, worthwhile, and whole.

Her continual acting out of her sex and love addiction led us to refer her to long-term treatment. She could not follow the rules in an institution, so the odds of her being able to follow the rules at home or in school seemed quite slim. In fact, her persistent but not flagrant or violent transgressions seemed in some way to be a behavioral means of telling us that she was out of control and that she needed us to provide her with a safe environment because she could not manage on her own at home.

Case 13: Jill

One of Jill's stories about her life sent chills down my spine. I sometimes tell myself that I've heard everything, but I was not prepared for the day that Jill told me about being molested in the same room, in the same house, in which her mother had been molested. I was shocked with the immense powerlessness and hopelessness that was communicated in this story. She was to return to that same house after treatment.

Jill came into treatment with the common problems of depression, truancy, family conflicts, and suicidal ideas. She was abusing alcohol and marijuana. She had low self-esteem. The year before, she had received some outpatient counseling. She did not do well in school, was not especially attractive or talented, and had little to be proud of about herself except for her gymnastics ability. She had been somewhat successful with this sport, but had given it up when she discovered boys. Jill raged at home and hit her sister. She was ashamed of her lack of self-control and childlike behaviors. She could not talk to her parents. Her father was on Disability Insurance, and Jill was afraid it would kill him if she told him about her drug abuse, anxieties, and problems. Her older brother had given up trying to help her. Her parents were overwhelmed and helpless. Her mother called her a "whore" and tried to control her with shame and guilt while treating her like "the baby" of the family. Her family worried a lot that she would get pregnant, and Jill worried a lot about it, too.

In treatment, she rarely spoke and made little progress. She was primarily interested in establishing a relationship with a male peer and was quite creative, devious, and persistent in this regard. She resisted the efforts we made to help her to trust and open up, and eventually she was discharged without much change. She was readmitted eight days later with an overdose. Her continued lack of progress led to a referral to long-term treatment. She lasted less than a month in the long-term program and was kicked out for having boys in her room. She came back to us in disgrace and was filled with shame and embarrassment. She opened up a bit more; for example, she told us that she had been raped at age twelve and that she had been physically abused by a boyfriend.

Jill was stuck in a childlike, dependent role with adults and was obsessed with finding a man to save her from her troubles. Her "little girl" role was supported by her mother, who was also an abuse victim. Her mother seemed unable to set any appropriate limits for Jill, and her father was too sick to try. Finally, against our advice, the family decided that she would do better living with her brother, who would provide her with discipline, structure, and rules. She was pulled out of treatment in time to start the new school year.

Jill lasted only six weeks at her brother's place when she became self-mutilative and burned herself with a curling iron. She was not attending school, was driving her brother crazy, and was in an obsessive relationship with a rather unhealthy male peer whom she had met at the hospital over the summer. This boyfriend was to be her salvation of course—but since he lived closer to her mother's house than her brother's, Jill had to find a way to get home so that she could go out with him. She became suicidal and self-destructive because she was afraid that she was pregnant by another boy and that her newfound love would reject her. Back in treatment once more, she again refused to cooperate, and within a week her mother had decided to take her home and "give her another chance." At this point, Jill told me that her sex life was "none of your business" and seemed proud of her ability to manipulate her parents to get what she wanted.

Case 14: Debbie

Debbie's male dependency drove her parents crazy. She and they fought about her inability to have a life outside of a relationship. She would promise to change but never did. Her love addiction led her to a rape, to an unwanted pregnancy, to having to live with her grandmother, to shame, guilt, and self-hatred, and eventually to hospitalization.

In her written assignments, she articulated examples of her feelings of powerlessness over her relationships:

When a guy asked me to have sex with him, I could not say no.

When my boyfriend starts giving me hickies and I cannot say no.

When my boyfriends try to get hot and heavy and it starts, I cannot say no.

When my boyfriend tells me to get something for him and I'm tired and he knows it, I cannot say no.

When they tell me "I love you" and I think they really mean it, so I would make love to them.

When I do not feel well about myself, I get a guy to tell me or to be around.

Being unable to say no, Debbie's life became increasingly out of control and unmanageable. She listed a number of painful consequences of her active addiction:

Instead of doing what I wanted to do, I always listened to the boyfriend.

I could not handle the fights and would constantly worry.

I always worried about him not me or other things that I should be focusing on.

My self-esteem was always up and down and I had no control of how to feel.

My father and I always fought about guys.

I would tell my parents that I would not go near him again and I would anyway.

I told my parents that I would be more careful with guys but I wouldn't.

My boyfriend broke up with me and I started a fight with my parents.

I told something to my boyfriend and he told his friends and I felt so bad.

I had sex with my boyfriend and he told everyone and I felt bad.

I hated myself because I got raped and it was my fault and he laughed at my face and told his friends that I wanted to do it.

I felt so low going with my mother to get an abortion and it should have been my boyfriend.

I felt bad killing the baby.

I didn't care about myself or pay attention to myself.

These are traumatic and painful experiences for a seventeen-year-old young woman. Her parents were at their wits' end with trying to find a way to get her to be more careful, normal, and honest. They would talk to her and appear to reach an understanding, but she was unable to live up to her promises. Her parents felt more and more betrayed, which led to increasing frustration, anger, and eventually rage. They saw her as a vulnerable, needy girl who was being taken advantage of by every boy she dated. Of course, she developed "a reputation," and the boys who were attracted to her expected her to be "easy." Like Debbie herself, her parents too felt powerless to protect her from this abuse, and they pleaded with her to change.

Debbie rarely exhibited much insight into the dynamics of her addiction, but in one essay she wrote,

I need a good feeling "fix" from a relationship because there is no other way I can figure to feel good about something. I do feel good about myself but just one topic ("men"). I cannot understand why I feel like this. I want a good, healthy relationship with guys and I'm sick and tired to need guys to be there for me. I don't like this hollow feeling. When my boyfriend tells me that he is going to marry me, I think it's going to be great. I always end up with the wrong men all the time and I always go back to them. I also deny the fact that this is a problem. I wanted to change my father to be warm and loving but it never ends up that way. I go for the same guys as him.

Debbie attempted to discuss this with her father in a family session, but both of them were so uncomfortable that the issue was avoided.

Her struggle for sobriety was an intense and painful one. She was easily triggered by all kinds of stimuli in herself and in her environment. As part of her recovery process, we tried to identify some of her triggers, that is, the things that got the addictive process rolling. We made a list from Debbie's responses:

A guy staring at me or coming up to me—I automatically think that he likes me.

If I see a cute guy, I will try to get his attention.

A guy who follows me around.

A guy who whistles at me or drives by in his car.

A guy smiles and keeps looking back at me.

Guys who call me up.

When I look at old pictures of boyfriends.

Letters from them.

Looking at other couples and wishing that was me.

Thinking that someone still likes me.

Thinking about relationships.

Looking at guys.

Cologne #1.

Talking about relationships.

Looking at guys' eyes.

Magazines.

Guys yelling "babe."

Getting a note from a guy.

Reading novels [love and romance].

Girls talking about their boyfriends.

My ex-boyfriend's clothes.

Love songs.

Someone telling me about a guy who likes me.

Thinking about old times and wanting to call them.

As I read over her list, I felt overwhelmed. I had the thought that she would have to be locked in a closet for the next ten years. She did not have a chance, especially around other adolescents who do or are interested in most of the things on her list. And her family felt the same way. How could she survive in an environment so filled with stimuli that were potentially dangerous for her?

In fact, she was not surviving very well. Her addiction and the related detachment and numbing allowed her to disconnect from her pain. When she wrote a history of her relationships, she chronicled a number of romances that all ended the same way. Finally, she said,

I am stopping here because it's making me feel real bad about myself. I had bad relationships with guys. I could not picture me how it hurts alot and I hope I am getting to the point where I should be more aware. I mean I am now but in the future and try to look back and that list and say to myself. Look how I felt when I was writing about my history of relationships. I think honestly to know what to do because I screwed up when I was 14 years old. I rather have a nice life in my late teens and 20's. Out of ten, five I had sex with and the other five had bad arguements relationships weren't good even though we didn't have sex. That's horrible to think that's enough for me. That's my terrible life of relationships.

Debbie did not have the time to reflect while she was in her active addiction. When we encouraged her to look at what her life was like, she did not like what she saw.

EXHIBITIONISM IN A GIRL—CASE 15: BETTY

Betty's peers helped her keep her sex and love addiction secret for some time. She came into treatment for a cocaine dependency. She obviously had difficulties with men and could not seem to stay out of a relationship. However, the extent of her compulsion to connect with males was not known for a while because her peers were both fascinated and amused by her acting out. Finally, after a rather intensive investigation by staff, one of her peers told us that Betty was "flashing the boys." At first, we did not know exactly what he was referring to, so he explained to us that she would expose her breasts when the staff were not looking. Her compulsive exhibitionism was well known to the adolescents on the unit, but it was a secret well kept from the adults despite its obviously unhealthy nature.

As Betty began to work on these behaviors, her painful story emerged:

I came from a dysfunctional home. My dad is an alcoholic and there was always constant arguing in my home. My parents were divorced. I feel a strong need to be loved and have stayed with a boyfriend even though he put me down and even hit me. I thought it was my fault that I had done something wrong because I was put down when I was growing up. I would do anything, like it was a challenge, to make that guy love me. I depend on a person with whom I have a relationship with. If they leave, I'm lost and try to replace the person because I can't stand being alone.

In another essay, she wrote, "I have a strong need to feel secure and having a boyfriend is a temporary way to make me feel secure." Betty's words speak clearly. Her need for love was a huge hole that was never filled. As she tried desperately to get the love that she needed, she experienced more and more negative consequences in her life.

Betty herself identified many of the damaging effects of her "male dependency," including these:

I was irresponsible at home because I was either not home or I was talking on the phone with some guy.

I would be thinking about living with a certain guy when I should have been thinking about my job.

I used cocaine and it took my mind off guys on and off because cocaine also made me feel secure.

I found myself staring at guys when the guy I like is not around even if I don't want to be like that.

Even when I say I love a guy and I don't want anyone else, I find myself looking and flirting with other guys when that person is not around.

I say I won't go out with a guy for a while and never follow through with what I say.

Sometimes when I know a guy is just a little interested in me [and] if I am even just a little bit interested in him, I might do or say something sexual to him.

I put my hand between a guys legs just cause I felt like doing it.

I had wanted to be with a certain guy and was with him without taking any precautions.

I slept with a guy even though I wanted to wait to get to know him a little better.

If a guy I like alot is in the room when I'm supposed to be doing work, I get side tracked and stare at him or talk to him or day dream about being with him.

I had a fight with another girl because she had liked my boyfriend.

I got into fights with my mother about her giving me a hard time about me going out with a certain guy.

I got pissed off because the guy I liked had hurt my feelings, so I punched a hole through my closet door.

When I do things I regret later, it makes me feel aweful about myself.

I got pregnant.

I got suicidal.

I went out with the wrong kind of guys and a couple of them hit me.

My mother went looking for me because I did not come home because I was with a guy.

My friends that did not hang out with older guys, so I didn't really have those friends too much anymore.

My friend's boyfriend was flirting with me because I was flirting with him and I ended up not being friends with her anymore.

A boyfriend dropped me because I was flirting with his friends.

A girl I was friends with didn't want anything to do with me anymore because she said I am a slut.

I fooled around with my friend's boyfriend and she still was my friend because I told her I was so drunk and it won't happen again which I lied because I knew what I was doing. I just thought that he was hot, so I kissed him.

I was called "bitch" and "whore."

A guy I would go out with had used me because he would say things I wanted to hear and then when I slept with him, he dumped me.

I want to always have a boyfriend even if I have to take someone else's away.

I would cut school to be with a guy.

I would lie to them to keep them.

I was talked about by people I didn't hang out with.

I only wanted guy friends.

I stopped having interest in other things besides guys and drugs.

I made my parents feel bad because I ran away to live with a guy.

I got pregnant with a guy I had only gone out with for two months and he left me. I wanted to die.

I started thinking that I was a slut.

I didn't really want to acknowledge God.

Betty's sex and love addiction had affected every part of her life: her self-esteem, her relationship with her parents, her friends, her schoolwork, her job, and her relationship with God. She had lost control in so many ways—pregnancy, punching a hole in a door, abandoning friends, abusing drugs, skipping school, fighting with friends and family, and running away. Finally, she was so compelled that she would undress in front of her peers in order to get her sex and love fix. Her feelings of emptiness, worthlessness, and loneliness were so intense that she responded in the only way she knew how. She got attention in a sexualized way.

FULL-BLOWN ADDICTION

Case 16: Harold

At sixteen, Harold's life revolved around sex. He was a mixed-race adolescent who was depressed, truant from school, stubborn, and explosive. His parents felt confused, hopeless, and angry. He had started abusing drugs at age eight, and by twelve had undergone his first inpatient hospitalization. After that, he had been in another month-long psychiatric treatment and a six-month residential program for drug abusers. Nothing had worked. No one, however, had addressed his sexual issues.

Harold had *lots* of issues, in fact: learning problems that needed special education intervention; asthma; a club foot; parents from differing racial and cultural backgrounds; hyperactivity; and conduct-disordered behavior (stealing, drug dealing). By the time I met him, his sexual acting out was out of control. He had become obsessed with two of his female peers on the inpatient unit and had made a small peephole between his room and the girls' room next door. When asked to complete a sexual addiction inventory, Harold shared with us a large number of behaviors: compulsive masturbation; voyeurism; exhibitionism; masturbation to the point of self-injury; looking at pornographic books, magazines, and videotapes; sexualizing people; participating in phone sex; one-night stands; multiple relationships; anonymous sex; inappropriate touching and fondling; sexually explicit talk and jokes; flirting and seductive behavior; pretending to touch people by accident; an obsession with oral sex; tying others up and being tied up during sexual encounters; and sex with a consenting minor.

His addiction was so present that he could not participate in treatment. When asked to write about this problem, Harold wrote,

My obsession with sex is effecting my treatment by the way that all I think about all day is having sex not focusing on my treatment but on having sex mainly with Sue but really with most of the girls in all my meetings. I sit there and undress Sue not hearing what is going on in the group but fantasizing about having sex in lines to go to lunch or school rubbing up against them the way they smell drives me crazy. Sometimes I cannot think and if I am thinking it is how to get laid in here planning it and also fantasizing about Nancy. I cannot concentrate on any of my problems only sex.

His difficulty with getting help was obvious to everyone, and a source of great frustration. He was still in an active addiction even while confined in the hospital.

Harold went on to explain his sex and love addiction in more detail:

My obsession with sex started when I was very young around first grade. I was all ways infatuated with females and their bodies. I remember there was a girl who lived across the street from me, we used to play doctor and truth and dare. I was only 8 and I was all ready trying to have sex. Then, there was a girl who lived two doors down from me. We used to get naked and play with each other's body parts. This went on for 3 years until I was 11. Then we started having sex. I couldn't produce sperm yet but it still was the greatest feeling I ever had. When I turned twelve, I went to a new school and all the girls there liked me. This is also where I had a homosexual experience. All day I would finger and feel the breast of this girl Kim and during lunch we would sneak into the locker room and have sex. After I got out of that school, I went down the shore for the summer and it seemed like all the girls loved to have sex. I was having sex so much my genitals were starting to hurt, but I wouldn't stop until the pain was so unbearable and I was doing five nights out of the week sometimes seven. When I came back from the shore, I started hanging around with sluts and doing nothing but having sex. Then, I found that when I did coke, my penis would get harder then usual and stay hard for hours on end. So I started having sex even more but it still wasn't enough. All I thought about all day was sex. Then, I started calling them 900 numbers and masturbating around 10 to 15 times a day but the urge wouldn't go away. I tried things to get my mind off sex but nothing would work. All I thought about was sex all day every day. When I told people, they just said that I was a pervert. I was proud of it. All of my relationships were based on sex. I never knew there were such things as sex addicts but I loved sex. When I look for a girlfriend, I didn't care what they looked like or if they were nice but only if they would have sex with me. I always like the girls that would have oral sex with me. My one girlfrend said she wouldn't have sex with me until we were going out for a month, so I broke up with her. I also used to crank call people's houses and talk dirty to them over the phone. This would get me off. I was also always worried about the size of my penis if it was big enough and if it was as big as every one else's.

His too is a painful story of hypersexuality that is medicating great pain and abuse.

Harold's sexual history included being raped at age eight by a man he did not know, being sexually molested by his babysitter at eleven, masturbating ten times a day when he was fourteen, and tying up sexual partners at fifteen. He made his own pornography by filming his sexual contacts. He was a sexual predator with girls whom he saw were emotionally vulnerable. He was extremely jealous, possessive, and violent. He swore that he would stop, only to escalate to a more extreme behavior.

Case 17: Claire

Claire was a spunky, worldly, fifteen-year-old Hispanic girl who was in her third pregnancy. Her charming smile, intelligent banter, and seductive manner belied a background of abuse and deprivation. However, when she became violent, enraged, and capable of harming herself and others, it was then that she showed us the horrible nightmare she was living. Claire was obsessed with sex and love. She pursued drugs and men with a maniacal zeal. No one could control her—even in the highly restrictive hospital environment—unless she wanted to be controlled. Her treatment was confined to her hospital stays because she was noncompliant with recommendations for long-term residential care and with outpatient therapy.

Claire could not communicate very well in person, but she was able to say more of what was on her mind in her daily journals. Her profound hurt, abandonment, and attachment to men are chronicled in these entries. About her father, she wrote,

Today, I seen a man who looks like my father. Well, how my father would look like if he were still alive. What really got to me was that I always wonder what he would be like if he were still alive, or if he would have gotten clean. Everybody tells me that he died and I still don't believe it. I want to see my father and talk to him. I wish that my father wouldn't have done the things that he did, that way my mom wouldn't have left him and she wouldn't have met Harry [her stepfather who molested her]. I feel like he fucked me over. He left me. I want to know if he loved me and why did he do the things he did.

Most of the adolescents with whom I work have feelings like these for their parents. They desperately want them to be healthy people who could care for and nurture them. They want their parents to remain together. They want their parents to be drug free, nonviolent, and involved in their lives.

About her mother, Claire wrote, "I have alot of feelings towards my mom because I always felt she wasn't protecting me the way she was supposed to. I felt like she didn't protect me from my stepdad. She makes me angry when she says she doesn't know what to do because she never knows what to do. I don't know what to do either. I'm scared too." It was very hard for Claire to get in touch with her anger toward her mother, especially when her mother was present. However, she acted out her rage by being totally out of her mother's control. And if fact, her mother subtly supported her acting out; for example, the mother was excited about Claire's pregnancy and was unable to consider any other alternatives than Claire's taking care of the child. Her mother had been overwhelmed with the violence of Claire's father, and went to a shelter for battered women. She even progressed to the role of counselor to other battered women. Nevertheless, she was not able to develop a healthy parental relationship with Claire.

Claire's stepfather did the most damage. Her words speak powerfully to her pain: "My stepfather was nice when I first met him. Little by little, he started changing. He began to hit me and call me names. My mom was always working and she didn't know what was happening. Then, he started to molest me. It felt very weird. He scared me, frightened me. I'm very angry with him. I just feel like killing him." Her picture of the stepfather's domination and control continued:

When I was little, we would celebrate Holidays. Everything would be fine untill somebody brought beer. People would drink until they noticed my stepdad was getting drunk and they would start to leave cause they knew what was coming next. I would go upstairs or just stay downstairs and wait. Once everyone was gone the shit started. It was like living in a war zone. He would say that my mom was flirting when she wasn't, my mom was not like that. Then, he would come and start with me for anything, he would even bring up things from my past like grades in school. He was sick. When I would stay downstairs and wait, it was because I didn't want him to hit my mom like my dad did, plus I knew he would wake me up anyway so he could complete his routine. I hate him so much. Just sitting here remembering this makes me feel like it just happened again.

It became obvious to us that Claire was suffering posttraumatic stress syndrome from the "war zone" inside her home.

She went on to elaborate about the effects of her stepfather's behavior on her peer relationships and trust level:

When I was growing up, I never had friends because I wasn't allowed to. My stepdad didn't let me because he said everybody was a bad influence. So, when he was out of the picture, I tried to make friends and I did, but the friendships didn't last long. We would fight, argue, resent each other, and it keeps on happening. I still don't know how to keep friends, I'm trying to change. It feels weird because I want a friend that I can trust but I don't trust anybody.

Her inability to bond with any nurturing adults left her unable to connect with peers as well. She was alone, felt worthless, and turned to compulsive behaviors like sex and drugs to medicate her pain.

When Claire could no longer tolerate the pain, she left home.

When I ran away from my house for the first time, I started selling drugs for some guy. I would buy my clothes and my food. I started selling to get high and I wouldn't buy any clothes anymore. I really got hooked on dust, that really fucked me up. I didn't sleep, eat, and I didn't care how I looked. I was living in a whorehouse with five other girls. The owner of the house was 18 years old, the guys would pay her to screw the girls. Everytime she asked me to do that I would tell her no. Then, finally, she told me to leave and I left and went home.

Claire overdosed at the age of ten. She was locked in her room, beaten, and sexualized by her stepfather. He touched her breasts and stomach and rubbed up against her. Finally, she told her mother and they took her stepfather to court. He escaped prosecution by disappearing and had two bench warrants out for his arrest.

Despite this intervention, her sex and love addiction had begun to grow. She described the frequent combination of sex and drugs:

I had a problem when I went to a party and I started drinking. Things started to get out of hand. I started fucking around with this guy, but somehow I ended up leaving with someone else. I went to his house and I slept with him. After that we never spoke again. I felt stupid because people that were at the party would laugh when they would see me, so I never spoke to them again. I felt hurt, embarrassed, stupid and slutty.

Addicts do not learn from their mistakes. They keep expecting different results from the same behaviors. For example, Claire wrote about a partying incident that occurred as her addictions escalated:

Something that has been bothering me is that, one day not too long ago, I was on my way to buy some pills and on my way, I met this guy and we started talking. He invited me in his house. We started to drink and take pills, some of his friends came over and that's all I remember. I went into a blackout period. When I started coming too, I was in a car and got dropped off at my friend's house at 6:00 A.M. Everytime I think about that night, I get upset because I don't know if I slept with him and his friends or just him. I feel dirty, sleasy, nasty, whorey, disgusting, skanky, and slutty. I feel very ashamed, after that incident, I started hating pills and liquor.

However, this was not enough to get her to stop drinking, drugging, and sexing. Claire's problems continued to escalate and she was more and more isolated and alone: "All my life people have called me names. My stepfather called me a little bitch, slut, and little whore. He really got upset. Then, the guys talked shit about me and put me down. That's why now everytime someone calls me names, I get very angry. Sometimes, I feel like killing someone. It hurts alot to hear stuff like that." Her sex and love addiction was noticeable to others, and they were not kind with their interpretation of her behavior. Lack of control over her male dependency led her further and further away from her peers.

I have a problem with fucking my friends over. I feel really bad because I slept with my girlfriend's boyfriend. I know she would have never done that to me. I was high once again. I feel so ashamed. The next day, I didn't even want to see him again. I didn't want to see her because I thought I was going to break down. I love her like if she is my sister. I wanted to just disappear.

As her pain grew, so did her dependency on drugs, sex, and men.
In a treatment effort to facilitate her separation from a particularly destructive relationship, when she was thirteen, she wrote this letter to the former boyfriend.

I'm writing you this letter because I'm scared if I see you I might try to do something to you. Lately, I've been thinking about you alot and everytime I do, I get angry and upset. You really hurt me. You said alot of things to me that I thought you would never say. I know we had a really sick relationship. I played you wrong with alot of people, even people that you know. I guess I love you, but I wasn't satisfied, is that I wanted more attention, especially from other guys. I knew you knew about me doing that, but

I still had to deny it because I didn't want you to leave me. The last time we broke up, I thought I was going to die. I never thought I would get like that for a man. You really changed when you met Sue "Bitch." You told me that your feelings for me would never change, but then you treated me like dirt for that bitch. What messed me up the most was that I used to be your number one girl and somehow that changed because then I became your piece on the side. When we broke up, I didn't know what to do about the feelings, so I started to do more drugs. I just went down hill from there. Well, I'm letting you go now.

Unfortunately, this habit was not so easily kicked. Later, she lamented, "I found out a few days ago that my ex-boyfriend broke up with his girlfriend. It brought up alot of feelings for me. My first reaction was to try to call him. I cared about him alot, but he hurt me alot. But, I still love him. I want him back so bad. I'm very confused because I don't know what to do. I'm hurt, angry, happy and confused." Her attachment to her boyfriend sounds a lot like her love/hate feelings for her father.

Claire's obsessing with this boyfriend caused her tremendous pain and killed her unborn child. She told the story:

When I was thirteen, I had a miscarriage. The baby was by Sam. I went to this club and Sam was there with a girl. That really made me pissed. I started fighting with the girl. She was pregnant too. I wanted to kill the girl. She went unconscious. After they got me off of her, they took me home and I was bleeding and I lost the baby. I was really hurt, upset, angry, and I felt stupid for getting into a fight and putting my baby's life in jeapardy.

The insanity did not stop there, however. At fourteen, she was pregnant again.

When I was 3 months pregnant, I got jumped by four Black girls because of my ex-boyfriend Jim. He had 2 kids by one of the girls. I thought I was going to loose the baby. I was scared and angry. I was angry because I could have lost the baby because of my stupidity. Right now, the reason why I haven't been [sexual] with anybody is because I don't want my baby to get hurt because of me.

Her intentions were good, but her impulse control was not. Claire was transferred from our hospital to a home for unwed mothers. She lasted there only one day because she attacked another resident who was "bugging" her by calling her names like "drug addict, bitch." Immediately, the staff there discharged her. On our unit, her stay had been threatened by her compulsive need to be in relationships with male peers despite frequent confrontations, consequences, and therapeutic interventions.

The cycle of abuse was continuing in her life: violence, rage, lack of control over aggressive and sexual impulses, dependency, low self-esteem, feelings of worthlessness, and hopelessness. She was trapped on a wheel that she could not get off. She was terrified to let go of sex and drugs and was unable to trust anyone enough to allow them to help her learn to let go.

Case 18: Bess

Bess was a sex addict who, in her middle teens, was referred to us for treatment because she was depressed and out of control. Her grades in Catholic school had dropped. She had given up her interest in athletics. She was withdrawn, sullen, and noncommunicative with her mother. She and her mother had verbal battles about Bess's behavior—especially her constant contact with innumerable boys. She had suicidal ideas and fits of anger and rage. Her psychological testing supported her diagnosis of depression. Because of her shame and guilt, the exact nature of her problem was not immediately evident. Initially, she was shy, guarded, and evasive. She had a profoundly sad and hopeless look on her face.

In her written history, the pain of her sex and love addiction spoke loud and clear:

The first guy I ever had sex with picked me and my friend up off the side of the road one day. We were together for about two weeks and had sex maybe three or four times. I didn't have any feelings for him. I just wanted to have sex and he was just a good opportunity to do that with. After that I haven't had any other relationships. Not that that was really a relationship though. I would just meet guys and just be casual sex partners. Sometimes after work I would have sex with some of the guys I worked with. Some of them gave me money and others didn't. If I just had sex with one person after awhile it wasn't enough. I would have to go out with in between 4–15 guys at a time. Over the summer things got really out of control. I can't sit here and name every person that I've been with because most of them told me fake names and I can't remember a lot of them. I would go out maybe five days a week with 3 or 4 different groups of people. One time I took count and in 11 days I was with 45 different people. Some repeats, but a total of 45 different people. Guys would just come down my street, literally cars filled with them asking me to go out. Practically all of them I never even met before. We would just go to the woods near my house and I would have oral sex with them then regular sex. A lot of times they would do acid or smoke pot while they were waiting. They would call me a bitch and tell me to suck their dick or to "fuck them like the pig that I was." At the time I didn't care because I knew that was true. After I came home from going out a couple hours later I would sneak out and go out to have sex again. One time, we went over this guy's house and they made a video tape of me with all of them. I was really angry but I couldn't do anything about it because they threatened not to take me home alot of times. And everything just went along like that. It was fun for awhile. It wasn't fun anymore. I would just think about the things they said and how worthless and nothing I felt like and how my friends talked about me and things my mother said to me and nothing I did made me happy.

Her addiction was clearly out of control.

As we spoke about her acting out, Bess indicated that she preferred to have anonymous sex. If she knew the person or made some sort of personal contact with them, then she could not be sexual with them. The sexual contact had to be with someone she did not know. She felt terrible shame and guilt about her behaviors. She thought of herself as a bad person and did not think that she was sick. Her harsh self-criticism actually reinforced her need to act out in an effort to soothe her pain.

She was surrounded by judgment and rejection.

Many times my counselors and parents have told me to stop my sexual behaviors. One of the most obvious reasons is for my health. I have endangered myself to the risk of diseases, AIDS, pregnancy, and everything else having unprotected sex. Another type of health reason is that I had become real run down plus I wasn't getting hardly any sleep. I had deep circles under my eyes and I wasn't keeping up with my appearance. They also told me to stop my behaviors because it is inappropriate and ruined my reputation. Also there is a constant stream of guys calling my house and coming over even while I am here and my mom always gets mad when this happens. When they told me these things I would always get mad or just tune them out when someone told me something I didn't want to hear or have to think about. There have been other times though when I just agreed with what they told me but just continued to go about in the manner I had become accustomed to and just blocked out all of my feelings.

Bess was not able even to hear the concern of others about her because she had become so entangled in her sex and love addiction. Acting out meant everything to her. She loved "having a reputation" and the attention of all of these men. This was her drug and she needed more, more, more.

She was preoccupied with sex. Bess said it this way:

A lot of times, well most of the time, if I'm not really concentrating or giving my absolute full attention to something, I am thinking about sex. Sometimes it's remembering certain experiences or planning new things, or talking about either of those two things. Once I start thinking these thoughts, it's very difficult for me to stop. And then, I jones [have cravings] until I can do what I was thinking about.

Sex was the only thing that had any real power in Bess's life and she was afraid to give it up. In fact, we had a great power struggle over her letting go of her list of phone numbers. She had a huge stack of boys' phone numbers (only their first names) at home. Part of her recovery involved going home, getting the pile of numbers, and giving them up to me. She obviously got high when she got them, and did not want to let go.

How could a young girl turn out like Bess? What made her this way? The answer to these questions was only initially covered in her inpatient treatment. Her parents were both homosexuals and were in active relationships with partners of the same sex. She lived with her mother and her mother's friend. Bess's father, who was separated from his wife but not divorced, had a close male friend who often visited and stayed the night in her father's bedroom. Neither of her parents had ever acknowledged their sexual orientation or lifestyle directly with Bess. She knew, but she did not know. Her father agreed to tell her the truth during her first weekend in treatment. The secret was not a secret to Bess. She knew and had suffered greatly as a result of her parents' sexual preferences. She reported teasing, humiliation, and rejection by her peers at a young age—and the devastating isolation that went along with that. She was alone both inside and outside of her family. She did not have permission to speak about her feelings about her parents' sexuality and certainly did not feel able to talk to them about her own sexual issues (e.g., was *she* homosexual?). Her behavior did her talking: there could be no doubt that she was heterosexually oriented. Though Bess could not say this to her parents in words, her actions spoke volumes. She was able to get attention from men and declare her sexual preference. She was able to express her rage at the family's sexual secrecy with her own blatant sexuality. *She* was not going to be a hypocrite or phony to the world. In fact, there was an element of revenge in her behavior: the pain she suffered as a child because of her parents' sexual preferences was now back on them because of her sexual proclivity.

She enjoyed the irony of this reversal.

SEX WITH ANIMALS—CASE 19: DON

A consultation was requested for Don because he exhibited an obsession for sexual activity with animals. He had been referred to the hospital because he was becoming more isolated, was doing poorly in school, and was explicit about his sexual encounters with his dog. He indicated to us that he had been sexually molested by his father "many times," but was reluctant to give many details. At eighteen, Don had become so preoccupied with sex that he could not function.

Reports from his family and outpatient counselors indicated that he had been sexually involved with a girlfriend and had written many graphic letters to her about their past sexual contacts as well as his fantasies about the future. The girl's father had seen at least one of these and had forbidden her to be in touch with him. In fact, his girlfriend had also become uncomfortable with the intensity and nature of his sexual demands on her. She had begun to refuse sexual activity—which he had great difficulty accepting. He persisted in "always asking" for sex, even after their relationship had ended.

Don indicated that he had begun masturbating at around age six. There was some sort of association in his mind between masturbation and dirty diapers. He compulsively masturbated and believed that he would not be able to fall asleep without doing so. He had also begun writing about his masturbation to stimulate himself—a form of his own private pornography.

Don found that animals also caused him to become sexually aroused, although he did not have any idea how this fixation developed. He had a sexual experience with a dog about which he said, "I had a better sexual feeling with the dog [as opposed to his girlfriend] because I could spend time with the dog." He bought stuffed animals and engaged in sexual acts with them. He plastered the walls of his rooms with pictures of animals. He started becoming aroused by "whales and polar bears." He spoke openly about his sexual preoccupations and activities to friends and adults in a way that seemed provocative and exhibitionistic. Finally, he purchased a dog for sexual activity.

He was more circumspect about his sexual attraction to children. He did acknowledge an obsession with diapers and an association with his masturbatory activities. He also indicated that he had thoughts about being sexual with children and that he watched pornography depicting sex with children. He denied any overt activity with children at this point.

Don's sex and love addiction horrified the adults who learned of it. His family and counselors were at their wits' end trying to find some way to make him stop. The external pressure to change seemed to fuel his addiction even more. He seemed to flaunt his preferences and to challenge the adult world to try to control him. His arrogant, narcissistic, "you can't change me" attitude hid a terrible sense of guilt, shame, and self-loathing. He reported feeling extreme hopelessness and despair. He felt out of control and unable to stop his sexual acting out. Don was almost paranoid in his thoughts about other people, and he saw himself as losing touch with reality. He had lost weight and was putting himself in dangerous situations. His self-esteem was gone, and he felt he was going against his own values and beliefs. He had lost his faith, felt abandoned by God and believed that he had lost the respect of others, including his girlfriend and his family. He thought of himself as blowing academic opportunities, wasting money on "buying diapers for my animals and alot of condoms," giving up hobbies and activities, and losing important friendships.

Don's sex and love addiction had taken over his life, and he found himself in the strange position of trying to hold onto it while still having other things and people in his life. Friends and family were clearly telling him that he was not acceptable the way he was. Still, he felt both unwilling and unable to let go. He hated himself, on the one hand, and hated others, on the other hand. This great internal conflict resulted in symptoms of depression and increased sexual compulsion as a form of self-medication. He had developed rather complex and, in his mind, justified rationalizations for his sexual contact with animals and desperately tried to convince others that his behavior was normal and should be tolerated. When he was not able to win others over to his way of thinking, he became enraged, belligerent, and hostile. He dared people to try to stop him. His need to force his sexual preferences and activities on others resembled his own sexual abuse. That is, he had been forced to endure unwanted and damaging sexual advances from his father at "any age"; and now—in a role reversal where *he* had the power—he was pushing his sexual needs onto others, including his girlfriend and the people with whom he flaunted his sexual attraction to animals. Don's behavior, then, could be interpreted as a reenactment of his own sexual abuse. He was not clear about the role of animals in his early sexual development, but it is possible that he did not originate the idea of being sexual with animals. He may have been introduced to sex with animals by someone else. He had indicated that there was also sexual abuse by another person: "someone else did [molest me], but I don't know who." His memories of this or these events was not clear, but Don's behavior suggested other forms of inappropriate sexual stimulation in addition to what happened between him and his father.

COMPULSIVE MASTURBATION—CASE 20: DENNIS

Dennis was an insecure, inadequate teen who was controlled by his mother. She was aggressive, overweight, and tough. She tended bar for a living. His father was not at all involved in his treatment, and his mother was overly involved. Dennis was a "mommy's boy" and was desperate to keep her approval. He had difficulties in school and was not able to perform well athletically. He had few friends and was considered "weird" by his peers. He had few sources of self-worth and few relationships that could nurture him. He was frightened easily but tried to put on a front of bravado in order not to be teased too much by his male peers. He was raised Catholic, but then dabbled in Satanism—probably because of the lure of power in the dark rituals.

Dennis came to my attention because his roommate in the hospital complained about Dennis's frequent masturbation. As a rule, most of the teenagers with whom I talk will make it clear that they do not masturbate and that they think masturbation is bad, weird, unhealthy, or abnormal. Even the sex and love addicted adolescents described in this book—who, by their own admission, masturbated compulsively—did not have their peers coming to me with concerns about the sex addicts' self-stimulation. So, Dennis's need to masturbate so frequently and so obviously that he made his roommate uncomfortable was a rare event on the unit. And even when he and I talked about the complaint and what he should do about it, he was not able to find some way to masturbate more privately. In fact, he became more anxious, self-conscious around his peers, ashamed about his behavior, and driven to act out sexually. One time, he felt compelled to masturbate in the public bathroom as the unit was assembled to go out to lunch. His peers figured out what he was up to and humiliated him terribly. Still, he was not able either to stop or to masturbate privately enough that his activity could be kept to himself. His out-of-control masturbation almost drove him out of treatment entirely.

In his addictive behavior inventory, Dennis indicated that he saw himself as sexually obsessed and that he spent a great deal of time fantasizing about sex. He had an illusion that somehow something would change and his sexual problems would miraculously evaporate. He saw sex as a way of having power over others, and he thought that he had to be sexual to feel good about himself. He tried to rationalize away the consequences of his sexual addiction—for example, being the laughing stock of the unit because of his compulsive masturbation. He often felt depressed, worthless, and hopeless after a sexual encounter. When he tried not to be sexual, he had great difficulty maintaining abstinence for any length of time. He thought sex was love.

Much of his sexual preoccupation and acting out was focused around compulsive masturbation, but he engaged in other behaviors as well. He looked at sexually explicit magazines and was particularly interested in child pornography. He collected pornographic materials. He sexualized people and materials that were not sexually explicit, such as advertising catalogues. He looked for sexually suggestive moments of television and in films. He participated in anonymous sexual encounters and engaged in voyeuristic activities. He frequently attempted to touch or fondle other people inappropriately. His talk was filled with sexually explicit jokes and comments. He made inappropriate sexual advances to people and occasionally made inappropriate phone calls. He touched people as if by accident.

Dennis acknowledged having had rare incidents of forced sexual contact. He used drugs and alcohol to enhance his sexual activity and to take sexual advantage. He became interested in sadomasochistic sexual activities and practices and preferred to cause harm, rather than to receive it. He indicated that women's vaginas were a fetish for him.

His sex and love addiction led him to depression, suicidal thoughts and feelings, homicidal urges, extreme hopelessness and despair, emotional instability, feeling out of control, low self-esteem, guilt, shame, isolation, fear, and emotional exhaustion. He put himself at risk with his sexual behaviors including the possibility of unwanted pregnancy, self-abuse, and involvement in potentially dangerous and abusive situations. He felt lost, alone, and spiritually bankrupt—without God or any sense of a Higher Power. He was angry with God, had lost the respect of his family, lost his girlfriend, was unable to sustain friendships, and was failing in school. His life was a great big mess. And the worse it got, the more he wanted to medicate himself with masturbation.

GOOD LITTLE GIRLS

Case 21: Samantha

Samantha was a senior at a private school who always dressed in black, binged on alcohol, and had a history of suicidal ideas and attempts. As a child, she had been the perfect daughter. She was smart, did well in school, was polite and quiet, and reflected well on her lower-middle-class parents. They had done a good job of raising such a "good little girl." When her parents brought her to us, for treatment, it was ostensibly because her one point of praise from them—her grades in school—had collapsed. Obviously, she was depressed. She reported problems with concentration, anhedonia, increased appetite, isolation, crying spells, and irritability and anger. She felt lost, confused, and worthless.

Samantha's low self-esteem was evident in a number of areas. She saw all her personal value as being based on her academic performance. She did not see herself as having other gifts or talents, such as attractive looks or athletic ability. She denied Satanic involvement but had self-mutilated herself by carving anarchy signs in her arm. Her consistent suicidal ideation and attempts were another indicator of her lack of self-worth, as well as of a great deal of inner pain that she could not share with others. She had overdosed three times. After her first suicide attempt, her parents did nothing. After her second, she managed to get outpatient treatment. Finally, after her third suicide attempt, she came to the hospital. She was not functioning in any area of her life at that point; that is, she was failing in school, was socially withdrawn, and has disconnected from her family.

Her parents were difficult to figure out. Her father was disabled from an accident, but no one on our staff was ever able to get enough details to have a good understanding of what had happened to him. He was quite frugal with money yet sent his daughter to a private school (with scholarship aid). He had purchased a new car, but he never allowed anyone to drive it—and so it sat in the garage at home while they all rode around in an old car. Samantha's mother never spoke up to the father. She was quiet, withdrawn, and seemed depressed. She seemed similarly rigid and emotionally inexpressive. Samantha was their only child; in material ways, she appeared to have been spoiled, although she also experienced her father's withholding of money. Affectively, she seemed to be starved for love. She could not remember her parents holding her, and they were not demonstrably affectionate now.

In therapy, Samantha—much like her parents—had trouble opening up. She was anxious, somewhat perfectionistic, and dependent. She seemed deeply sad, lost, and empty. She could not tolerate any sort of compliments, and she reacted to them like they made her stomach turn. She was able to give her peers excellent feedback that was both insightful and empathetic, but she was not able to give the same to herself. Behind her depressive exterior was tremendous insecurity, helplessness, and fear. She did not want to try antidepressant medication, which was suggested because her depression was so obvious that it was painful for us to observe in our interactions with her; but she had a craving for alcohol. As her urge to self-medicate became clearer, she was switched to a group that incorporated chemical dependency recovery with psychotherapy.

Alcohol was not Samantha's only dependency. As she progressed in therapy, her sex and love addiction became more evident. She had a boyfriend who was a freshman in college. Shortly after her admission to the hospital, her pregnancy was discovered. She was stunned and horrified. Her religious background suggested that abortion was not an option; and indeed, she was certain that her parents would not support that choice, even though it was her immediate thought. She was also sure, however, that she was not ready to take care of a child and did not really feel emotionally equipped yet even to take care of herself. Her intense attachment to her boyfriend emerged as she struggled with this major life decision. She desperately needed to talk with him and was overwhelmed when he was not available. Unfortunately, her boyfriend was not supportive. She felt alone and abandoned. Surprisingly, her parents rallied around the idea of terminating the pregnancy; the procedure was then completed in a short amount of time. Notably, Samantha did not show much feeling around this event—particularly, grief at the loss of the baby.

Her male dependency became even more apparent when she was discovered having a relationship with a male peer. She was actually involved with him before her relationship with her boyfriend deteriorated. In fact, she had been restricted from this young male soon after her admission and had denied any lingering feelings for or contact with him. This young man whom she chose was drug dependent, superficial, manipulative, and "a user." She invited him to take her to her school prom because she became panicked when her boyfriend acted aloof and distant about her pregnancy. Rather than waiting to see how things worked out or if she even would feel like going to a prom in a few weeks, she needed that fix immediately. She lied about this when asked and only began to tell the truth after the young man left treatment.

Samantha was confronted with her inappropriate behavior and her relationship dependency. She reacted with rigidity and denial, and tried to rally her parents to her side with arguments about how normal her behavior was for adolescent girls: what girl would not be terribly invested in having a date for the senior prom? Samantha threatened to leave treatment immediately if we did not stop questioning her about her choice of partners and her intense need to have a boyfriend at all cost. She wrote this in her daily feelings log two days before she left:

I feel so alone today. It seems like I am the only person who believes in me—believes that I won't drink for my prom. [Her chemically dependent peers had questioned the safety of even going to the prom, because of the prevalence of drugs and alcohol.] I don't expect people to agree with my decision, but I would like some faith in me. I realize that I am being stubborn and childish, but I haven't changed that. So, I don't think I'm ready to surrender completely. Someday, that time will come.

Sadly, her parents—in an effort to show their "faith" in her—supported her decision to take this young man to the prom. They got caught up in the idea of what a "normal" adolescent girl would feel like, as well as the thought that this was a one-time event in life. They felt a need to align themselves with her in a way that polarized them against the treatment team. The parents wanted her to be well without expecting her to go through the pain that recovery entails. After all, Samantha was their "good little girl." She relapsed with alcohol after her discharge, and stayed in the relationship with the young man from treatment until he cruelly rejected her. Then she quickly reunited with her original boyfriend, whom she had kept waiting in the wings. Indeed, she was beginning to destroy her image of being a good little girl. Driven by the painful emptiness in her relationship with her parents, Samantha was determined to keep a boy in her life despite the obvious heartache that she had already been through with her depression, pregnancy, and tendency to be dependent on chemicals to alter her mood.

Case 22: Cindy

Another high school senior, Cindy bounced into treatment. At first glance, she appeared good looking, sparkly, and knowledgeable. In fact, she could have been mistaken for a staff member at times. She was serious, responsible, conscientious, and determined. She worried about whether she would be home in time to participate in the school play. She was critical of her peers who did not take staff corrections seriously and who horsed around rather than becoming involved in treatment. She was the "ideal patient"; that is, she was well mannered, followed the rules, never complained, and was the first one in line—a genuine good girl.

Cindy was born with a birth defect that made sexual intercourse impossible for her. She discovered this on her own a couple of years before we met, when she and her boyfriend attempted to have sex. When she questioned her mother, her mother told her that Cindy had been born without a uterus and fallopian tubes. This syndrome meant she could never have children, but she probably could have surgery done that would at least allow her to have a relatively normal sex life. Her mother, however, had never pursued the surgery, which might have been done when she was five or six. Cindy's parents had divorced when she was three. Her father, mother, and stepfather all drank heavily, although she hesitated to call them alcoholics. She alleged that her parents were physically abusive to her. She also suffered from asthma dating back to the same time period (eighth grade).

Cindy herself had begun to use drugs heavily after the discovery of her physical condition. She drank, smoked marijuana, used LSD, and snorted cocaine and "crank" (methamphetamine). She had a nine-month period of sobriety prior to admission and was attending counseling and AA and NA meetings. However, she had become increasingly depressed over the summer. She attempted to overdose in June after her stepbrother overdosed on alcohol in May. She continued to have suicidal ideation, insomnia, loss of appetite, and early morning awakening. Things were not going well at home and she was living with a friend from AA. The apparent trigger for her referral to the hospital was an increasingly obvious and destructive "authority problem."

On admission, Cindy was depressed, agitated, anxious, confused, and defensive, but she could be charming, polite, and "good" whenever necessary. She seemed quite rigid and demanding in a quiet way, although she would quickly back down if confronted. She was withholding, distrustful, and fearful. There was a smoldering anger in her. She felt it was particularly unfair that her mother, her school counselor, and even the female friend with whom she was living had conspired to push her into treatment. However, when the crucial moment to protest came—when she had to sign the voluntary commitment paper for admission to the hospital—she became the good girl and signed involuntarily, to all appearances at least.

After she started trusting some of the female staff, she began to reveal the difficult story of her life. She had been neglected and abandoned by both of her parents. Her mother was physically abusive to her—and, like a small child, Cindy was still afraid to make her mother angry. Cindy was a people-pleaser and an actress. She was the best little girl in town with adults. But it was a different story with her peers. She did not get along with any of them. She was hypercritical, isolative, and rejecting. She became enraged in group therapy sessions and would storm out in hysterical tears or violent anger. Peers, in turn, had a great deal of trouble tolerating her. She was parentified, and so they refused to trust her or allow her to get close. She felt out of place and wanted to leave. She saw her peers as dishonest, hypocritical, and childish; they saw her as narcissistic, grandiose, and self-centered. The difference between her interactions with adults and with peers made some staff wonder if she were a multiple personality. She seemed like two different people. They wondered if she was acting or if she had any control over her behaviors.

One of Cindy's primary defenses seemed to be fantasy. Her sex and love addiction took the form of a romance addiction. She fantasized about finding her "Prince Charming" who would take her away from the pain in her life. She could spend hours a day inside her mind. She loved television soap operas and Harlequin romance novels. And Cindy used the same defense to avoid dealing with the reality of her abusive and alcohol-dependent mother and stepfather. She finally agreed to have a family meeting—which she had been refusing to do and her mother had been avoiding—so as to begin the process of dealing with the issues that surrounded her neglect and abuse. All along, Cindy had been refusing to meet with her mother, let alone go home to live. But after one family session, she was almost immediately ready to return home—despite the fears of staff, friends, counselors, and sponsors. She seemed like a child who had found her dream: to return home.

So we gave Cindy a therapeutic pass from the hospital to test the waters at home. She had requested an alcohol-free environment at home—which is the usual suggestion made by treatment staff for an adolescent who has a problem with chemical abuse and/or dependency. As it turned out, Cindy's stepfather was drinking at home while she was there for the visit. But she managed to twist this around in her mind to mean that this was the last time he would do this and that, since she was not technically residing in the house yet, he had not violated her request and would honor it in the future. Clearly, she was in fantasy land and not in touch with reality.

Cindy's need to distort reality—combined with her mother's denial and minimization of her own problems—led me to think that this was a potentially dangerous situation. Cindy's substance abuse, depression, and suicidality coincided with her discovery of her birth defect and inability to have normal sexual relations. Her romance addiction was likewise triggered by this traumatic event. I had no reason to believe that all of these issues were resolved in one family meeting, so I decided that I had a duty to report Cindy's mother to the authorities for child abuse and neglect. In particular, I warned the state's children and youth department that Cindy's life was in potential danger unless her mother would follow through with our suggestion that Cindy have the surgery if medically recommended. Fortunately, the authorities agreed; a year after my report, I received a letter stating that the surgery had been successfully completed under the supervision of state authorities. Hopefully, Cindy's chemical dependency and sex and love addiction tendencies were reduced by the attention paid to this major trauma in her life. Cindy was indeed a good girl, but her pain was hidden in her rage and need to self-medicate with drugs, alcohol, and romance.

Case 23: Joan

Joan was another girl whom anyone would be proud to invite into their home. She was energetic, engaging, and playful, but she could also be serious and sincere. When I met her, she was a junior in high school who loved animals—especially horses.

Joan had become increasingly depressed after Christmas. In February, she attempted suicide by cutting herself. She was taken to the emergency room of the local hospital, but no follow-up treatment was obtained. One of her friends overdosed in March. By May, Joan started seeing an outpatient therapist. She had lost almost forty pounds in six months and was clearly underweight. She fought a great deal with her mother and blamed her father for "always putting me down." Finally, she was suspended from school for fighting with a peer.

Upon her admission to our hospital, Joan's depression and chemical dependency became obvious. She tested positive for cocaine and marijuana. She reported a history of alcoholism in her paternal grandfather, but no problems with substance abuse on the part of her parents. Initially, she was dysphoric, angry, irritable, and emotionally labile. She could be quite friendly and cooperative or she could fly off the handle and be selfish, hostile, and withdrawn.

She seemed quite anxious and jittery; she was easily overwhelmed and often tearful. She reported feeling quite "confused."

However, she did appear to become involved in the treatment process and was gradually less defensive and less anxious. She seemed to be opening up and talking about her situation—especially her difficulties with her father, whom she found to be quite rigid, rejecting, critical, and hurtful. She was a "good patient," at first glance, and was making progress in terms of earning privileges and taking responsibility.

Her good-little-girl image shattered when she was discovered to be having a relationship with Harold (see Case 16). Even when confronted with the relationship, Joan was not able to give it up. She tried to manipulate the staff and create an appearance of compliance with the rules, but her peers were trying to support her efforts to get honest and so they continued to tell her about her "male dependency" with Harold. She was hurt and enraged that they would not go along with her sneaky efforts to pass notes or otherwise communicate with him. She seemed to have no appreciation of how sick Harold was and how destructive the relationship would be for her. She was like a moth drawn to the flame. The more we tried to help her let go, the harder she fought to hold on. She got excited by the Romeo and Juliet quality of their forbidden love. He, of course, fed into her fantasies with promises of great fidelity and love in the future when they were freed from the constraints of controlling staff.

The source of Joan's intense love addiction became more obvious during family therapy. Her parents presented as she did—that is, overly "good." Her father worked in an auto body shop, and her mother was a hairdresser. They were concerned, involved, and cooperative. Her mother seemed somewhat overprotective and intrusive, but she seemed to have a "good heart" and positive intentions for her daughter. Her father was a bit more strict, straight, and did not seem to understand his daughter's rebellious behavior. The most telling comment he made still rings in my ears and makes me shudder. We were discussing Joan's drug problem when her father suddenly announced to all, "Drug dealers ought to be shot." Somewhat confused about where he was coming from, and believing that he was expressing protective feelings toward his daughter, I asked Joan's father whether he would feel the same way if he discovered that his daughter had sold drugs. She had, in fact, sold drugs as part of her drug dependency, although she was not a large-scale drug dealer. She had sold to many friends as a means of getting money for her own drugs. The father stunned me by saying that, if his daughter sold drugs, then she ought to be shot too.

The family session quickly degenerated from there: Joan ran crying from the room, and her parents started to fight with each other. Joan's mother was trying to defend her husband on the one hand—by telling me he did not really mean what he had said—and attack him, on the other, by yelling at him for his harsh comments. Their fight continued after the session—through the lobby and out into the parking lot. Joan was crushed, but also felt a bit vindicated because her father's extreme criticism had been evident to others as well as to her mother.

In her sex and love addiction, Joan was chasing this rejecting father by choosing men who would use, abuse, and abandon her like her father had. She was blind to this, though, and pursued the relationship with Harold even after her discharge, despite our strong advice to the contrary. Her parents were so locked in their own struggle that they were unable to let up long enough to unite in helping their daughter. Finally, after a few weeks of stringing her along, Harold dumped Joan and moved on to a new conquest. She was devastated and humiliated, but she continued to fan the flame with fantasies that he would learn his lesson and return to her true love.

NEEDY GIRLS

Case 24: Lisa

At fifteen, Lisa was lonely, needy, and struggling to find someone to hold onto. She had little contact with her father. Her mother was quite needy, dependent, and had parentified Lisa. Her older sister sexually abused her. She had been in foster care for a year and a half. She was referred for treatment by the state's department of children and youth. She felt worthless, lost, and alone.

Lisa was chronically depressed but had become even worse just prior to her hospital admission. She was not eating or sleeping and had trouble concentrating. She was angry, irritable, and had crying spells. She tended to be agitated and anxious, and needed a lot of reassurance. She was skipping school, staying out late, and running away. She medicated her pain with food, relationships, sex, and drugs. She abused alcohol, marijuana, amphetamines, caffeine pills, and "rush." She was obese and thought of herself as "fat and ugly." Her self-worth was terrible and she often wondered why she was alive.

In treatment, Lisa was childlike and dependent with adults; she was shy and guarded with her peers. She seemed to be hyperreactive and intensely sensitive. By the third week, we gave her an assignment to write an essay on "how being a 'perfect patient' is my trying to be 'superwoman.' " This was followed by another essay assignment, on "why I protect my addiction by hiding my urges to use?" Trust was a major problem for Lisa. Self-esteem was another huge issue. So were relationships. As she began to open up in therapy, she started talking about her chemical dependency and her sexual acting out. She was promiscuous and "male dependent." Shortly after revealing her pre-admission behavior, she was discovered passing notes to a male peer and was placed on restriction from the males. She was quite competitive and hostile toward her female peers, and related in a sexualized way with the males. She appeared desperate for nurturing and yet unable to get what she needed. She seemed competitive with female peers and dependent with males. With adult staff, she was just needy.

Lisa's conflicts with her female peers were related to problems with her sister and her mother. Her sister had victimized her sexually. Lisa was preoccupied with this molestation and yet could not talk about it. One evening, she approached a female staff member hysterically and asked the staff member to read her story:

The first time my sister ever touched me was when I was at home and she was watching me and we used to play house all the time and she would make me be the baby and she would be the mom and she would make me suck her fucking tit. The second time I remember is we were at home again and we were playing and she was rubbing my vagina and was rubbing and rubbing. The third time was when a friend of mine was over and she made me feel her and she felt me and then my sister felt the both of us. The other times we were at my aunt's house and we had to sleep over and she was sticking q-tips up inside of me. And another time when I was up at my dad's house and this would happen every week she would finger me and play with me and would play with my tits.

Finally, after divulging the severity and extent of her abuse, she was able to calm down and enter more fully into treatment.

The next crisis centered around Lisa's mother. Her mother worked in a supermarket as a cashier and did not have a car. She was about 150 miles from the hospital, so it was difficult for her to visit or attend family meetings. Other families traveled similar distances and, despite the three-hour ride, managed to come down every weekend. Lisa's mother never visited and, in fact, made Lisa feel guilty for wanting her to come and be part of the treatment. She got mad at Lisa for not calling her—when, actually, the mother had access to a toll-free 800 number at work. Lisa's mother was as overweight as Lisa was, and had many physical complaints. The mother too was male dependent and used her male partner as an excuse not to visit Lisa—for example, saying he was sick and she needed to take care of him. The mother presented herself as a victim, and Lisa felt the need to care for and to "fix" her mother. Thus, Lisa was parentified and placed in the caretaking role, so she never got her own needs taken care of, especially by her mother. One time, her mother was supposed to come for a family therapy session with the county social worker; but on the day of the session, she was "too sick" to travel. Lisa was crushed and blamed herself for her mother's irresponsible behavior; she thought, "If I did not have these problems, then my mother wouldn't be under so much stress and would not have to be traveling all over the world to help me."

Lisa's experiences with her sister and her mother—these two needy and abusive women in her own family—drove her outside the house to seek comfort and solace. She looked to food, alcohol and drugs, and sex and relationships to fill the great inner void that she felt. She was asked to write about how she got into a relationship on the unit:

Well when he first came in I thought he was cute and I didn't say anything to him but hi how are you and said my name was Lisa. Then later on that night we were sitting in the ot [occupational therapy] area and I was sitting at one table and he was sitting at the other and he kept looking at me and I kept looking back then he mumbled something to me and I didn't say anything back to him. Then later on that night it was like really start to talk to him not of any importance. Then Saturday, we were talking and he asked me about something in this magazine and then later on that night I was asked by him if I would give him something and really understand what he said and I said yes. Then on Sunday he finally got off the unit [i.e., was allowed to go outside the building] and I made sure I sat by him and when we were sitting there he started to play with my leg and I just moved it away and started to laugh and then I put it back and he did it again. I didn't say anything and he said some smart stuff and I said to him don't say that because I can't have relationships for you because of my self-esteem and he said he didn't know what I meant. Then I told him I would tell him when we got back to the unit and I explained to him what the program said about relationships and then he said what if I am to see you when you get out and I said I will be in long-term [treatment] and you can see me then and we can only be friends in here. And then I told I was getting really jealous of him because the way he was talking and looking at Susan and Lori. I also told him that I was extremely pissed off when I couldn't sit by him. when he made eyes at me and I felt lonely and scared and I hate myself and I need someone to make me feel good about myself. And I'm really doing this on my own. My family and my fucking mom isn't here and I need someone to attach myself to, so I don't need to feel so lonely.

Lisa summarized her sex and love addiction well in those last few lines. She wanted to be a good girl and follow the rules, but the pull of the promise of attachment and filling her emptiness and loneliness was too much to resist, especially when she was still actively being neglected by her mother. Lisa's father had abandoned her; but she learned that by being sexual and seductive she could get attention from the male peers, who seemed to be less threatening to her than her female peers, based on her previous experiences with women.

Lisa was taught that other people could indeed meet her needs; but these people were also objectified and sexualized. So, in the context of a relationship, she could get her cravings for worth, contact, specialness, and value met and all she would have to do is be seductive and be seduced. Despite being surrounded with caring and nurturing adults at the hospital, Lisa had to turn to a male peer to fill the hole in her soul. The rush and excitement of that flirtation, the anticipation of the touch, and the fulfillment of the fantasy pulled her away from the pain of treatment: dealing with her substance abuse; focusing on her sexual abuse, admitting to herself that her mother was not there for her; and examining her male dependency. Her neediness was obvious to everyone, as was her anger, jealousy, competitiveness, people pleasing, and perfectionism. Her sex and love addiction was hidden—the secret "stash" that she hoped would really fix the pain.

Case 25: Pam

Pam was a puzzling young woman. She tried hard to be a "good patient," and the staff responded positively. She was engaging and intelligent. She came from an upper-middle-class, suburban family and looked the part of a private school student. But she had a dark side that was well hidden and only became evident when you knew her for a while. Pam seemed needy and grateful for attention, but somehow all of our positive reenforcement never seemed to click. She could not let go of her unhealthy ways of getting her dependency needs met—Satanism, drugs, and relationships—despite having an overly involved mother and attentive staff.

Pam was fifteen and had already tried to end her life twice. In September, she had been hospitalized in a local community hospital when she overdosed the first time; she overdosed again the following March, and ended up being hospitalized in our psychiatric hospital. A breakup with her boyfriend triggered the second suicide attempt. She had become depressed, lethargic, anhedonic, isolated, and hopeless. Her school grades dropped and she was suspended for truancy. She was abusing alcohol, marijuana, LSD, and "ecstasy." She overdosed on Fuerocet, which had been prescribed for her migraine headaches. She also suffered from asthma.

Pam's parents had divorced when she was three. She was the oldest of three children. Her mother remarried, and Pam reported having a "decent" relationship with her stepfather. Her natural father was involved to some degree, but she described their contact as "distant." Her relationships with her siblings appeared to be all right; but, again, there seemed to be some detachment and lack of closeness. Her mother was anything but distant. In fact, she seemed overly involved with Pam and yet strangely unclear about what was going on with her daughter. The mother seemed to have no clue as to why Pam should be so depressed and preoccupied.

Pam had a major problem with trust, intimacy, and self-esteem. She was so guarded that she seemed paranoid about anyone finding out what was on her mind or what sorts of things she was up to. She could not tolerate any sort of positive feedback or affirmation, but she could not really explain why identifying her gifts was so painful for her. Clearly, her father did not act as if he thought she was special. But her mother—perhaps, in part, to compensate for what the father did not do—was quite positive, enthusiastic, and complimentary about Pam and her special talents and abilities.

Pam indicated that she had always had a difficult time with her peers, and her mother confirmed this. No one really knew why, but Pam felt odd and left out most of her life. She had artistic talent, but her art pad was filled with dark, depressing drawings of skulls, death, and Satanic symbols. At home, her room was painted all black and she often wore all black clothing. She was preoccupied with death and depression. She felt hopeless and was certain that she could not be helped. Her interactions with staff were typically dependent, needy, and bottomless. Nothing seemed to fill her up, especially when it came to nurturing from adults.

Her drugs of choice were "fantasy" drugs: hallucinogens like LSD, marijuana, and "ecstacy." She also was obsessed with men. Her male dependency was kept well hidden, much like her Satanic involvement—but her relationship dependency was kept even more secret than the devil worship. She had an intense relationship dependency going on prior to her admission. She was obsessed with a seventeen-year-old young man who strung her along for sex and companionship until someone better came along. When he dropped her, Pam's world fell apart and she did not want to live anymore. Even after she stopped feeling suicidal, she still fantasized about reuniting with "Teddy" (her playful, fantasy name for him). She could not imagine life without him even though he had hurt her and was no longer available.

In the hospital, her struggles with her sex and love addiction became more evident than they had been on an outpatient basis. She had managed to keep her dependency problems more secretive she was under less restrictive supervision and observation. One of her initial assignments in our program was to let go of the trappings designed to attract men: her jewelry, fancy hairstyling, and makeup. Shortly thereafter, she was asked to write an essay on the "two sides of Pam." Because she was reticent in participatory situations, she was given a behavioral assignment to speak in each group or meeting and get a note signed by staff indicating that she had completed the requirement of sharing something. She was also asked to "write a secret daily and give it to your doctor [psychologist]."

Next, Pam was told to write an essay on "what male dependency means and how it applies to you?" She struggled with these therapeutic tasks and made little progress. She seemed desperately needy, but she was not able to take the first step in therapy, that is, to become a bit assertive, take a little initiative, be at least somewhat responsible for her negative thinking, feeling, and behaving. There was a terrible struggle going on inside of Pam between the part of her that wanted to stay small, childlike, and dependent (as she often was with her mother and with boyfriends) and the part that wanted to become independent, wanted to feel good about herself, and wanted to develop her own identity independent of those on whom she had so far depended.

Her daily secrets reveal this fight within her. Four weeks into treatment, Pam wrote, "I like someone in here, and have for a long time, and he knows. I've gotten other people involved because I've never really felt comfortable talking to him. I was told that I would receive a note from him, although I know what will be in it already." She could not be direct or responsible, but instead was compelled to act out in a passive/aggressive way that required negative behavior on the part of her peers. Her neediness was so strong that she could have gotten them in trouble too, but she was just too frightened even to talk directly to the young man in question. Her addictive acting out was discovered: "I was confronted last night about receiving a note, and I automatically lied, so I got consequences." One of these consequences was a "male restriction," which was intended to separate her from males for a time so that she could think more about her actions, rather than react on impulse. Rather than feeling like she was being helped, however, she "felt like a slut by being put on male [restriction]." Fortunately, Pam did begin to experience some of the benefits of this therapeutic intervention: "I didn't know how to deal with my feelings, like not talking to him was going to kill me. I talked it out with staff and then went to the gym. I realized that, even though he was there, I could have a good time with my friends without thinking of him!" This was the beginning of recovery for Pam. She started to feel like she could live and enjoy life without one of her main dependencies. She would have to learn that she could have a life without a man, without drugs and alcohol, without depression, and without Satanism.

Case 26: Janet

At the age of fifteen Janet's sex and love addiction had left her with a four-month-old boy, a history of broken and abusive relationships, horrible self-esteem, and a great emptiness. She grew up in the suburbs. Her father was distant and he abused drugs. Her mother had a history of depression and substance abuse that had led to psychiatric hospitalization. Janet hated her mother's current male partner. In the past, Janet had been molested and sexually assaulted. Now, she was sexually acting out and was drinking a lot. She felt guilty, ashamed, and needy, but she was afraid to ask adults directly for caring. Instead, she acted out in ways that got adults to intervene and take care of her.

She came to our hospital because she had attempted suicide by cutting her wrists. After being seen at a local, general hospital emergency room, Janet was transferred for inpatient psychiatric care. This was her second attempt on her own life. Earlier, she had tried to overdose on aspirin. She had trouble eating, sleeping, and concentrating. She reported crying spells and had stopped caring how she looked. She had become hostile and verbally abusive at home and at school. Her grades had dropped and she had begun to be truant from school. She was confused, overwhelmed, and hopeless.

Janet was also kind, cooperative, and attractive. She wanted to please and responded to attention from adults. She was anxious, impulsive, and insecure. She had profoundly low self-worth and was deeply inadequate and easily overwhelmed. Her psychological testing indicated that she had a modestly low IQ, a depressed mood, immature coping skills, and sexual preoccupation. She tended to be somewhat defensive about her acting out and, in fact, lied initially about her drug abuse. She minimized the risks involved in sexual acting out, and projected blame onto her parents for her problems. She seemed to react well to the structure and support of the hospital environment and began opening up about her life and her experiences.

As Janet became more honest and revealing, she wrote for us a relationship history that documented the progression of her sex and love addiction:

1. *Bill*—My relationship with Bill was nice. He was my first boyfriend and I really liked him. He was my next door neighbor. My mom liked him and everything. But my girlfriends had something to say, because he was white [and Janet was black]. It was fine and everything until I moved and then soon after he moved too. I kissed for the first time with him. We frenched-kissed. We never had sex.

2. *Jim*—My relationship with Jim was very odd and messed up. We started going together in 6th grade and we would go together for that whole year on and off. When summer come, we just split apart until school started again. We went together in 6th and 7th grade and we make a pack to our friends that we weren't going to go together, so we didn't and I moved. Me and Jim's relationship was almost like a marriage or something. We would argue, fight, get jealous, and all the other stuff husband and wife would do even buy things for each other. It was pretty messed up but I think, I think he was my first love but I'm not sure. I really, really cared about him alot, a whole lot. We also never had sex hard to believe now for me.

3. *Juan*—My relationship with Juan I think was wrong from the beginning. I had broke up with another boy and I still cared about Jim. Juan was very rude and ignorant. He treated me like a shit on a stick. And I still went with him. I put up with alot of stuff from him, but I didn't give up until later on. He was real cute and I liked him alot too and I told him I loved him but I don't think he loved me. We were having alot of problems between us about old girlfriends and boyfriends and we just broke up. He embarrassed me in front of the whole cafeteria. He told me on the microphone to give him his shit back. That hurt me and was very upset and angry. I used to wear his necklace with his name on it, but my mom didn't approve of that. But one thing we didn't do was have sex either.

4. *Sam*—My relationship with Sam wasn't meant to be either. I went with him for no reason. I liked him alot but it wasn't enough to go out with him. We were at a game and I went inside the school and Juan, Jim, Bill, and Don asked me out and I took him serious and he wasn't serious after awhile. And broke up with Sam just to go with a guy who was just playing around with me. We didn't go together very long (me and Sam). We definately didn't have sex either.

5. *Carl*—My relationship with Carl was very good. I think he was my first willing sex was with him. I really, really loved him. We were really close and we would have sex all the time. He and I lived in the same area like two minutes away and I would see him every day at school and at home. We were entirely too close. We were like were married or something. we fought sometimes and had alot of good times. He would interfere by my school work and my social life. He left pretty soon after and my social life was back to how it was before. It was like my whole life and time was all dedicated to him. He had a tremendous effect on me when he left me. He messed me up. He left me and went down South. When I found I was pregnant, he didn't try to get back up to me. He just stayed and got into trouble and try to forget about me. It was fine between us until he left. Girls didn't like me for going with him, but I went with him anyway. We never really fought that much except one time and we weren't really going together. I was just playing with him and he took me serious and we just started arguing and then I slapped him and he slapped back. That was it.

6. *Rick*—My relationship with Rick was I don't know. He said he really liked me, but I didn't think that he did. He would say he was coming over and wouldn't come. He would have me waiting all that time for nothing and when he said the reason, he said he wanted to be with his friends. Then, later on, he would say stuff in the relationship like I'm smothering him. And he needs space. I would try everything and anything in my power to get him from not being mad or upset with me. I cried and pleaded with him. He would hurt me constantly over and over again. I wanted to break up with him in a way and in another way I didn't because I thought I loved him. Remember, I was stupid and afraid to let him go, so I didn't for awhile. I felt miserable, hurt, confused, angry, and sad all at once. When I told him to break up with me, he told me I was cramping his style and I was smoothering him. He just didn't like me anymore. Then, one day on Friday, he was angry at me and I just told him if he doesn't want to go with me then just say it. And, after awhile on the phone, he broke up with me. I still liked him and everything, heck I thought I loved him. I gave myself to him a few times and I thought of it as being special and meaningful. I cried when he broke up with me and I haven't seen him since. I miss him, but he doesn't miss me. He has a new girlfriend and he just forgot about me. He really didn't care after all. My friends told me to give it up, to leave him alone. I think they said this because he was treating me like dirt and I was letting him. I feel that they were right most of the time but sometimes I thought they were wrong. I didn't react nice. I was very upset and angry, but after all she or they were right. I didn't want to admit it but I did.

7. *Stan*—My relationship with Stan was great until I screwed it up. We were great together. He was a virgin. I later on found out I was his first but he wasn't mine. I started drinking and eat and licking cocaine. I had sex with him when I was drunk for the first time. I really liked him alot, but I didn't

love him. I drank beer and got stupid and did something with somebody else besides him and he forgave me at first until too many people found out and then he changed. He started acting rude and stupid. Then, he started hurting me. He said he loved me and that he still cared for me but he had to think. He would kiss me one minute and then play me off like a dummy. He was playing mind games with me and it was messing me up really bad like something fierce. It probably would be good and everything until I messed it up. I guess I did that because he treated me nice and with respect and everything and I just couldn't accept him. He was just too nice and I had to mess it all up.

Janet's history sounds much longer than from fifth to tenth grades. Notice that she tried to make it sound more positive, fun, and caring than it really was. She focused a lot on whether or not the particular relationship was sexual. She described herself tolerating abuse—physical, mental, emotional, and sexual— which is what she had been subjected to as a young girl. She was desperately needy and hoping that somehow, some way, things would work out and she would really feel loved and accepted. Her dependency was evident in her need to please and her inclination to be "husband and wife" or "smothering." Notice the progression from bad to worse until she was left abandoned with an infant. She felt lost, alone, worthless, and in need of a way out. Men—with all of their excitement and promise—had left her this way, so the only other escape route was suicide. She had learned from her parents that her needs would not be met. She had high hopes for romance and love, but again she was disappointed— until she could take no more.

TOUGH GIRLS

Case 27: Connie

Connie was tough. Life had made her that way. By the time I met her, she had been abandoned by her natural father, physically abused and molested by her stepfather, raped, had a severe car accident, and suffered the murder of her mother. Connie was of mixed races—half white and half Hispanic—and was only sixteen when I met her. She lived with her aunt and uncle, but she hardly ever listened to them. The courts had ordered her to treatment because she was caught receiving stolen goods as part of a scheme to get money for drugs.

Connie thought she was living life in the fast lane. I thought she was on the run. She was depressed, suicidal, and hopeless. She had tried to kill herself twice in the past year. She could not eat, sleep, concentrate, or function at home or in school. She was truant and unable to keep up her grades. Connie stole, ran away, and lied to her aunt and uncle. She had lost thirty-two pounds in two months. She was stubborn, bored, and pessimistic. She abused alcohol and drugs—including marijuana, LSD, amphetamines, cocaine, and crack—and had injected drugs intravenously twice. She was suffering a post-traumatic stress disorder (PTSD), with distractibility, anxiety, hyperreactivity, and nightmares. She had no sense of having a future. She had sex with whomever and wherever she pleased. No one told her what to do.

Connie was tough as nails on the outside, but inside she was scared, lost, and alone. She was determined to keep her inside hidden, too—especially from her peers. She was withdrawn, isolative, people pleasing, and avoidant. Because of the tragic death of her mother, most people allowed Connie to maintain this tough facade and did not try to find out what was underneath. She often engaged in power struggles with staff. At times, in private, she would regress into a hysterically sobbing child, but usually she was aggressive, in control, and suspicious. She seemed to have two sides to her personality. With authority figures, Connie was a "nice girl." With her peers, she showed her angry, vengeful, sadistic side. Occasionally, she would become panicky and over-whelmed with anxiety; but most of the time, she was hard, distant, and aloof.

Connie's treatment was long and difficult. She was sent to long-term residential care after two and a half months of inpatient psychiatric treatment without much improvement. Her sex and love addiction became more obvious in the less structured long-term setting. She had alluded to a history of promiscuity, many boyfriends, and unusual sexual experiences; but she was in a period of abstinence when she first entered our hospital. In long-term treatment, she became more obviously sexual and obsessed with having a relationship. She could not follow the direction of treatment staff, and continued to act out in relationships and sexually despite a variety of interventions by staff.

Her sexual and romantic activity triggered her memories of sexual abuse, and she came back to our hospital because she had regressed into a catatonic state. She reported losing time, having "blackouts," and nightmares. She had also returned to depression, anxiety, and suicidality. With female staff members she began to talk more about her sexual abuse. She was terrified of dealing with these issues because her stepfather had repeatedly told her she would be killed if she told anyone. But Connie had begun to realize on her own that her male dependency and her highly sexualized behavior were related to her sexual abuse. She knew she used sex and romance to distract herself from her pain. She was able to see that she had few coping skills other than getting a sex and love "fix" to process her feelings and experiences from the past.

When she got sober from chemicals, her sex and love addiction became more intense. She had attributed her extreme sexual activity and inability to maintain relationships to her chemical dependency; and in many ways they *were* intertwined. However, in her residential treatment, she was not doing drugs, but she was still doing sex and love to the point where it was interfering with her treatment. She thought she could stop whenever she wanted to, but she discovered that she was not able to let go of her seductive, flirtatious, and sexualized behaviors even though she had the intention of not acting this way any more.

She felt great shame and guilt about the problems she had caused her aunt and uncle with her sexual and romantic liaisons. They had tried to talk with her about her reputation and the danger in which she was placing herself, but she had ignored them and laughed them off as "old-timers" who could not understand the needs of modern teenagers. She had continued the same pattern with the residential treatment staff. Whenever they approached her about being out of control, she got angry and defensive and refused to listen to what they were trying to say to her.

Eventually, the whole front collapsed and Connie was again feeling like life was not worth living. She had suffered enough pain for more than one lifetime and she could not imagine things getting any better. The emerging memories of sexual abuse were enough to overwhelm her defenses and leave her feeling intensely alone and filled with shame and dread. Even her sex and love activities were not enough to keep these experiences at bay. Being tough was all that she had to hold onto, and now even that was slipping away.

Case 28: Mindy

Mindy had been an intravenous drug user for two years when she turned sixteen. She was street wise, tough, and down to earth. She obviously had a good head on her shoulders; but she had been so preoccupied with family problems, her own psychological hang-ups, and drug dependence that there was never any time for academic learning. Despite this lack of attention to schoolwork, she did well in school whenever she put her mind to the work. She was friendly, cooperative, and polite, but she would not do anything that she did not want to do.

On admission to our psychiatric hospital, Mindy was depressed, withdrawn, angry, agitated, and hostile. She cooperated minimally with the intake interview. A drug screening indicated that she had been abusing Valium, cocaine, and marijuana; she admitted to abusing alcohol, methamphetamine, and heroin as well. She had trouble eating and had lost twenty-seven pounds. She was not sleeping well. Mindy could not concentrate, felt bored, and was anhedonic. She had anxiety, panic attacks, and crying spells. She felt ashamed, guilty, worthless, and hopeless. There were increasing conflicts with her mother and stepfather. She ran away, stole from the family, and lied to them. She was truant from school. Her life was out of control.

Immediately, Mindy fought with the staff and threatened to leave treatment. She seemed to feel better about herself when she was fighting with some authority figure. She had a severe physical and psychological withdrawal from the drugs, but actually she appeared more dependent on her drug-abusing girlfriend, Carol, than on the chemicals. She was not allowed to call Carol (This was a privilege she could earn by working in her treatment.) Yet, despite our efforts to police her phone calls, Mindy found a way to get in touch with the friend. When confronted, Mindy became enraged, threatening, and explosive. She could not imagine life without Carol and would do anything in her power to maintain the relationship.

As she became a bit more trusting of the staff, Mindy shared with us that, prior to her treatment, she had developed a suicide plan and was self-mutilative. She also engaged in high-risk sex and shared needles—both activities that could have led her to HIV/AIDS. Carol's boyfriend was HIV positive, and he was Mindy's major drug connection. She had concocted elaborate con games with Carol to fleece people of their money so that the two of them could have the cash for drugs. They were both quite proud of their ability to manipulate people and to get what they wanted.

Mindy was terrified of connecting with her feelings. She loved to play power games with adults and peers alike, and she was determined to win. She was quick to run and often seemed a likely candidate for an elopement from the hospital (i.e., running away). She listened in groups, but rarely shared. She became close with a few peers, but was always quite private and secretive about her alliances and emotions. No one knew where she really stood. She apparently wanted to stop using drugs, but she did not want to have to let go of any control—and she definitely did not want to have to be open, vulnerable, or less than tough.

Over time, the source of her hard exterior became more clear. Mindy shared with us, finally, that she had lived on the street and in abandoned cars as a child because the family was homeless. Her father was sick and disabled. He probably drank too much. He abandoned his family, and her mother was overwhelmed with trying to care for the children and find food and shelter. Mindy was parentified as a child; she wound up taking care of her mother and siblings. She had no time for play or joy. Life was harsh, and survival was the name of the game. Mindy was profoundly neglected; but when she was encouraged to allow herself to talk about how painful this was for her, she became quite defensive of her mother. Afraid that we would think her mother did not love her, Mindy felt she had to stick up for her mother and deny her own pain.

Sometime after the homeless period, Mindy's mother found another man and remarried. Mindy's stepfather adored her; she went from being neglected to being spoiled. As a result, she developed into a confusing combination of hard reality and entitled princess. She would switch back and forth between these two extremes of self-denial and self-indulgence. Any sort of deprivation would trigger an aggressive desire to gratify her every need. Her grandiosity and narcissism compounded themselves when she felt the need for whatever she wanted whenever she wanted it. Mindy's mother often went along with her mood swings; the mother would be angrily defensive when she thought we were not being fair to her daughter, and overly indulgent when she thought Mindy might be suffering in any way. Probably, Mindy's mother was overcompensating for the time when she could not meet her daughter's needs and adequately take care of the family. However, her protectiveness and indulgence were counterproductive to Mindy's therapy process, which was designed to help her give up her addictions by, first, letting go of (self-destructive) control.

Her sex and love addiction was rather well hidden through much of her inpatient treatment. There were clues, however, to sexual acting out and possible prostitution. In addition, she tested positive for hepatitis. Mindy seemed unable to conceive of practicing safe sex. Her relationship dependency was obvious with her girlfriend Carol, but she did not appear to latch onto any of the boys. Only after discharge did she immediately attach herself—to an older man. She was in love within days of her discharge and was living with this older man within a month. He allegedly was sober from chemicals, but there was an active sexual exchange involved in their relationship. Safe sex was not practiced—despite the education she had received in the hospital. Mindy was afraid to say no because she could not afford to lose him. Eventually he led her back to drugs and ultimately back to the hospital. Despite her tough facade, Mindy was putty in this man's hand; she could not admit to her powerlessness and ask for help until she had again fallen to the bottom.

When she came back to the unit, she felt overwhelmed with shame and guilt and could not make eye contact with anyone on the staff. She hid in her room for two days and wanted to run. She was again suicidal, filled with self-hatred, and out of control. She had become so dependent on the relationship that she had lost her sense of self, her recovery from chemicals, and her self-esteem. She hated her own dependency and consequently was driven to act it out in a reenactment of her childhood neglect and abandonment by a male. Her mother felt driven to rescue Mindy and was not able to set any limits or realistic expectations of her. Her husband realized that Mindy's mother was part of the problem, not part of the solution. But his loyalty to the mother interfered with his ability to tell her that she was hurting her daughter, not helping. Consequently, she assisted Mindy in leaving treatment again—against medical advice and without any clear plan for the adolescent's survival at home.

Case 29: Beverly

"Wild" was the most commonly used word to describe Beverly. She was fourteen going on forty. She got high from placing herself in dangerous situations—such as "copping" drugs in the scariest part of town. She was proud of her toughness and eager to meet any challenges to her image. She was filled with bravado and quick to prove herself to others. Her list of traumas and outrageous behaviors was lengthy.

Beverly's father had been shot when she was a child. The circumstances were mysterious, and Beverly's mother would not clarify them for us. She told us that he had been accidentally gunned down in a restaurant in a Mob-related shooting. Beverly had tried to commit suicide at least nine times, including overdoses and cutting herself. She was self-mutilative and had numerous scars on her arms and legs. She bit herself. She would become hysterical and agitated to the point where no one could calm her down. She ran away from home and was truant from school. She had been in the juvenile detention center, foster care, and long-term residential treatment (although she stayed there only a few days). She had been in our psychiatric hospital for three months the year before. Stealing her mother's car and running off with a boyfriend had triggered that admission. Beverly had been in outpatient treatment since she was eleven. She fought with her peers and teachers. She assaulted a police officer the month before her second admission to the hospital. She was verbally abusive and threatening to everyone, including her mother, sister, and stepfather. She was anorexic, abused drugs (marijuana and cocaine) and alcohol, and acted out sexually. She had been arrested for driving under the influence when she stole her mother's car. After her first hospitalization, she managed to stay sober from drugs for about nine months. Then she was raped, at age thirteen. Three months before she came back to the hospital, she had a miscarriage.

In treatment, Beverly was depressed, angry, suicidal, and homicidal. She wanted to keep everyone away from her and did not think that she deserved to live. Beverly was hostile, threatening, and intimidating even though she was not a large person. She made it clear to her peers that she was not someone to mess with, and they gave her a wide berth. She was needy, demanding, aggressive, and intrusive with staff. She had her favorites and would treat them well; to those whom she did not like, she was caustic, sarcastic, and abrupt.

Finally, she began to talk about the Satanic rituals to which her father would subject Beverly and her sister, in the family basement. She could not talk about much of what happened, but it was obvious that she had been terribly traumatized and terrified as a small child. She remembered being tied up and being referred to as the "devil child." She continued to play this role with her family and the rest of the world. Her sister was the angel: she got good grades in Catholic school and was pleasant and cooperative at home. Beverly's mother could not figure out why one of her daughters was so "good" and the other so "bad." Beverly's younger sister hated Beverly for being so abusive to her and so disruptive of the family's life; she did not want her hospitalized sister to come home, because she was certain that the chaos would return with Beverly. In the highly structured environment of the hospital, Beverly was able to control herself most of the time; but even there, she had explosive and self-destructive outbursts, as well as spells of sexual and relational acting out.

Having wild sex and multiple relationships was one of the ways in which Beverly ran from her pain. She was never without a boyfriend and had many prospects waiting in the wings in case a relationship failed. She could not be committed sexually to a partner and had many hurtful encounters with men over this. It left Beverly feeling like a "slut." Her behavior was out of control and she felt driven to be with men. Her highly sexualized appearance, behavior, and reputation was scandalous to her family, which was (now) quite conservative and modest. Her miscarriage was marked with shame and disgrace. She tried to act tough and as if she did not care; but underneath her hard exterior, she felt a great deal of shame and guilt. She had wanted a baby to love her unconditionally, because no one else did. She felt unacceptable and unloved by her mother and stepfather, and used and abused by her boyfriends and sexual partners. Beverly was lost, alone, and holding terrible memories. But she was determined never to trust anyone or show her vulnerability.

Case 30: Brenda

Brenda came from a middle-class, African American, Christian Fundamentalist family that was horrified by her sex and love addiction. She plunged into it at age thirteen. She was told that she had been sexually abused by her mother's employer when she was six, but she did not remember anything of that. She had not even begun dating until she was a teenager. Yet, by the time she entered treatment at age fourteen, she had been with thirty-eight sex partners.

Brenda was obsessed with sex, and fantasized about past and future encounters all of the time. She let go of friends, school, religion, and family to pursue abusive and highly sexualized relationships with men, deluding herself into thinking that the next relationship or even intimate activity would be different from the painful contacts previously. Brenda felt that she had to be sexual to feel good about herself. She tended to deny and rationalize the negative consequences of her acting out. She had sex when she did not even feel like it. She thought she had to follow through with sexual activity whenever she engaged someone by flirting or being seductive. She was desperate and tense in her brief periods of abstinence. She looked for love through her sexual activity—and she constantly worried about something happening to her partners.

While she thought that masturbation was "disgusting" and did not engage in the behavior, Brenda did masturbate sexual partners, participated in the making of home videos of sexual activity, and occasionally engaged in phone sex. She had been in numerous relationships and one-night stands. She had affairs outside of her primary relationships. She participated in anonymous sex frequently. She seemed to "always be drawn towards my partner's best friends." Occasionally she would expose herself in school yards and showers. She brought sex into her jokes and social conversation. She made inappropriate advances to guys. She had been raped by one partner. She infrequently used alcohol or drugs as part of her activity. At times, she was the recipient of physical harm or pain during sex, to intensify the gratification.

All of this left her suicidal, homicidal, filled with despair, alone, and feeling like two people. She had lost her goals, self-esteem, religion, and self-respect. She was unwanted in her family, had lost friends, and failed in school. She had given up her hobbies and other interests. She stole, lied, and did "alot of serious fighting for certain guys. I started sticking people up. I sold drugs for about a month."

Brenda wrote an essay on how her relationships had interfered with her life:

Most of my relationships are with older guys (19–26) and they're not in school or they don't have real jobs other than selling drugs so I would cut school in order to be with them the whole day. It was like a schedule in my relationships. In the morning, he would do his rounds (drugs), then so-called lunch, shopping and whatever the night called for. Meaning, I probably wouldn't come home, so I wouldn't go to school the next day. Some of the guys are real party like people, so every night that's a party night he gets drunk, so I'm his girl, I'm supposed to get drunk or just drink along with him. So I end up drunk and half high walking in the house at 2:00 A.M. in the morning arguing with my mom when that can all be avoided. My sexual life can all around be avoided because it's too soon. I could be working, going to the 11th grade, but I have to spend all my hours in "*bed*." I've all ready had an STD [sexually transmitted disease]. I've risked many of times being pregnant. I've had many physical problems from having sex because everything was going so fast. I've missed alot of fun getting together with girlfriends. Alot of my promiscousness has caused all my arguements with my mom too.

Brenda also wrote some descriptive comments about the progression of her sex and love addiction. She started, "I had my first relationship at 14, but afterwards it seemed like it was any guy. I could not longer control my relationships of what I would do or wouldn't do. I got close to one guy and he just left me for no reason." Then, "I started having alot of different partners, so I was trying to hide causing me alot of secretive running around, lying, stress. Many guys started calling my house and I would deny knowing them." As things escalated, "it was like a different guy every other day and each time I got interested in more and different sexual activity. I started staying out real late or it became an overnight thing." At its highest level, "it was like more than one guy in a day." She added that "it had been like one guy I would be with three or four times a day or, if it was a one night stand, it would be a different guy that same day." There was a period of de-escalation: "my partner got involved with some kind of murder, drug case, so I was trying to be with him through this, so I was spending alot of time with him. My mom thought I was getting too caught up, so she sent me to South Carolina. In South Carolina I was so worried about him, I didn't get into another relationship." Her sex and love addiction led her to go against her own values: "I started sticking people up, then selling drugs all to get him what he wanted that was where I broke my limit because I never thought I would threaten a person's life or take something that belonged to someone else." Obviously, her life and addiction were way out of control.

She wrote a history of her sex and love addiction:

Well, when I graduated from eighth grade, I got into my first older relationship. He was 27 and sold drugs. I met him on my way to school. In the beginning, he was nice, then he changed and because of his change, I refused to have sex with him that's when he raped me and started physically abusing me. That relationship ended because he got put in jail for drug related reasons. I've only been in like 4 or 5 *relationships* but have had sex with 38 different guys. Most of my relationships were all the same except one. But I'm too scared to continue my relationship with him because he's too good to be true. And the 38 different guys I've been with, I've been with during relationships or in between. One guy I went with for material reasons only because my mom was mad at me, so she wasn't doing any thing for me. So, He bought my school book, clothes or just things I wanted, but I got out of that relationship before he asked anything of me because he was my girlfriend's boyfriend. Another I stayed with about 5 or 6 months, he was cute, he drove, he had money, friends. He lived alone. He was 21. He used to call me names, beat me well not really beat but constantly slapped me around and I stayed because he was *everything* I wanted. I fought with girls for him, missed school for him, paid no attention to my mom for him. But, we broke up because he felt it was time to move on. That relationship hurt me when it ended because I found myself caring for him. But mostly they all were the same. I just don't know why.

She wrote this about her most destructive relationship:

My most abusive relationship was with Chuck. We would argue every single day and most of them would turn physical. He never left marks so my mom could not tell, but, sometimes, the next morning, I would be in such pain that I wouldn't go to school the next day for fear he may be waiting for me. We would fight over little things like what time I had to meet him somewhere, talking to his friends or he likes me always to look neat. It was usually when I tried to defend myself or call him names that it would turn physical. There were so many reasons I didn't break up. I was "scared" I may be pregnant. I didn't know how to, in his own way, I felt he cared about me because he was willing to support and protect me. After awhile I got used to him; not hitting me but seeing him everyday, taking me out and arguing but not fighting. We finally broke up by I finally came out and "accidentaly" said I hate you and that he treated me like shit. He said is that how I feel, well fuck you and he left. Sometimes, I see him and he says we could of had it and *I think* we could have.

Brenda's friends tried to help her, but to no avail:

Alot of my girlfriends, close friends of his or close friends of mine would say why do you take that. Like name calling, demands and plain disrespect. I would mostly feel embarressed by what was said because in front of my friends, he would say fuck you bitch or the work I did last night was no good. Only one girlfriend has ever seen me physically hit and she will take that to her grave not to tell any of my close male friends because they *are real friends* and they may overreact about it and I don't want anything happening. But, when she saw what happened, she told me I deserved better because I even had guys on the side that treated me better than he did and I was just plain worth more and she in a way threatened to tell if it kept happening. I then did start to feel like I was shit because he continued to do it until I guess he thought I had enough and he up and left as usual. So, I really didn't respond to my feedback about my relationships because it continued.

Brenda's sex and love addiction took off like a cocaine addiction. Unlike some of the other girls described here, she did not get involved with sex and love until she was thirteen. However, by the next year, she had already suffered many of the most damaging consequences of a sex and love addiction. When I met her, she was ready to kill—herself or someone else—but had no idea of how to escape from the hell into which she had so quickly slid.

CHILD MOLESTERS

Case 31: Will

Will was referred for psychiatric help from a drug and alcohol rehabilitation program. He had been sent there because of his drinking and huffing glue. Nine years before—when he was six—he had been hospitalized for five or six months. He had also spent a month in another residential program for boys with conduct disorders. Will's behaviors were certainly troublesome. He set fires, lied, stole, fought with peers, did poorly in school, and had problems with authority figures. He was depressed, suicidal, hyperactive, anxious, and agitated. He had terribly low self-esteem and felt insecure, inadequate, and worthless. He had few friends, and his family did not seem to care much about him.

Initially, Will presented as disheveled, disorganized, and hopeless. He made poor eye contact, lacked interest in treatment, and was easily distracted. He was minimally cooperative and spoke in a monotone. He sat slumped in his chair and seemed to be quite concrete in his thinking. He came across as quite limited intellectually, confused, childlike, and regressed. He made little progress and refused antidepressant medication even though he seemed quite dysphoric. He tended to blame his family for his problems. They did certainly seem to be contributors, since they did not cooperate at all with the family therapy. They sabotaged meetings and were not even available for a conference call.

Will fantasized a lot. He thought about his mother. He wished that he was home. He was quite helpless, childlike, and regressed for a fifteen-year-old young man. Since his verbal and written skills were quite poor, we asked him to do a daily drawing about his feelings. Almost all of his drawings were done in black, leaving a sense of profound depression. On top of one picture of himself and a friend, Will wrote, "I feel good we are have fun." On another, he put, "Why I get in trouble I feel bad." He pictured himself, his brother, and his father fishing, and captioned it, "we are fishing I feel homesick I miss my mom and and brodar." The next day, he drew a huge dark cloud covering the sun above a drawing of his father standing with an envelope in front of a mailbox. Over the top, he wrote, "I feel hurt becaues my Dad did not write me and that hurt I cryed." Another picture was of a small stick figure in a big square, above which he put, "I feel contfuge This is me in the emm room I do not know what wrong whit me I am stuck."

Will's depressing artwork communicated that he was an infantile adolescent who was overwhelmed, lost, and incapable of coping with life as a teenager. He was "stuck" trying to get nurturing from the other family members—who, for their part, had no idea of how to help him. He had been severely traumatized as a child. Neglect, abandonment, and sexual abuse were some of his issues. Will could not talk them out, so he acted them out. He was aggressive with peers, fought with authority, abused drugs, and was obsessed with sex. The latter was well hidden, while the former problems were evident to everyone.

At some point along the way, Will had either been taught or else discovered for himself that sex was the best drug of all for relieving emotional pain. He masturbated compulsively and acted out sexually with other children. He was able to control himself in a hospital setting where he was under close supervision. But at home, where he could come and go as he pleased, it was much easier for him to be sexually active with the other children in his neighborhood. Apparently, there was a conspiracy of silence among the adults about this behavior of their children—because there were no reports, questions, or other indicators of his sexual molestation, other than what he told me in the privacy of our individual therapy sessions. Will did not consider what he was doing to be sexual abuse, even though there was three or four years' difference between him and some of the boys with whom he had mutual masturbation. Actually, he had been having sex with boys from the neighborhood since he was five or six, some of them considerably older than he. He did not think of himself as a sexual abuse victim in these experiences. He thought of them as fun, normative, and enjoyable, and could not see where hurt was being inflicted on him or anyone else. Will certainly thought he was being abused when grown-ups hit him, but he did not have a concept of sexual abuse. He had no desire to let go of any of his sexual behaviors and was angry, hostile, and defensive when I suggested to him that these were part of his problem, much like the alcohol and the glue sniffing.

Case 32: Steve

Steve was almost the exact opposite of Will. He was arrogant, outgoing, narcissistic, and wiser than his years (at least in his own mind). And while Steve was only two years older than Will, he seemed much more mature, was physically twice as big, and acted in a dominating fashion with peers or adults. Actually, Steve's grandiosity hid a low self-esteem and feelings of inadequacy and worthlessness. He went to great lengths to show others that he was superior to them and that he was in full control of himself.

Of course, this was not true and, in fact, he had a great deal of trouble controlling his sexual impulses. He was also obese and had difficulty managing his food intake. Both of his parents had eating disorders—in this case, compulsive overeating. Steve had been in individual therapy since he was first caught exhibiting himself at age fourteen. He was in an outpatient sex offenders group for two years. His inability to control his exhibitionism had led him to feeling depressed, suicidal, and hopeless. His first suicide attempt was made soon after his grandmother died. His second was shortly after his girlfriend broke up with him. He had been having sex with her two or three times a day, and that seemed to help decrease his urge to expose himself. Their breakup sent him into a panic: he imagined he would end up in jail because he could not stop his exhibitionism. He was asked to leave Catholic school because of it, and later was suspended from public school for the same behavior.

Steve blamed his problems on an incident in which he had been sexually abused when he was eleven or twelve. A friend of his mother's was staying at their home and had come into Steve's room and fondled his genitals. While this was obviously traumatic for Steve, it did not appear to be powerful enough an incident to have triggered the intensity and type of sexual obsession and acting out in which Steve engaged. He had become driven to expose himself to girls four and five years his junior. Despite his contact with the juvenile justice system, his psychotherapy, and his shame, he could not stop acting out sexually.

Steve tried to present himself as someone who was eager for treatment and recovery. However, his behavior was not consistent with his words. For example, he twice completed an inventory on sexual addiction (developed by Sexaholics Anonymous, 1985), and each time he answered it somewhat differently. There were only twenty questions, so his inconsistency was rather surprising. On one, he indicated that he thought he needed help with his sexual thinking or behavior; while on the other, he responded negatively to this question. On one, he reported that he had tried to stop or limit what he thought was wrong about his sexual behavior; on the other, he did not indicate an attempt to change. On one, he responded affirmatively to a question about whether he felt guilty, remorseful, or depressed afterward; on the other, he denied these feelings. On one, he thought that his pursuit of sex had made him careless about himself and the welfare of his family and others; but on the other, he did not see this as a problem. On one, he mentioned that he had been arrested for a sex-related offense; on the other, he did not check this off. On one, he indicated that he masturbated or had sex with others even when sex with his primary partner was satisfying; while on the other, he did not agree with this statement. On both, he checked that he felt the "right relationship" would keep him from lusting, masturbating, or being promiscuous and that he would be better off if he didn't keep "giving in" to his compulsions. His overall mixed response was difficult to interpret. My experience with this questionnaire suggests that most people who take the inventory twice will respond much more consistently; for example, they might agree on eight of ten items that they checked, rather than the two of six items in agreement that Steve had.

On a questionnaire about relationship addiction (Norwood, 1985), Steve identified with coming from a dysfunctional home where his emotional needs were not met. He also indicated that he was used to not having love in interpersonal relationships and being "willing to wait, hope, and try harder to please." He saw himself as taking more than half of the "responsibility, guilt, and blame" in relationships and being "more in touch with your dream of how it could be than with the reality of your situation." These responses suggest strong psychological dependency as well as feelings of insecurity, inadequacy, and worthlessness. He was childlike, grandiose, and narcissistic—which made it difficult if not impossible for him to have mature relationships with girls his age.

On another sexual addiction inventory (Carnes, 1988), Steve indicated that he very often fantasized about past and future sexual experiences. He also tended to think that things would change next time—for example, "I'll find the right person." He often rationalized or denied the real consequences of his sexual acting out—such as going to jail. Steve often felt desperate and pressured with anxiety when he refrained from acting out sexually. He acknowledged his compulsive masturbation, which he infrequently performed in his car. He periodically used and collected sexually explicit magazines and videotapes. He cruised television and movies for sexually suggestive moments. He also sexualized people and magazine images.

Steve's reason for referral was his compulsion to expose himself, and he was referred by someone from the court system. He had periodically exposed himself in public places. He admitted to one experience of voyeurism, when he used binoculars to watch people through windows. He frequently brought sex and sexual jokes into his conversation. He made inappropriate advances and phone calls. He touched people as if by accident in order to get a sexual thrill. He admitted to very frequent cross-dressing and transvestism—behavior that only revealed on the second sexual addiction inventory. He had not been able to share this with me face to face. He was particularly attracted to young girls and had exposed himself to a thirteen-year-old just prior to admission. He was sexually active with a girl four years younger than himself.

Steve thought of his family as being "very open about sex" and said that they talked about it. However, his idea of talking about this was probably like his idea that he could control his behavior if he tried. He wrote, "I always said it wasn't a problem, and that I could control it, and stop whenever I wanted." In reality, his family was encouraging his sex and love addiction by housing one of his girlfriends—which made frequent sex quite available. Also in reality, he was acting out despite individual, family, and group therapies focused on his offending behaviors, as well as the experience of being arrested and sent to detention.

Steve was filled with shame, guilt, and embarrassment. So, he developed coping strategies to disconnect himself from these painful feelings. For example, he wrote, "I never would admit it [sex and love addiction] and be honest before here [the hospital] except I admitted what I did." In fact, he admitted what he got caught doing and kept the rest of his sexual acting out a secret. Steve did not tell his outpatient therapist about his sexual molestation of a thirteen-year-old girl or about his tendency to cross-dress and compulsively masturbate. He did not reveal his obsession with pornography and his tendency to sexualize people wherever he was. Initially, his acting out led him to feel suicidal. But he found that he could act out in other ways besides exposing himself, and this helped him to manage his sex and love addiction while not risking jail. When one of these ways failed—that is, he broke up with his girlfriend—he quickly resorted to exposing himself as part of his acting-out pattern.

Steve indicated that he had been in a period of euphoric recall about his sex and love addiction: "it happened during my outpatient therapy, and because of my wanting the good old days I got put on inpatient for help." Probably because his mother was so controlling, Steve had difficulty accepting therapy. He wrote, "I have always had a problem with turning my life over to someone else." Unfortunately, this hang-up led to greater and greater consequences for him and for those whom he victimized. Steve tended to see his sex and love addiction as limited to his exhibitionism. He described a typical day as "two or three hours of obsession, an hour acting out, three hours covering up my acting out, and five or six hours feeling shameful." His outpatient treatment, family reactions, and legal interventions also focused on only the one aspect of a much larger problem. Steve himself said, "I often think about sex or sexual related things in my head or I daydream." But his recovery was not seen as needing to address his cognitions, his sexuality, and his behavior in a comprehensive package. And Steve was not about to tell the outpatient therapists, his family, and the authorities about this mistake. He was determined to protect as much of his sex and love addiction as possible.

The stories I have shared with you in this chapter represent roughly half of the sex and love addicted adolescents with whom I worked during a three-year period. They were about 15 percent of my caseload; I was working primarily with dually diagnosed (in this instance, depressed and chemically dependent) teenagers who were with an inpatient program for adolescents in a private, for profit, psychiatric hospital just outside a major urban area in the United States. My clinical sample is obviously biased by these factors—and probably by others that I have not yet identified. Nonetheless, if I found sex and love addicted adolescents in my work, there are probably many unidentified sufferers of this difficult disease. These case studies may stimulate clinicians, and others in a helping position, to take another look at adolescents through the lens of sex and love addiction.

4

Treatment Tools and Technology

The treatment of adolescent sex and love addicts is in an embryonic stage. This is largely due to the lack of recognition of this disorder. Until fairly recently—as indicated by my own experience described in the Introduction—professionals have hesitated to classify adolescents even as chemically dependent. The idea of suggesting that an adolescent is a sex and love addict may not occur to most treatment specialists. Since sex and love addiction is not yet established as an official diagnosis by, for example, being listed in the American Psychiatric Association's *Diagnostic and Statistical Manual—III—Revised* (1987), it is not surprising that people who work with adolescents are hesitant to establish treatment protocols and programs for a disease that may not even exist. However, as I have demonstrated in Chapter 3, the suffering is clearly present, and clinicians who treat teenagers are struggling to develop therapeutic interventions that can help adolescents who exhibit compulsive sexual acting-out patterns and excessive dependency on relationships. The sex and love addicted teenagers described in Chapter 3 were in a treatment environment, but it was still only by chance, that is, my presence in the treatment facility—that they had the opportunity to identify their sexuality and relationship addictions and to learn some ways of working with this type of difficulty. Hopefully, this book and this chapter in particular will assist therapeutic professionals who have sex and love addicted adolescents in their programs to develop effective treatment approaches to this potentially deadly disorder.

The main thrust of treatment is to reverse the addiction cycle (see Chapter 2), which will be reviewed in the first part of this chapter. There are three main elements in the treatment and recovery process: psychoeducation, psychotherapy, and support groups. Each of these three areas will be presented in subsequent sections with sufficient detail as to enable therapists to incorporate aspects of this approach into their own style and experience.

There is no right way or even acknowledged path to follow. This book is an effort to carve out a domain; but I expect that, even by the time this is being read, there will be improvements on the tools and techniques described in these pages. I do not propose to present in this book the definitive word on sex and love addiction treatment for adolescents. Hopefully, this will be a starting point that will be used by others to generate effective and successful treatment and recovery. I have been encouraged by the openness and hard work of my adolescent clients who want to end their suffering and find a way to live more normally. They deserve the attention and expertise of informed professionals and the community at large. At present, most teenage sex and love addicts are shamed, ridiculed, misunderstood, and rejected by adults and peers alike. Many do not even see their own agony as a treatable condition and believe that they are morally bankrupt and the cause of their own suffering. They need the approach presented here, as well as the improvements that will inevitably come with more study, work, and examination of the issue.

One of the most exciting things about any recovery process is the energy and creativity that gets unleashed for the recovering people and the professionals alike. New ideas, innovative approaches, and practical wisdom are greatly needed by everyone in the recovery endeavor, no matter what the source of the idea or approach. The synergy that happens when people feel safe enough to talk openly and honestly about their struggles, compulsions, obsessions, and addictions releases powerful and transforming emotions, insights, spiritual experiences, and behavioral changes that are, as they say in the recovery community—"beyond our wildest dreams." In order to create these discoveries for our teenage sex and love addicts, the addiction cycle needs to be reversed.

REVERSING THE ADDICTION CYCLE

While treating adolescents does require some special knowledge and techniques, the basic principles of sex and love addiction recovery (Griffin-Shelley, 1991, 1993) apply at any age. The roadmap for recovery can be envisioned by reversing Patrick Carnes's (1983) addiction cycle, as shown in Figure 4.

Working from the top down, the place to begin is with acting-out behaviors. Then the despair and rituals are addressed, followed by the role of preoccupation in maintaining the addiction. When some sobriety has been established in these areas, the treatment can focus on unmanageability and distorted thinking. Finally, family-of-origin issues such as core beliefs and childhood trauma can be uncovered. Obviously, this is an oversimplification of a complex process. But approaches that start at the bottom—that is, family-of-origin work, without adequately addressing the addiction issues in the past seem doomed to failure. Unfortunately,

Figure 4
Reversed Version: Childhood Trauma and the Addiction Cycle

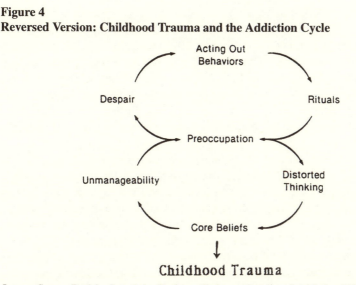

Source: Carnes, Patrick, *Out of the Shadows: Understanding Sexual Addiction* (Minneapolis, MN: CompCare Publications, 1983), p. 15, "The Addictive System." Reprinted with permission.

when this happens, the addict was usually seen as the one who is to blame because he or she is "not trying" or "not working hard enough" to make the therapy successful. Until recently, the intense and powerful role of self-medication provided by the active addiction has not been appreciated by treatment professionals or clients, especially in terms of the addiction's potential to undermine all efforts to change. Treating a sex and love addict without establishing some sobriety is like treating an alcoholic who comes to the sessions under the influence.

Managing Acting-out Behaviors

The goal of any addiction treatment is to stop the destructive behaviors. For sex and love addicted teenagers—as seen in the case examples presented in Chapter 3—this may mean stopping compulsive masturbation, telephone sex, anonymous sex, involvement with pornography, one-night stands, multiple relationships, dependent relationships, or obsessions about sex and love. Usually, prior to treatment, the sex and love addicted adolescents have already attempted a number of strategies to cut down on, cut back, or eliminate the behavior in question. For example, they may have thrown away a collection of sexually explicit magazines or videos or broken off a relationship that they considered overly dependent. Exploring the ways that they have sought to cope with the problem on their own will give the therapist a better idea about other approaches that may be successful, and will give the clients a sense of self-worth because they have exhibited a desire to change and have made efforts (albeit unsuccessful) in the right direction.

Stopping the acting-out behavior is important because of the issue of self-medication and numbing feelings. Addictive behaviors change the individual's brain chemistry (Lord, in Griffin-Shelley, 1993) in such a way that the system is flooded with activating or sedating chemicals. As a result, the person is "high." Just as a therapist would not attempt to do therapy with a client who came into his or her office intoxicated or under the influence of drugs, so too any attempt to do therapy with someone under the influence of an active sex and love addiction is usually ineffective and frustrating to both the client and the therapist.

One client comes to mind, in particular. He was usually quiet, shy, self-effacing, and depressed. At one session, he came in energetic, buoyant, talkative, and animated. Since I was so struck by the personality change, I inquired about what had happened just prior to the session. He told me that he had encountered a young woman who was nice to him when he bought something, and that now he was fantasizing about dating her and eventually marrying and settling down. My client was on a stimulant high much like cocaine that had little to do with the brief encounter with this woman and even less to do with reality. Our session was enlightening to me because I had never seen him in this condition, but we were not able to accomplish any work on his addiction because he was not even sure at that point that he really was sex and love addicted. Perhaps, he thought, what he really needed to make his life better was a relationship with the young woman. Therapy was irrelevant to him at this point. Later, he "crashed" from his high and was able to reengage in the therapy process.

Often, complete abstinence or elimination of sex and love addicted behaviors is not possible in the beginning. But usually, the major acting-out behaviors that need to stop can be agreed upon, and a commitment to working toward sobriety can be established. For example, in Chapter 3, Dennis (case 20) was able to agree to try not to masturbate, and Don (case 19) committed to not being sexual with animals while in the hospital. Similarly, Jane (case 12) and Connie (case 27) agreed not to have boyfriends while in treatment. They may not have been able to maintain their commitment completely; but their failures, temptations, and trials could then become a regular part of their treatment. That is, it became all right for the therapist to inquire as to whether they had been flirting, masturbating, or acting out in any other ways, and it was expected that the client would report any difficulties with maintaining sobriety.

This initial phase of treatment is often characterized by some sort of confrontation about the behaviors. An adolescent sex and love addict may be confronted by his or her peers in a group session or community meeting about inappropriate sexual behaviors or involvement in a relationship. The teenager may have been challenged by his or her parents or staff about their sex and love difficulties. There may have been an encounter with school, community, or legal authorities that led to questions about the adolescent's behaviors. In most cases, the teenager does not come into treatment asking to stop acting out. Most adult sex and love addicts have to be confronted as well, so this factor is not predictive of eventual success or failure. Sex and love addicted behaviors are unhealthy coping mechanisms that need to be confronted in order to be changed. Most active addicts cannot confront themselves and need the help of other caring people in their lives in order to begin to change their acting-out patterns.

In terms of Twelve Step work, the beginning of recovery involves admitting powerlessness. Written work in a recovery workbook like Carnes's *A Gentle Path through the Twelve Steps* (1989b) can help adolescent sex and love addicts identify examples of powerlessness in their sex and love addictions. They might list things like having sex with someone when they had decided beforehand that they would not be sexual that evening or with that person, or flirting with their best friend's boy or girlfriend even though they knew the behavior would threaten their own relationship with their friend. Admitting powerlessness is difficult for anyone. Our culture stresses the importance of independence, power, and control. Acknowledging deficits in self-control and/or independence is likely, then, to receive negative reactions and to be questioned or judged. Teenagers are keenly aware of these judgments and have a strong developmental need to fit in with peers and to feel accepted and acceptable. Saying that they feel powerless puts them in a position where they are vulnerable to exclusion, rejection, and judgment from the very people from whom they need acceptance.

Likewise, the idea of being unable to control some aspect of their person or behavior threatens the adolescents' sense of omnipotence and invulnerability. Again, in terms of teenagers' normal developmental stages, adolescents are not yet fully in touch with their limitations, their mortality, and their deficits. They are beginning to have these experiences—for example, they may lose a peer to a drunk-driving incident or some other type of accident—but such losses are not part of their normal experience. Really being able to grasp and own a sense of powerlessness over sexual and/or romantic impulses, then, becomes an unusual and especially difficult task for an adolescent.

Addressing Despair

When acting out ceases at least temporarily, feelings emerge that have been suppressed by the intensity of the active addiction. Among the most common of these feelings are depression, feelings of worthlessness, and despair. Sometimes, the despair of suicidal thoughts and/or actual attempts to end their life will drive the sex and love addicted teenagers into treatment. The cycle of the addiction has brought them to feelings of hopelessness because acting out is no longer doing the job. They are desperate to change and will promise anything, even going into a hospital.

Once the initial suicidal feelings have settled, another type of despair sets in: the grief of letting go of their acting out, which may have been their best source of comfort, their sole coping mechanism, or their only sense of having any value to or connection with others. There is a grieving process that recovering addicts go through, and it resembles normal grief. When sex and love addicts give up their addiction, they experience the loss of a lover, the emptiness of losing a trusted friend, the hurt of a broken relationship, and the pain of the death of a style of coping with life. Therefore, they pass through a period of denial, then anger, sadness, and finally acceptance. As with other grieving, these probably do not fall in succinct, separate stages; but the feelings, thoughts, and behaviors associated with grief occur in this context, and recovering people need to be supported and validated in terms of their experience of loss. Young people, in particular, may never have had any significant losses or grief and may not know what is happening to them. Or they may have had too many losses, so any other losses—especially the voluntary letting go of an addiction—can seem impossible, unfair, and overly harsh to them. Typically, their addiction is closely bound up with feelings of deprivation and neglect. The idea of choosing to deprive their inner self of a mood-altering experience that is so powerful and pleasurable is intolerable. They imagine never being able to enjoy anything for the rest of their lives.

The thought of never acting out again may seem unfair, impossible to achieve, or cruel and unusual punishment for someone who has already suffered a great deal. In addition, for adolescents in particular, the idea of stopping something "for the rest of my life" seems like an overwhelming and unattainable task. They cannot conceive of doing anything for the remainder of their years on earth (or, in this case, stopping the doing). Here, the recovery philosophy of "one day at a time" is helpful. Teenagers can relate to the idea of building something for their future. Sometimes, I will share with them some of the wisdom that was passed on to me by a recovering alcoholic who likened his recovery to building a brick wall. If one concentrates only on one brick at a time, before too long, the wall will take shape. If, however, one focuses on how far one has to go, one can lose his or her motivation and give up the project.

Cognitive therapy can be helpful with adolescents at this point, to help them examine their thinking more objectively. If they can identify the downward pattern of negative thoughts that leads them into despair, then they can work with a therapist on constructing positive thoughts that will create a happier mood. Mindy (case 28) had extremely negative, depressing cognitions that put her in an angry, hostile position with the world and helped her to justify acting out with drugs, sex, and relationships. Reframing her thinking helped her to be more optimistic and hopeful so that she had the energy to tackle the concrete steps of treatment and recovery.

In the second step in the Twelve Steps, addicts are encouraged to "come to believe in a power greater than ourselves that can restore us to sanity." An experience of faith—taking that "leap of faith" and believing there is some type of meaning or design to life, is another important antidote to despair and hopelessness. Such a step requires an exercise in trust that can be extremely difficult for young people who have been hurt by parental and authority figures in their lives. Most recovering people de-emphasize the religious overtones of this step and concentrate on forming some type of peronal spirituality. The sex and love addict may not be ready to believe in a formal concept of God, but he or she usually can see that there are other people who understand their problems and who seem to know how to get better. Having some faith in another recovering sex and love addict or in a therapist can be enough to further the process of letting go of hopelessness and making a decision to try to live differently.

The second part of the second step speaks of being restored to sanity. One of the important aspects of treatment at this point is to enable the sex and love addicted teenagers to get some distance from their addiction and to observe how "crazy" it is to keep expecting different results from the same behaviors. Mindy (case 28) expected that she would be able to find the boyfriend of her dreams—a man who would fix everything and take care of her—without her having to change herself. Instead, she kept finding herself in abusive, destructive relationships that made her feel worthless, vulnerable, and ashamed, but she never looked at what was wrong with her. Her insanity was in thinking that the problems in her relationships lay in the men that she chose, not in her inability to choose healthier men. When we get some distance from our "insanity," we usually can laugh at how ridiculous our behavior has been. Recovering sex and love addicts show their progress by being able to smile at the craziness of their active addiction. Such humor about oneself is, of course, great medicine for despair.

Ending Rituals

After a period of obsession and preoccupation, sex and love addicts enact rituals that alter their consciousness and enable them to act out. An important part of recovery, then, is identifying and changing these ritualistic patterns of behavior. For example, Tom (case 1) had an elaborate ritual of dressing prior to going out cruising the beach for sex. He could spend hours thinking about, buying, trying on, and examining his clothing in the mirror. Likewise, his hair, skin, and jewelry had to look just right before he felt comfortable going out. Once he was "on the prowl," he had certain places that he had to walk by, particular people whom he wanted to interact with, and special things that he liked to say to girls before he would try to "score."

The traditional addiction-recovery advice is to change the "people, places, and things" associated with the acting out in the addiction. For Tom, this meant that he needed to think about changing his public presence—especially those items most closely associated with his sex and love addiction, like his tank top shirts, his jewelry, his hairstyle, and his aftershave lotion. He also had to consider not going to his old "hangouts," such as the beach or the local singles bars. Furthermore, he had to decide about the friends with whom he spent time, because most of them lived a similar lifestyle to his and would encourage him to return to his previous behaviors. Faced with these seemingly overwhelming changes, Tom seriously considered giving up recovery and taking his chances with addiction. He could not imagine that at his young age he should have to make such dramatic changes. He wanted to deny it at first; then, he wanted to bargain with it; then, he got angry and felt abused; next, he felt sad and despairing; and finally, he came to some acceptance of what he needed to do in order to establish some sanity and manageability in his life.

Recovering sex and love addicts need to examine their exhibitionistic and voyeuristic tendencies. The way they dress and talk may be subtle ways of letting other people know that they are available for and interested in sexual and/or romantic encounters. Flirting and sexual talk, innuendo, and jokes are all behaviors that will get reactions from others. The nature of the reaction will tell the sex and love addict whether the other person is a potential partner for sexual or relational acting out. When someone is turned off or pulls away, the sex and love addict looks elsewhere. When someone responds in kind, the sex and love addict knows that there is a possibility of a "score" either now or in the future. Sex and love addicts are almost always cruising, intriguing, and taking "rain checks" for future activities. These behaviors are important parts of their acting-out rituals and need to be stopped for recovery to have a chance.

Tom (case 1) was not only good at showing himself off (exhibitionism), but he was skillfully able to get women to tell him intimate details of their sexual and romantic lives. He was voyeuristic in this way. He "got a hit" when other people exposed intimate information about themselves to him. He created the illusion of intimacy, caring, and friendship so that he could secretly get high on their revelations. Some with tendencies similar to his joined in on the stimulating activity. Others would have been shocked if they knew he was using them for his own gratification. Tom used women as sex objects and as fuel for his erotic fantasies, with no intention of ever being really close or available to them. This was a strong part of his ritual, and it protected him from truly feeling vulnerable in a relationship with a woman.

Adolescent sex and love addicts need to examine the environments that they frequent, since many such "places" are part of their ritual. Music and drug and alcohol use can support or even create altered states of consciousness. Popular music even speaks of being "addicted to love," or of obsessions with sex and love. The image presented suggests that such addictions are the ultimate expression of "true" love and passion. Typically, adolescents are steeped in this music; they know the words and melodies by heart. Drinking and drugging facilitates social interactions among teenagers—as it does among their adult counterparts—and reduces social anxiety, inhibitions, self-consciousness, and insecurities. Thus, alcohol and drugs function as a "social lubricant" and are present (even though they are illegal for most teenagers) at the majority of adolescent gatherings and activities. Sexual and relational acting out is usually blamed on the influence of chemicals, which can be an easy excuse for a sex and love addicted teen. In determining the presence of a sex and love addiction, chemical-free behaviors need to be examined since romantic and sexual acting out will occur even if there are no drugs or alcohol involved. Often, when chemicals are not available for some reason, the sexual and relational acting out increases. The mood-altering effects of chemicals and music can be achieved through manipulation of sex and love.

The third step of the Twelve Step program encourages recovering addicts to "make a decision to turn our will and lives over to God as we understand Him." This decision step requires "turning it over," letting go of control, and acknowledging some sort of Higher Power. Alcoholics Anonymous has sayings that summarize this philosophy—for example, "Let go, let God"; or, perhaps a bit more concretely, "Get out of the driver's seat." What these sayings are suggesting is that the recovering sex and love addicts give up their unhealthy rituals, their dysfunctional coping mechanisms, their efforts to alter their moods, their desire to change their states of consciousness, their escapist behaviors, their illusion of control, and, ultimately, their addiction.

For teenagers, the idea of turning their will and lives over to anyone is counter to the developmental tasks that they face. Erik Erikson in *Childhood and Society* (1963) posited that the fifth stage in his eight stages of man was the development of "identity" (p. 261), and he saw this as the main task of adolescence. The establishment of a sense of self-independence as separate from one's parents, family, cultural, ethnic, or racial status, neighborhood, religion, or country is seen as a significant developmental milestone for adolescents. Taking the third step in addiction recovery can appear like the surrender of one's identity and the submission of oneself to the will of others. What is really being asked of adolescent sex and love addicts is that they let go of their false self, their phony identity, and their addictive image so that they can discover their real self, their true identity, their ritual- and compulsion-free personality. Letting go of their rituals, then, can allow them to go through the developmental stage that they are in, to grow into independent, self-confident young adults. Conversely, holding onto addictive patterns will block development, inhibit their growth, and keep them stuck in an adolescent phase of personality development.

Preoccupation/Obsession/Fantasy

Sex and love addicts have developed their ability to escape into their own minds to the point where most of the time it is not obvious to other people what they are really doing. They can be sexually or romantically preoccupied, obsessed with acting out, and excited by fantasy and still function at work, appear "normal" at home, and sustain some level of manageability in their lives. Their skill at dividing their minds is an important safeguard for them. Obsessive thoughts provide self-soothing, relief from pain, distraction from feelings, and protection from attack. This sort of intellectual defense—technically known as "splitting"—is developed to give the person a buffer between themselves and the abuse and neglect that they experienced as a child.

Young children live in fantasy a great deal of the time. As we grow older, one mark of maturity is the ability to grasp and cope with reality. Those people who cannot overtly let go of fantasy are seen as childish, immature, and less able to deal with life "on life's terms." Sex and love addicts learn this, but they also have learned the power of being lost inside their own mind. In our own mind, we have all the control. We have the power to make things the way we want or need them to be. In the outside world, we may have little control, influence, or safety. In our own mind, however, we can create worlds in which we are in charge, safe, cared for, and nurtured. If safety, love, and affirmation are absent in a person's world as a child, he or she may learn to cope by creating fantasy worlds, and may get in the habit of using that skill long after childhood.

Six, seven, and eight year olds can be quite skilled in fantasy, obsession, and preoccupation. An eight year old whom I met once told me that he "hated" his mother. His parents slept in separate bedrooms—which indicated some marital problems. His mother was overly controlling, intrusive, overprotective, and nagging. His father was distant, superficial, and preoccupied with sports when he was not working. This young man asserted himself in control battles with his mother over food, social activities, and friends. He also followed his father's example and lost himself in the fantasy worlds of video games and sports. His friends identified him as a "Nintendo addict." He could play for hours. He collected baseball cards, autographs, and sports memorabilia. He watched all sorts of athletic contests on television. His preoccupation with sports and video games insulated him from the trauma at home and provided comfort, control, and consistency internally when there was little nurturing and much chaos externally.

The roots of sexual or romantic fantasy, obsession, and preoccupation are probably deeply fixed in childhood. This probably was a main coping strategy for the sex and love addict way before sex and love came on the scene. Some sex and love addicts—especially those who were sexually abused at an early age—identify sexual or romantic obsession as having been with them as young as first grade; but this tends to be the exception rather than the rule. Nonetheless, most sex and love addicts can trace to their childhood their pattern of using fantasy, preoccupation, and obsessive thinking as a means of coping. Rather than letting go of this coping style as they grow up, sex and love addicts learn to hide their fantasy life and to cover up their dependence on this way of dealing with painful events and affects. They become skilled at appearing like they are realistic and mature. They develop a false self that fools the world and keeps their inner, real self protected from harm.

Adolescent sex and love addicts—while they have already learned to keep their mental life secret—are not yet as good at hiding their obsessive, preoccupied self as their adult counterparts are. However, the adolescents are still quite protective of this part of themselves and will only reveal it if they are in great pain or if they have a trusting relationship with someone. Getting this addict part of the adolescent into treatment can be the difference between success and failure. Some teenage sex and love addicts—for example, Cindy (case 22) and, at times, Bob (case 8)—could appear to be involved, sharing, and open when, in fact, they were still leading a double life in treatment. They only share what is already known about them; they keep their sexual and romantic lives separate. Since sexual and relational development is such a significant part of adolescence, talking about sex and love should be part of any treatment process. Adolescents who act as if these are not issues for them are hiding, manipulating, and covering up. Adolescent sex and love addicts have a good reason to be secretive. They are filled with shame, self-loathing, guilt, and embarrassment about their difficulties with sex and love. They feel out of control and cannot risk showing this to others. They are also quite dependent on this means of coping, so they cannot risk exposing it to someone who might suggest that they change.

The antidote or cure for obsession is to "get out of your head." The first step is to attempt to stop the fantasies and obsession. Most sex and love addicts know that they have to stop behaviors, but they often do not realize the integral role of their mental preoccupation in setting the addiction cycle in motion. They need to be educated about the role of fantasy in acting out. This can be done through bibliotherapy (i.e., reading recovery materials), discussion in one-to-one or group sessions, or more formal lectures. They will often discover the need to let go of fantasies in their own efforts not to act out on their bottom lines. For example, Dennis (case 20) realized that he could not indulge in sexual fantasies without masturbating. Having the fantasy without following through was too frustrating, so he decided to give up the preoccupations and daydreams that he had entertained himself with for much of his life.

Another needy teenager, Lisa (case 24), found it almost impossible to let go of her fantasies. In her case, we tried a whole array of interventions to help her to bring herself fully into the present. We worked on awareness and relaxation exercises like deep breathing, clenching and releasing muscle groups up and down her body, and taking an inventory of feelings from head to toe. We experimented with present-centeredness exercises such as describing the room in great detail, or using her senses—touch, smell, sight, and taste—to examine an object in the room.

We had her doing activities that required concentration, such as making something, drawing her feelings, or putting together a collage of her feelings. We encouraged her to make eye contact with others, to talk about whatever was on her mind, and to share her secrets with others. We suggested that she write letters, lists of secrets, descriptions of painful events in her life, or journal entries to get things off her mind. We pointed out that she could read sex and love addiction recovery literature if she could not get positive thoughts in her own mind, so that she would have the words of others to counter her own internal voices and preoccupations.

Stopping the obsessions requires both mental discipline and alternative forms of self-soothing. Eliminating fantasies without having something positive to replace these important coping strategies will not be effective. While these teenagers need to learn to say no to their impulse to obsess, at the same time they need to have positive activities that will have the same mood-altering, nurturing effect. The suggestions mentioned in the preceding paragraphs will help to reduce anxiety, to create good feelings, to bring the adolescent more fully into reality, and to develop a sense of increased self-control and self-worth. Rather than feeling deprived by giving up obsessions, fantasies, and preoccupations, the teenagers in treatment will feel fulfilled by initiating healthier internal coping strategies and more productive contact with the external world.

As this contact improves, they will be more able to stand back from their fantasy life and look at it more objectively. As they feel less pulled back into the active addiction—the rituals, acting out, and subsequent despair—they will be less threatened by the power of preoccupation and less in need of a mental or addictive "fix." With letting go and establishing some distance, they will be more capable of interpreting the message of the fantasy. The stage of preoccupation, the obsessive thinking, and the elaborate fantasies hold the clues to what is bothering the sex and love addict. For example, Jane (case 12) had a distant, critical mother who abandoned her and a father who was too close to her and allowed her to sleep in his bed. Jane's obsession with finding a male who would "make it all better" was an expression of her need for parental nurturing and affirmation, maternal love, paternal boundaries, and unconditional acceptance. Because her needs in a relationship were so overdetermined, they were overwhelming to her and to her partners. The result was a repeated reenactment of intense bonding with a male, rejection, abandonment, and criticism from others for her problems with dependency. The more these relationships failed, the more intense her fantasies, preoccupations, and obsessions became. They led her to more complex rituals and more dangerous acting out. The active addiction brought her despair, suicidal depression, and total unmanageability in her life, in spite of the intensive structure and treatment of our program. Letting go of her fantasies, obsessions, and preoccupations was crucial to her getting well. Allowing herself and others to examine her secret mental life—her inner addict—was a way out of the chaos and pain.

Distorted Thinking

In the upper circle of the addiction cycle, trauma begets negative core beliefs about the self (see Figure 3 in Chapter 2). This low self-esteem leads to distorted thinking. In the earlier example of a sex and love addicted client who came to a session on a fantasy "high," distorted thinking led to the fantasy that produced a rush of good-feeling chemicals in his brain. This young man's intrusive and controlling father and distant and now-deceased mother left him with a legacy of inadequacy, insecurity, anxiety, and low self-worth. He saw himself as bad, unworthy, and unlovable. These core beliefs about himself made his thinking abnormal. When a woman was nice to him, he distorted reality and believed that she was making sexual and romantic invitations. He experienced normal civility as a "come on." His twisted thinking then led to fantasies of sexual encounters and eventually to thoughts of lifelong commitment. When he revealed his thoughts to women, they recoiled in horror and reacted to him as if he were insane. They perceived his thinking as "crazy" and were afraid of him because they did not know what he might do. His distorted thoughts were seen by women as a threat; in their minds, he was capable of stalking them, raping them, and possibly killing them.

And he was surprised by their reactions. He did not see himself as harmful in any way. He was hurt by the implications. He wanted to be close to them and, yet, his addictive thinking was driving them away. They did not want him around and complained about his flirting, the innuendoes in his conversation and behavior, and the discomfort they felt at the way he looked at them. They were particularly struck by his strange thoughts and the extreme way that he distorted reality in his mind. He appeared normal at first; but when he shared with women what he was thinking, he seemed "out of his mind" in their eyes. There was a psychotic quality to his thinking. That is, he seemed out of touch with reality. He had created scenarios in his mind that did not correspond to anything real, yet he believed his thoughts more than he believed the feedback that he was frightening people and that they could not tolerate being around him.

This case is also an example of the narcissistic, grandiose distortions in thinking that addicts exhibit. As their addictions progress, addicts become more childish, demanding, self-centered, and infantile. In Twelve Step programs, the active addict is referred to as "His (or Her) Majesty the Baby" because of the need for instant gratification and the anger and rage that is unleashed when these needs are not met. The sex and love addict's world becomes more and more private, secretive, and selfish. Probably because of traumatic experiences with caretakers, the sex and love addict does not trust anyone to meet his or her needs. The addiction becomes the only reliable source of nurturing, relief, or support. The addict's thinking becomes infantile and self-centered. Their needs are the only needs that matter and they do not care about others, nor do they really see anyone else's needs. To someone who does not understand the addictive process, this lack of empathy for their victims is often the most troubling aspect of sex and love addicts. Their preoccupation with themselves makes others angry and often feeling used, left out, manipulated, and abused. The addict's selfishness seems unwarranted, unnecessary, and at times even out of character. Partners want to love the distance away; they want to forgive and to feel that the addict's apologies are sincere and heartfelt; they want to be really close, yet the addict always seems to find a way to create distrust, hurt, and self-doubt.

Sex and love addicts make a great effort to disguise the narcissistic nature of their thinking because they are afraid that they will not be able to manipulate others if their selfishness is discovered. Staying in control is the key element in the relationship. When sex and love addicts feel in control, then they can be aloof, unavailable, and rejecting. But when the partner takes control—for example, he or she decides to give up the relationship—then the sex and love addicts will try desperately to find a way back into the partner's heart. They can be extremely charming, kind, caring, loving, sensitive, and intuitive in order to get what they need. All of this is pseudo-intimacy. The excitement of the chase is what keeps the relationship alive. Real intimacy is too threatening to the addict's narcissistic needs.

Recovery, then, requires a letting go of control, getting out of "the driver's seat," surrendering, following direction, and giving up narcissistic and grandiose thinking. Bonnie (case 5) bragged that she had a "personal judge" who would make sure that she got whatever she wanted. She arrogantly told staff members what to do, how to do it, and why they were wrong or mistaken, fully believing that she knew better than they did how to do their job helping people recover. She had never maintained any sobriety from drugs, sex, or relationships, so she was in no position to judge others. But she did it anyway. In order for her to get into treatment, she needed to let go of her facade of control, of being a know-it-all, of having all the answers. The reality was that she had no answers for herself or anyone else; but for her, letting go of control felt as if she were saying that her abusive father was, in fact, right about her being stupid, worthless, and self-centered. She could not tolerate the humiliation of being in a vulnerable position with others and admitting she was not in control. Her abuse had taught her never to trust anyone and never to give up her power, even if she had to distort reality to maintain the illusion of control.

Of course, underneath Bonnie's grandiosity lay a profound sense of worthlessness, self-hatred, and low self-esteem. Her thinking in this area was just as distorted as her grandiosity and narcissism. Nothing I could say would convince Bonnie that she ever did anything well enough. She cringed when given any sort of compliment. I made an effort to catch her doing something right—which was not actually all that difficult. When I would make a big deal about the support she gave to a peer, an insight that she had about herself, or a well-written essay, she looked as if she wanted to melt in her chair. She was quite adept at trying to change the subject at times like these, but I would gently bring her back to her good qualities. She could not tolerate affirmations, nurturing, or praise—even though this is what she was starving for, especially from her father. Later on, through letters, she let me know that she thought I was a "great doctor," but she never let on at the moment that she was listening or appreciating my efforts to point out her positive qualities, to recognize her efforts to grow and change, and to boost her self-esteem by identifying her worth and value.

Carl (case 9) was much like Bonnie. He had many outstanding positive qualities. He was intelligent, sensitive, humorous, athletic, and handsome. His grandiosity and self-centeredness, however, provoked both peers and staff to want to "put him in his place." They were furious with his avoidance of his own issues and his preoccupation with appearing totally in control at all times. He was totally out of control at home and had destroyed property, been arrested a number of times, spent time in involuntary hospitalizations due to his danger-ousness to others, and could not let go of sex or drugs. But whenever he was under scrutiny of any sort, he could act like the perfect child. His phoniness and dishonesty drove others wild. They could not tolerate his narcissism and his need for control.

Underneath this smooth facade, Carl was frightened, ashamed, sad, and alone. He felt like a "bad person," a monster out of control. He had no self-worth and could not accept any positive support from others. When he was given a compliment, he looked for the other person's ulterior motive. When he was affirmed, he rejected the effort to reach him. When he was nurtured, he wondered what people wanted from him. He did not believe that anyone could love him as he was. He thought that people gave him love because they expected something in return. His thinking was so distorted that it seemed almost paranoid. His inferiority complex—well hidden under his grandiosity—left him in a schizoid position, without any close relationships with anyone.

Other types of distortions in thinking that adolescent sex and love addicts may employ include:

- **Denial**—The classic symptom of addiction; sex and love addicts will not admit they have a problem, even in the face of overwhelming evidence that they do have a serious and life-threatening difficulty.

- **Minimization**—Sex and love addicts make a molehill out of a mountain; when total denial does not work, they try to present the problem as small, unimpor-tant, easily taken care of, and minuscule in comparison to real difficulties.

- **Rationalization**—Sex and love addicts are experts at making up excuses, of fabricating stories, of conjuring up half-believable explanations for things that disguise the truth, rather than bringing it to light.

- **Projection**—When all else fails, blame someone else; sex and love addicts become adept at putting the responsibility for their problems on other people, on institutions, and/or on society in general, rather than admitting that they are at fault.

- **Intellectualization**—Sex and love addicts live in their heads and cannot allow themselves to feel anything; feelings seem too unsafe, while thoughts can help to maintain the illusion of control.
- **Detachment**—Sex and love addicts can disconnect their behavior from their self, so they are capable of acting in a robotlike manner when they sexualize or objectify someone else as part of their acting out; they feel safe not being connected.
- **Compartmentalization**—Sex and love addicts can separate things in their minds into discrete compartments so that they do not have to feel troubled by such things as putting a partner at risk as a result of unsafe sex while acting out.
- **Splitting**—Sex and love addicts can divide themselves into disconnected parts internally and externally; this allows them, for one, to manipulate others to be on their side, especially when they feel under attack.

All of these intellectual defenses are used by most people to some degree, in order to protect the self from experiencing overwhelming pain. However, sex and love addicts have made running, avoiding, hiding, disconnecting, and detaching from pain a way of life; they will use any and all of these defenses in order to protect their addiction, their method of coping. Each defense in its own way contributes to the overall distortion in sex and love addicts' thought processes. Such a major distortion in thinking often takes a great deal of effort to sort out and unravel.

Adolescents may not be sophisticated at using these defensive strategies, but nonetheless, the defenses are present in most teenagers who have become addicted. Straightening out their cognitions, unraveling their distortions, and clarifying their thinking processes can be a significant contribution to their overall recovery. Pointing out their denial, rationalization, or compartmentalization will help the adolescent sex and love addicts think more clearly and will improve their decision making. The cognitive distortions of addicts drive normal people crazy. Identifying their twisted thinking for family members, and discussing the role such manipulation plays in addiction, can assist the family in overcoming their anger and distrust and help them truly to support the recovering addict. Peers are usually in the best position to spot "stinking thinking." Often in meetings or in therapy groups, other recovering addicts will quickly spot manipulations, "cons," and cognitive distortions, because they too have had the same sorts of thoughts.

Claire (case 17) found it easy to confront her peers when they were lying and manipulating. She could detect dishonesty and cognitive distortion almost immediately. But she infuriated her peers because she could not see these same problems in her own thinking. For example, she was able to spot another female's denial about a brother's sexual abuse and use of minimization and rationalization to justify a boyfriend's physical abuse. When the focus was on Claire, however, she denied her mother's responsibility for her stepfather's sexual abuse and made excuses for her mother's rejection, abandonment, and helplessness in the face of ongoing physical abuse by Claire's biological father.

Dissociation is another form of intellectual defense and cognitive distortion that is used extensively by sex and love addicts. Associating means finding the connections between things. Dissociating means breaking the connections or links between things. Under extreme stress such as a medical emergency, people can disconnect from their physical pain long enough to complete acts of heroism. Under emotional stress, people can learn to separate themselves from the painful experience. An extreme example is the victim of sexual abuse who disconnects from her body and observes the event from the ceiling of the room. Multiple personality disorder is the result of extreme trauma that—to be survived—requires extensive use of dissociation to the point where different personalities exist within the same person. Sex and love addicts have learned to dissociate enough to allow themselves to act out in sexual and/or romantic ways that are inconsistent with the rest of their personality. They have developed to some degree a "split personality" à la Dr. Jekyll and Mr. Hyde.

Recovery, then, requires the integration of these two parts. The addict and the rest of the person need to associate with each other. This can be a difficult job since most sex and love addicts come to hate their addict side. They loathe the part of them that demands immediate gratification and acts out without regard to the long-term consequences. They want to kill, dismiss, destroy, bury, or otherwise get rid of the addictive tendencies that have created so much trouble. They call this part "stupid," "childish," "slutty," "whorish," "selfish," and "disgusting." They may be able to set this part of themselves aside for a while; but in order truly to recover, they must eventually come to love the addict within themselves and understand the addict's pain and the message of hurting. There can be not in-depth healing without learning the hidden story driving the acting-out behavior.

Bess (case 18) acted out through anonymous sex with boys. She was the town "slut" and her name probably appeared on walls in men's bathrooms with messages like, "To have a good time, call Bess 000–0000." Her vehement heterosexuality was a loudly communicated protest against the environment of secrecy and dishonesty that her parents had created about their homosexuality. Bess was enraged with them and the situation they had put her in, and she could find no other way to cry out in pain. Her recovery took a giant step forward when she could put her pain into words and could tell her parents directly what she was acting out in her sex and love addiction. Until this point, Bess had been dissociated from her true feelings. She had out-of-control sexual behavior that was threatening to destroy her life, but she had no idea why or how this addiction came about. She had dissociated from her pain so that her words said one thing

("I'm fine—don't bother me") and her behavior said something else ("Help—I'm drowning in sexual shame"). Her recovery was strengthened when she could stop dissociating and could connect her behavior with her pain.

Unmanageability

As their addiction cycle repeats itself, the lives of sex and love addicts become increasingly unmanageable. The habit of using preoccupation, addictive rituals, and acting out sexually or romantically to self-medicate, and the subsequent despair that drives addicts to repeat the pattern, will result in increased self-centeredness, isolation, and loss of control over the rest of their lives. In fact, their inability to manage their lives is usually what brings the sex and love addicts into treatment. Most often, especially for adolescent sex and love addicts, other people notice their lack of control and encourage or even force them into some type of treatment.

Unmanageability affects all aspects of the addict's life. Each person's pattern has individual differences, but damage is done in all areas. Some examples of loss of control are easier to spot than others. Examples of unmanageability include the following:

- **Physical**—Sexually transmitted diseases (especially exposure to or contraction of HIV/AIDS); injuries from fights that become physical; engaging in high-risk activities like driving at excessive speeds; physical injuries from sexual activities such as compulsive masturbation or use of sexual "toys" or objects; and unwanted pregnancies.

- **Mental**—Inability to concentrate; paranoia; obsessions; low self-esteem; negative self-talk; critical and shaming inner voices; and distorted thinking, as described in the preceding subsection.

- **Emotional**—Depression; anxiety; panic attacks; shame; embarrassment; humiliation; self-hatred; patterns of other compulsive behaviors with food, money (gambling, spending, debting), shopping, work, chemicals, prayer or religion, and scrupulosity; and suicidal and homicidal ideas and actions.

- **Social**—Decreased or failing academic performance; demotion or discharge from employment; isolation from or conflict with peers and family; change in peer group; association with people who use and abuse drugs and/or alcohol; legal charges for sexual behaviors and/or obsessive relationships (e.g., stalking); and involvement in abusive relationships.

- **Spiritual**—Decline in or ending of attendance at religious functions; anger at God; loss of faith; involvement in cults and/or Satanic activities.

No one will have all of these symptoms of addiction, or examples of loss of control, in their lives. The more severe the sex and love addiction, the more serious the unmanageability in the addict's life.

As adolescent sex and love addicts start to recover, they will begin to experience a discerned increase of manageability in their lives. They will be able to reduce their risk of getting AIDS, end abusive relationships, begin to communicate with their families, develop supportive friends, and get back into school. Therapists and support people need to focus on and highlight these accomplishments for the recovering person. Twelve Step programs know how important it is to recognize and affirm the small steps that build a recovery and that restore control to a person's life. For example, one day of sobriety is celebrated and acknowledged as much as one week, one month, or one year. Even simply attending a Twelve Step meeting is seen as a wonderful event and is enthusiastically cheered by other recovering people. By contrast, family members, friends, and therapists can often be insensitive to the effort that it takes for an adolescent sex and love addict to achieve any sobriety at all. People who do not understand addictions are typically impatient, critical, and annoyed by the sex and love addict's great need for support, and his or her slow progress. This is the nature of the disorder and needs to be accepted.

Accepting gradual progress in recovery does not mean ignoring the warning signs of slips and relapses. The recovering addict needs a balance of encouragement and detachment from those who are helping. If they wear "rose-colored glasses" and ignore instances of unmanageability, this can contribute to the addict's regression back into an active addiction. "Codependency" is the word most often used to describe friends, partners, family members, and therapists who are "too nice" and fail to confront the sex and love addict when they exhibit dysfunctional, unmanageable, and addictive behaviors, thoughts, attitudes, and feelings. Open communication between the addict and those who are supporting him or her is the best antidote to insensitivity, expecting too much, impatience, and codependency.

One of the biggest problems that recovering adolescent sex and love addicts face is boredom. This is a difficulty for adolescents in general. As they make the transition from child to adult, there is a period where their freedom is increased but is not unlimited. Likewise, while being more responsible is expected of us as we grow older, responsibility remains somewhat limited for teenagers. Learning to cope with freedom and responsibility is a major task; it is an important element in identity development. Spreading their wings and exercising their freedom and responsibility is exciting for adolescents. Excitement is a natural "high." Teenagers discover that they can get high on sex and love, chemicals, money, competition, anger, and aggression. A psychologist friend of mine who works with male adolescents, some of whom are sex and love addicts, in a residential setting shared with me his observation that the boys he works with would get high on fights, sex, or drugs with equal interest. The crucial factor seemed to be the availability at the moment. Whatever would relieve the current boredom was the addictive mechanism of choice.

Learning to live with the "normal" highs and lows of life without the wild roller-coaster ride provided by addictive acting out can be the greatest challenge to a recovering person. Adolescents are especially susceptible to this need for excitement because they are only beginning to discover the mature joys of adulthood while they need to give up the instant gratification of childhood. Unmanageability, then, for an active addict can be part of the excitement of the addictive coping style. Being out of control requires constant creativity, efforts to manipulate and control things, and unpredictability in their lives. Recovery requires planning, consistency, and predictability—which may seem boring, depressing, and uninteresting to a young person bursting with ideas and energy and few outlets for his or her creativity and control. Developing the capacity to appreciate life without unmanageability is a significant growth step for an adolescent sex and love addict.

Steps four through nine of the Twelve Steps provide sex and love addicts with an opportunity to examine the reasons for their life's unmanageability, as well as its effects on others. In step four, addicts are asked to do a "searching and fearless, moral inventory" of themselves; and in step five, they are encouraged to share with "God, ourselves, and another human being the exact nature of our wrongs." Step six involves being "entirely ready" for the "removal of all these defects of character," and step seven suggests that addicts "humbly ask God to remove our shortcomings." In step eight, a list is prepared "of all persons we had harmed," and the addict becomes "willing to make amends to the all." Step nine calls for making "direct amends" wherever possible, with the caution "except when to do so would injure them or others." The process of making and sharing their inventory, working on character defects, admitting to harming others, and being willing to make amends requires patience, maturity, and responsibility. It is a model for coping with human limitations and relationships that is applicable to a wide variety of situations beyond addiction recovery. It teaches the addict manageability.

Core Beliefs

Patrick Carnes (1983) identified what he calls four "core beliefs" that sex addicts hold:

1. I am basically a bad, unworthy person.
2. No one would love me as I am.
3. My needs are never going to be met if I have to depend on others.
4. Sex is my most important need.

These beliefs about the self must together constitute an obvious recipe for low self-esteem. These beliefs are deeply held and difficult to uncover and uproot.

Defenses like denial and narcissism hide the essential fact that the sex and love addict does not feel good about who he or she really is. Efforts on the part of others to improve the addict's self-worth—such as by giving affirmations—fail to become fruitful because of these underlying and undermining beliefs. Nothing positive can ever really stick for the sex and love addict when these core beliefs are present.

Adolescents are particularly damaged when they arrive at their teenage years with these beliefs already in place. Rather than discovering who they really are outside the context of their family, they spend most of their time and energy avoiding the pain of their low self-worth. Addictions can be numbing, distracting, preoccupying, and anesthetizing for the adolescent who comes into this growth period already overloaded with pain from childhood. Growth stops or is, at least, inhibited when the addictive process takes over.

Badness, Unworthiness

The deepest evidence of damage from childhood trauma (discussed in a later subsection) is the strong belief that the sex and love addict is essentially bad and unworthy. This feeling about oneself is the polar opposite of our society's belief in the basic dignity, goodness, and worth of each and every individual, no matter what the individual's color, skills, economic status, cultural or racial background, sexual orientation, or intelligence. Our religious institutions have championed the worth and goodness of human beings for centuries. Adolescents who hold the core belief that they are bad and unworthy, then, find themselves outside the bounds of our social and religious institutions. They see themselves as deviant, damaged goods, "perverts," monsters, less than human, and possessed by demons that they do not understand and cannot control.

An artistically talented seventeen-year-old sex and love addicted client drew a self-portrait. His drawing was a picture of his "addict" self. The pastel drawing portrayed a ghoulish, skeletonlike head colored gray and blue. There was no hair and the eyes were open, sunken, empty sockets. The nose was nothing but two brownish openings. The mouth opened wide to a reddish cavity that appeared ready to release a haunting scream. Below the head was a wall on which leaned one greenish-blue hand with long nails, poised to leap over the obstruction and capable of causing great harm. His "addict" had leaped over that wall, taken over his life, and left him alone, isolated, drug dependent, without a high school diploma, unable to work, alienated from his family, and filled with self-hatred, shame, and guilt.

In treatment, this young man had initially tried to hide the addict side of himself behind the wall again. He appeared to be the model drug-abusing patient until his sex and love addiction surfaced because he was acting out with female peers. He was encouraged to try not to compartmentalize, deny, and hide this part of himself, because he could not really recover without integrating his addict part into his whole self. The "addict" was at the center of his feelings of badness, unworthiness; and healing could not occur if it was not directed at these core beliefs. He was ashamed of this part of himself and felt guilty about the things that his "addict" part had done.

Shame and *guilt* are intimately connected with feelings of badness and unworthiness. Shame is the feeling that we are bad. Guilt is the feeling that our behaviors are bad. Healthy shame is a feeling of modesty and privacy. Healthy guilt is the knowledge that there are behaviors that are wrong. For example, parents in our culture normally cover their genitals when around their children. This effort to keep sexual parts of the body private is an instance of modesty. If a child accidently observes the parent's nakedness, most parents would feel embarrassed and ashamed that they had not taken adequate precautions to prevent the incident. Were such parents to expose themselves intentionally, they would feel guilt for engaging in seductive or sexually provocative behaviors. In the first instance, the feeling of shame is connected to the exposure of the parent's sexual self. In the second instance, the guilt is associated with inappropriate parenting behaviors.

Many sex and love addicts have grown up with shaming and guilt-inducing parents. Those who have experienced excessive shame feel, "I am a mistake." Those who have been given too much guilt feel, "I made a mistake." Some have too much of both. Shame can be a powerful tool in terms of enforcing parental control. Usually, parents who rely extensively on shame to control their children were shamed themselves as children. Shame-filled children feel that they are "bad" to the core. When they engage in "bad" behaviors (as all children do), they feel doubly awful about themselves. Their guilt and shame combine to produce profoundly low self-esteem.

Some parents are not able to acknowledge what a wonderful gift a child is to their lives. They see the child more as a burden than a blessing. All children are needy, and parents who do not know how to get their own needs met may resent the innate demands inherent in caring for a child. The child learns that he or she is not special and, in fact, comes to see himself or herself as worthless. Sometimes they even think that, if they were not around, their parents would have a better life. They can become parentified children who work hard to take care of their parents and to meet the parents' needs, rather than the other way around. Again, the result is a profound sense of worthlessness.

Al (case 3) felt like a burden to his mother. His father had abandoned him long before, but his mother struggled to raise him and was trying to pull herself out of poverty and drug dependence. Al had made a serious suicide attempt that had damaged him physically and mentally. His drug and sex addictions had overwhelmed him, and he was not capable of living sober, especially in the city where he lived. He thought that he could never do anything right; he couldn't even kill himself right. His sense of shame was deeply rooted in feelings of worthlessness. He was plagued with guilt because his addictions drew him to all sorts of "bad" behaviors, including prostitution and unsafe sex with older men. He thought of himself as thoroughly "bad" and not worth rehabilitating.

Al's therapy was focused on finding examples of his goodness and affirming his worth despite his protests to the contrary. He was kind and caring with peers and encouraged others to grow into honesty and truth. He felt too ashamed of his sexual abuse, involvement in pornography, and sexual acting out to be able to tell his peers about himself. Gradually, with a lot of support from staff, he was able to begin to share with others everything about him. The relief that he felt was tremendous. His secrets had been killing him.

Steps four through ten of the Twelve Steps address the issues of healing self-esteem. In the tenth step, recovering sex and love addicts are asked to continue taking a personal inventory—and when they are wrong to "promptly admit it." The effort to become open, honest, and true to oneself, then, is an ongoing process that continues as long as recovery does.

Unlovable

Sex and love addicts do not believe that anyone could love them as they are. Part of the reason for this is that no one really does know who they are, especially in the beginning of recovery. Secrecy and shame are such large parts of this addiction that sex and love addicts think they have many things to hide. They have a great fear of being found out and, then, of being truly rejected. If they can keep secrets, they can also keep the hope that they will eventually find someone to love them. Hiding their addiction also prevents them from having to experience the intense shame connected with their acting out.

As they long for unconditional love and acceptance, their addiction stands firmly in the way. When others try to love, affirm, and accept sex and love addicts, the addicts say in the back of their mind, "But they would not be saying these things about me or treating me in this way if they knew that I . . . (act out with anonymous sex, masturbate to pornography, have affairs on my partner, etc.)." The fact that they are out of control of their sexual and/or romantic lives is never far from their mind. Their sense of unworthiness, badness, and shame blocks them from receiving whatever love is actually available for them. While their sex and love addiction remains untreated and possibly hidden, they cannot ever feel lovable.

Pam (case 25) was obviously needy. She hung around adults because she craved their love and attention. She had a distant father, but her mother and stepfather tried to fill her up and make her feel special and loved. Nothing worked, however, and her mother and the other adults involved in her treatment were slowly going crazy. Pam had this bizarre attachment to a young man who was clearly not healthy and who treated her abusively. No one could understand why she insisted on pursuing love from him and refused to take the love that was available to her from people who really did care about her. Until her sex and love addiction was identified and treated, she would continue in this cycle of frustration, abuse, and lovelessness. She came close to killing herself more than once over a relationship, engaged in some strange cultlike rituals, and wore black whenever possible. Her family was frightened that they would lose her before the solution to her problems was found. Pam felt unlovable, and only when she began her recovery from sex and love addiction did she begin to put together the pieces of this puzzle she called her life. Her sense of being unlovable seemed to stem from her father's neglect and her mother's smothering behaviors. Both left her with low self-esteem and feelings of worthlessness. She thought that there was something essentially wrong with her because her father did not care and her mother treated her like she was incompetent, fragile, and in need of great protection.

Getting Needs Met and Depending on Others

Addicts do not like to see themselves as needy, dependent people. They fight the idea that they are dependent, using the many intellectual defenses described earlier: denial, rationalization, minimization, dissociation, and so on. Dependency is not valued in our culture—especially for men—so sex and love addicts feel inadequate, not as good as others, or damaged if they cannot live without a "crutch" such as an addiction. Depending on chemicals, sex, relationships, food, or money is seen as a sign of "weakness" in our society and dependent people feel a stigma for having this problem. Being independent is associated with being strong, powerful, and in control. Sex and love addicts want to appear as potent and as in control of their lives as anyone else, so they need to deny and hide their real problems with dependency.

Adolescents are in a developmental stage that expects growing independence from family and rewards the positive use of freedom and responsibility. If being dependent feels childish to an adult, for a teenager the position of being dependent is like being imprisoned in childhood, never to grow up. Consequently, sex and love addicted adolescents often attempt to appear overly independent and in charge of their lives. They can be phobic about any signs of dependency and appear fiercely independent when, in fact, the opposite is true. Some, however, acknowledge their strong tendency to be dependent and may even wear it like a badge of courage. Women seem more likely than men to be accepted in this dependent role, because of social stereotypes of men and women's roles in relationships.

Then, too, depending on others to get their needs met is almost impossible for sex and love addicts because they have been damaged in the primary relationships in which their needs should have been met. Typically, their families are physically, emotionally, and/or sexually abusive and neglectful. Growing up in a dysfunctional family, the children do not know the experience of having their needs met. On the contrary, many such children are expected to meet their parents' needs (e.g., for affection, appreciation, love, or perfect children) and are never allowed to express their own needs. Expressing needs may be literally dangerous or may simply receive no response at all from the people who are supposed to be paying attention. In either case, the children learn that they can not depend on anyone else to meet their needs. So, if their needs are going to be met, they are going to have to do it themselves.

Brenda (case 30) grew up in a home that was strict and religious. She was expected to behave and to reflect her parents' love for her by her good behavior. She was severely punished with shaming words and physical beatings when she was "bad." Her parents believed the biblical adage, "Spare the rod and spoil the child." They were supported in their parenting style by their church. Brenda grew up knowing that she was not supposed to have needs. Whatever needs she had for love and affection were well hidden from her own consciousness and from her parents. Unfortunately for her, these needs leaked out in indirect ways, such as her "bad" behavior. Each punishment further convinced her that she would not get her needs met from her parents.

When it came time for her to become interested in men, she went wild. She was desperately seeking the love that she had been starved of for fourteen years. She knew she could not depend on her parents for love, so she threw herself at men—who only continued to neglect and abuse her. If she could not get love, she learned that she could at least get held through acting out sexually. She could not depend on anyone to give her what she really needed, so she got what she could the only way she knew how. Her sexual and relational acting out only reenforced her feelings of badness, worthlessness, unlovability. She became convinced that she would never get her needs met and that she could depend on people only to hurt her more.

Building a therapeutic relationship with Brenda was difficult. She did not trust any adult to be different from her parents. She expected to be criticized, put down, and punished. In order for a therapy relationship to work, however, she needed to have some trust in the therapist and she needed to be willing to be dependent to some degree. Establishing such a relationship with a teenager who has been hurt by adults is challenging and requires patience and ingenuity. Brenda needed to know that we were going to be working together in a partnership and that she had some control over what happened in our sessions. She also needed to know that there were clear limits and that her therapist would act to protect her if she were dangerous to herself or to anyone else.

Sex (and Love)—The Most Important Need?

Unconditional love is the most fundamental and most important need for all of us. Convinced that they can never have this, sex and love addicts come to believe that sex and/or relational dependency is their most important need. They do not think they can live without it. Life without sex and/or romantic attachment is not worth living. They cannot imagine existing without an active sexual or relational component in their life. They picture life without sex and love as empty, meaningless, lonely, and incredibly painful. They have no idea that they could enjoy being alone or that they could live without sexual activity for a period of time.

Harold (case 16) could not live without sex. Even while he was in the hospital, he was constantly acting out. His sex and love addiction was discovered after he was found to have carved a peephole between his room and the girls' bedroom next door. The details of his addiction are described in Chapter 3. The short version is that Harold could not stop acting out long enough to find out what life was like without an active sex addiction. When he was not involved in overt sexual activity, his talk was filled with sexual innuendo; he was constantly intrigued with female staff and peers alike; he was always cruising for a potential liaison; no activity, interaction, or interchange was free from sexual overtones. He was constantly high on sex or seeking ways to get high. He could see no point in abstinence or letting go of his sexual activity. He tried to be more secretive and covert after he was caught, but he never considered attempting sobriety. His parents did not want to hear about his problem and acted like it was no big deal—which was exactly what he wanted to hear. They did not insist on his following through with any treatment recommendations; this suggested that there might be sex and love addiction issues in the parents' marital relationship. As some say, "the apple does not fall far from the tree."

The program of the Augustine Fellowship of Sex and Love Addicts Anonymous (1986) recommends that sex and love addicts confine their sexual activity to a committed relationship. What this means is that a recovering sex and love addict should be in a committed relationship first before becoming sexually involved with the partner to the commitment. Anonymous sex, casual sex, one-night stands, and sex with oneself are not encouraged.

An essential step in recovery, then, is to develop the capacity to have a committed relationship. Defining the therapeutic relationship as a committed one can be the foundation for learning what is required in such a relationship. Establishing clear boundaries such as time, place, roles, and responsibilities can be an important beginning. When boundary violations occur after this, they can be discussed in terms of their effect on the trust level and amount of commitment in the relationship. Outside the clinical setting, sex and love addicts can learn commitment from sponsors and meetings in the Twelve Step program of SLAA. Daily contact with sponsors, at least by phone, is the usual recommendation for developing this relationship. Sex and love addicts often have great difficulty making the choice to get a sponsor and then initiating the contact with the person whom they choose. Both therapists and sponsors play parental roles and represent an opportunity for reparenting experiences and learning healthy interactions with authority figures.

Peers in recovery offer a different type of commitment. We learn from our friends what an equal expects of us and what they will accept from us. Peers are not as accepting and forgiving as "good" parents or authority figures, on the one hand, and are potentially more loving and giving, on the other hand, because of their capacity for identification and empathy. The commitment between two recovering sex and love addicts involves equality and mutuality. There is a dynamic give-and-take that happens, typically, in therapeutic programs for adolescents. Sex and love addicts in the Twelve Step program can make commitments to SLAA meetings. For example, they can choose to take responsibility for the coffee—that is, make a "coffee commitment"—or commit to other activities such as chairing a meeting or bringing the program literature. Often, making a commitment to a group is the most that a recovering person can do initially. Individual commitments are too threatening at first.

All of the above are examples of relationship-learning opportunities that are nonsexual and nonromantic. It may be necessary to state this explicitly as part of the therapeutic relationship. That is, the therapist and the client agree that theirs will be a nonsexual, nonromantic relationship, and both parties commit themselves to upholding this contract. It is better not to assume that this agreement is understood or automatically expected by the client. In fact, as the therapy progresses, it may be necessary to return to this understanding and recommit to it as part of the contract's safety for both parties. Adolescents will at first find talking about sexual and romantic feelings to be quite frightening and uncomfortable within the therapy relationship. They may attempt to cover their anxiety with grandiosity or seductiveness. But it is important that the therapist not be fooled by these defenses into avoiding the topic altogether. The therapist needs to balance a discussion of sexual and romantic boundaries with sensitivity to what the teenager can tolerate, and not be too pushy or intrusive with the remarks.

Steve (case 32) was so engrossed in his sex and love addiction that even the threat of arrest for sexual offenses (i.e., for his exhibitionism) did not bring him into contact with the reality of his loss of control over his sexual acting out. He could not make a commitment to attend SLAA meetings or to come to group or individual therapy. He begged for help while he was in the hospital; but the minute he felt that the pressure was off from the courts, his commitment to his aftercare disappeared. His lack of attendance at outpatient group sessions was reported to his probation officer and nothing was done. Steve was never seen again. His parents had tolerated his having an active sexual relationship (many times a day) with a girlfriend whom his parents had taken in when she was thrown out by her own parents. Furthermore, his parents did not insist that he attend the self-help meetings or aftercare therapies. Without their commitment to helping him get the help he needed, he could not make a commitment to himself or to anyone else. He "talked the talk," but he did not "walk the walk."

Steps ten, eleven, and twelve of the Twelve Steps describe a recovering way of life that involves honesty, commitment, and priorities. Step ten suggests continuing to take personal inventory on a regular basis, and promptly admitting wrong. Step eleven encourages prayer and meditation to develop conscious contact with our Higher Power in order to discover His will for us and to have the courage to follow it out. Step twelve acknowledges the "spiritual awakening" that results in working the Twelve Steps and points toward "carrying the message" to other suffering addicts. Sex and love are not mentioned. The message seems to be that caring for themselves, being honest, being spiritual, and being committed to service will bring to recovering sex and love addicts the answer to their dreams. That is, they will feel good about themselves; they will have meaningful, committed relationships; their needs will get met; and sexuality will be in its rightful place in their lives.

Hopefully, recovery from sex and love addiction will eventually heal the core beliefs of the addicts. They will no longer feel bad and worthless. They will feel loved and loveable. They will be able to meet their own needs and, when appropriate, will be able to have dependable people in their lives to help them meet these needs. Sexuality will have an important role in their lives as part of a committed relationship, but it will not be their top or only priority.

Childhood Trauma

The topic of childhood trauma has filled many books—for one example, Judith Lewis Herman's *Trauma and Recovery* (1992)—and cannot be dealt with here in any detail. However, it is a key additional element in the addiction cycle that was not part of Carnes's (1983) original diagram. Since then, in research on a thousand sex addicts, Carnes (1991) found that 98 percent of recovering sex addicts described themselves as being emotionally abused. About 80 percent had memories of sexual abuse, and around three-quarters identified a history of physical abuse. While more research on sex and love addicts is not yet available, anecdotal reports and presentations at national conferences (e.g., the National Council on Sexual Addiction/Compulsivity—NCSA's national meeting) strongly suggest that sex and love addicts have histories of serious neglect as well as physical, emotional, and/or sexual abuse.

In fact, it is beginning to appear likely that sex and love addicts' patterns of acting out, and their obsessive fantasies, are reenactments of their childhood trauma. One example of this reenacting was a sex and love addict in our program whose acting out consisted of cross-dressing and having anonymous men perform oral sex on him. He had no memory of sexual abuse until after his mother died. Then, he had a flashback of his father dressing him up like a girl and performing fellatio on him when he was three or four. His sexual addiction had made no sense to him prior to this memory. He knew that he was heterosexually oriented, and he lived with his girlfriend. He also knew that his cocaine addiction had developed out of the sex and love addiction. And acting out had once almost cost him his life: Some men who recognized him as a man dressed like a woman had beat him up so badly that he had needed to be hospitalized. For some time, he had been wanting to stop cross-dressing, but did not understand the connection between his childhood and his acting out. He grew up fairly well off because his mother was a lawyer; he had graduated from an excellent suburban high school. He was attractive, intelligent, and "had everything" but peace of mind. He was driven by an internal demon that did not match with his external reality. Only when he recovered his memory of sexual abuse did he begin to put the pieces together.

Adolescents are in a difficult position when it comes to being ready and able to deal with their childhood trauma. Most of them are still living in the family that may have been abusive. They depend on those same parents to pay for therapy, provide transportation, and support their recovery. Unless there is overt, obvious abuse that justifies the intrusion of legal and human services interventions with the family, the teenager may still have to live with and relate to his or her parents, one or both of whom may have been neglectful and/or abusive. Unhealthy parental relationships are the breeding ground for abuse and neglect, so the adolescent in treatment is unlikely to find much support in the family for his or her treatment and recovery.

In addition to the external resistance of the family to dealing with underlying issues of neglect and abuse, the adolescents have their own internal resistances to bringing up painful issues from their past. Their sex and love addiction, plus any other obsessions and compulsions, as well as their intellectual defenses (e.g., denial, minimization), have all been designed to keep pain at bay. Having grown up in neglectful and hurtful environments, they have not learned healthy coping mechanisms for dealing with serious trauma. Their own growth and development has been interfered with by the presence of their sex and love addiction, as well as probably others. Their self-esteem is profoundly damaged and characterized by core beliefs that tell them they are bad, worthless, and unlovable. Unmanageability has ruined their successes and undermined their confidence in their skills and gifts. Without internal structures for nurturing and discipline, they dare not uncover material that is potentially overwhelming.

Tackling childhood trauma issues in therapy requires patience, trust, and commitment on the part of both the client and the therapist. Working on establishing a solid addiction recovery—the bottom circle of addiction in Carnes's schema—should provide a good foundation for this later, more difficult work. Some sex and love addicts cannot establish any sort of consistent recovery without some work on childhood trauma issues. They need to have a better sense that there is a hurting, inner child who needs their love and attention, before they can make the decision to let go of something that provides a quick fix, a powerful medication, and a complete distraction from these deeper, more painful issues. Other sex and love addicts cannot work on childhood trauma issues until they have been in recovery for at least a year.

Connecting sexual and relational acting out with childhood trauma can be a tremendous relief for the sex and love addict. Since their shame and guilt are so profound and their self-esteem is so low, they carry the full weight and responsibility for their addiction. They need to know that sex and love addiction is a coping strategy for dealing with childhood trauma that otherwise would have been so overwhelming they most likely would not have survived. However, it is an unhealthy strategy with many damaging side effects—for example, unmanageability—that they now need to change in order to renew their growth process and become mature adults. This is especially true for teenagers, whose options for coping are more restricted and limited than the choices available to adults.

PSYCHOEDUCATION

Addiction programs have traditionally offered psychoeducation groups to their clients. Classical psychoanalytic treatment encouraged the therapist to be a "blank screen" for the projections of the client; so, information giving by the therapist was discouraged because of its potential to "contaminate" the therapeutic process. Such analytic treatment of chemical dependency is generally viewed as a dismal failure. The approach of Alcoholics Anonymous has involved the sharing of recovery stories among peers who are suffering from the same disorder. As treatment centers developed that incorporated Twelve Step support groups, there was a need to integrate the traditional objectivity and detachment of psychotherapists with the grassroots subjectivity and attachment of anonymous programs. One example of this combination of approaches has been the widespread use of psychoeducation groups in addiction treatment programs.

Also, the development of counseling programs in graduate schools of education has further reenforced the idea that consumers benefit from education despite the potential for distortions. One phenomenon that has been observed in these graduate programs is that students imagine they have the diseases or conditions they are studying. This, then, has led to the fear that educating clients will produce more problems than it solves. However, in a simultaneous development, social movements such as consumerism has encouraged an open exchange of information between providers and consumers. This demand for "informed consent" have pushed health care professionals to provide more complete information to clients.

Teaching addicts about the possibility of relapse was one area that treatment professionals were hesitant to approach. If we tell an alcoholic about the high rate of relapse in chemical dependency, are we giving him or her "permission" to drink? Some alcoholics exhibit the distorted thinking that "it is not worth the effort to stay sober since I will probably fail anyway." Professionals have come to realize that they cannot take the blame for such a relapse, and that the education about relapse does not in itself encourage the behavior. In fact, the intention behind psychoeducation is the exact opposite. If consumers are informed in advance about some of the potential dangers, they are more likely to take the appropriate measures to protect themselves from relapse. Nowadays, most chemical dependency programs have a "relapse prevention" component, and some even provide specialized services for those clients who are at imminent risk for relapse. Psychoeducation is seen as an essential part of addiction treatment and relapse prevention.

Formats

The format for psychoeducation can vary depending on the type of treatment and the client population. The traditional form for education is the lecture, with students in rows and the instructor using a blackboard, newsprint, or handouts. While this format works fairly well for adults, it is preferable—even when lecturing—to set up a circle or semicircle of chairs; this helps to break down the isolation and distance between the teacher and the students. With teenagers—especially those in treatment to please someone else (i.e., their parents, the school, the legal authorities, or their girlfriend or boyfriend), or those uncertain as to their real need or problem—straight lecturing will most likely not communicate a lot of information. Most of these adolescents have had difficulties in school, and the formal classroom setting can turn them off even before any words are exchanged.

A discussion group or question-and-answer format tends to get the clients more involved with the information. When participants know that they are free to express their concerns or that they may even be expected to be accountable for the information (through questioning), they are more likely to attend to what is going on in the group. Again, circular seating will promote eye contact and verbal interactions among group members. Usually, the group leader needs to be responsible for structuring the group; so, the leader will present some material to stimulate discussion and will ask questions and encourage exchanges among the participants. Leaders will also make summary comments and keep the group on the topic under consideration.

Breaking the group into smaller groups for part of the session can facilitate sharing, especially when the topic is personal and people might be embarrassed to say something in the group as a whole. For example, I might divide the large group initially into groups of four and ask each group to make a list of "tools of recovery" from sex and love addiction. Then, after the small groups are done (and I have been moving around the room monitoring the small groups' progress), I will ask a group leader to present each group's discussion while, at the front of the room, I compile a comprehensive list of all of the tools that were presented by each group. After all of the groups are done, I will lead a general discussion of the similarities and differences between the lists made by the small groups. Often, there is a lot in common, which helps the groups to bond with each other; and yet, there are unique contributions from each. At the end, I affirm the participation of each person and group and point out the resourcefulness, creativity, and energy available in such a gathering of recovering people. Small groups can also be used for generating ideas on sharing more personal information, or for specific tasks.

A similar format to small groups is the use of dyads or triads. In this situation, we ask the participants in the larger group to pair up or to gather in groups of three for specific tasks. For example, the topic of the educational session might be "HIV/AIDS in recovery." One way to get the group members in touch with the seriousness of this issue for their own recovery would be to ask them to pair up with the person next to them and share with that person "the times that I put myself at risk for contracting HIV." Then, after each partner has had sufficient time to share, the group leader could ask in the large group whether anyone wants to share their dyad experience. Some participants will be able to share in the big group, while those who are not ready to speak in the large group have at least had the opportunity to speak with another person about an important aspect of recovery. Another variation of the same format would be to have people pair up with someone they do not know or know the least. This would help to break down some of the social barriers and cliques in the larger group and ultimately improve the overall cohesion of the bigger group. Adolescents appreciate when a leader understands that everyone is not able to talk in a group and that everyone can benefit from active sharing, instead of having simply to listen to the teacher talk.

Teaching brainstorming techniques helps to facilitate creativity and interaction in groups. When the members of a group brainstorm about a given subject, they need to be instructed that each person's contribution will be accepted without judgment. The idea behind a brainstorm is to generate of as many ideas as possible. Once the creative part has taken place, the group can go back and use critical and analytical skills to evaluate the quality of the particular ideas. The group leader needs to model acceptance by taking down on newsprint or the blackboard each suggestion exactly as the person states it. At this point, even the leader should not edit or change what is being offered. That comes later. The emphasis is on inclusiveness, not exclusiveness. Since adolescents are highly sensitive to issues of group membership and rejection (especially from peers), this format can help to involve quieter group members and to reenforce the norms of equality and mutuality in the group dynamic.

The final format suggestion is that of role playing. When a group uses role playing to learn about a particular topic, the group leader needs to facilitate the process by providing clear direction about the topic, the particular roles, and the length of time that the scene is played, and suggestions about how to process the information thus generated. This group technique is more powerful and difficult to do well than the ones listed above. Training is needed in order not to get into a situation that is potentially harmful to group members. In a role-play situation, the group leader might tell the group that "today's session will focus on learning to say no to a sexual encounter." The leader then would ask for volunteers to play the roles of seducer and victim. The players would need some additional guidance—say, about the setting, and about how to play the part. The group would then observe the role play and process it afterward. At that point, the leader would ask the protagonists how they felt playing the roles and, then, ask the group for feedback about the presentation. A group discussion or more role-play situations could develop. Adolescents enjoy this format because it makes the material more "real." Rather than being mainly an intellectual exercise, this format for educational groups can elicit strong emotional responses from participants—which offers them the opportunity to integrate what is in their head with what is in their heart.

Topics

There are a wide variety of psychoeducation topics that can be helpful to adolescents who are recovering from sex and love addiction. The twelve presented in this subsection are not intended to be an exhaustive list, but they are areas that so far seem to be the most relevant to treatment and recovery. And these twelve topics seemed to fall into four categories: initial identification of the problem; learning about the recovery process; special focus issues; and general information on normal development.

In terms of *initial identification*, the topics are the ones covered in Chapter 2. First, adolescents need to know the "what" of recovery: what is an addiction? They need some ideas about what the definition of sex and love addiction is and how we define addictions in general. Second, they need to be presented with the addiction concepts of tolerance, dependence, withdrawal, and cravings. Third, they should be made familiar with the terms "obsession" and "compulsion," the role of secrecy in maintaining addictions, and the existence of personality changes or dissociation. The adolescents have probably been exposed to many of these ideas, but usually not in any comprehensive presentation, nor directly connected to sexual and/or romantic acting out.

The next area of concern is *learning about the recovery process*. In these educational sessions, teenagers are exposed to information about the how of recovery. First, they should be exposed to the dynamics of addiction as outlined in the addiction cycle (see Chapter 2). In this segment, they should learn about the areas described in the beginning of this chapter: acting out, rituals, despair, preoccupation, distorted thinking, unmanageability, and core beliefs, as well as childhood trauma and neglect. Second, they need to know the Twelve Steps of Sex and Love Addicts Anonymous, with major emphasis on the first three steps.

Third, they should be able to identify tools of recovery such as identifying "bottom lines" and "triggers," the use of SLAA meetings and program sponsors, the importance of changing "people, places, and things," and the role of prayer and meditation. Fourth, they should be exposed to the idea that there are at least two stages of recovery: stopping the addictive behaviors, and uncovering whatever is driving the addiction.

There are some *special focus issues* that need to be highlighted in a psychoeducational program. First, the topic of shame needs to be dealt with directly, since it is such a powerful part of the addictive process, especially for sex and love addicts. Teenagers should be taught the difference between guilt and shame and the ways to ameliorate the intense shame that they experience at times in recovery. Second, the role of honesty as the "key to sobriety" must be underscored. With this disease, learning to be honest with oneself and one's peers can mean the difference between life and death. Third, the impact of trauma, the symptoms of post-traumatic stress disorder (PTSD), and the effects of parental neglect and abuse need to be explained so that the adolescents have a better perspective on what happened to them and why.

Finally, the teenagers need *general information on normal development*. First, they need to be educated about what normally happens for adolescents in the areas of sexuality and relationships. Their experience—and probably the experience of many of their friends—has been outside the realm of normal development. They did not have the boundaries or expectations that are usually imposed on teenagers, so they need help in reestablishing themselves in terms of healthy growth for a person their age. Second, they should be taught about safe sex. They need to hear about the role of abstinence in recovery. They need to know how to protect themselves and no longer be a danger to others. They need sex education. Typically, the psychoeducational groups dealing with sexuality are the most popular for recovering sex and love addicts. There is a lot of information that they do not have, despite their patterns of acting out that might imply more knowledge about sexuality and relationships than actually exists.

Psychoeducation is an essential element of treatment. Often—in outpatient settings, in particular—this aspect of recovery is neglected or nonexistent. Sex and love addicts have many developmental deficits that psychoeducational approaches can fill. Part of what good parents do for their children is to educate them. Adolescents addicts, in particular, require the services of treatment professionals who recognize their need for education, as well as for psychotherapy and support groups.

PSYCHOTHERAPY

Psychoeducation, psychotherapy, and support groups are the three basic elements of treatment and recovery for adolescent sex and love addicts. In this section, various types of psychotherapy will be examined: individual, group, family, psychopharmacological, bibliotherapy, and written assignments. Evocative therapies such as psychodrama, gestalt, art therapy, movement therapy, and recreation therapy will also be reviewed. In addition, various levels of therapeutic intervention will be looked at, including inpatient, residential, halfway houses, partial hospital programs, intensive outpatient, and traditional outpatient therapy.

In *Outpatient Treatment of Sex and Love Addiction* (Griffin-Shelley, 1993), my colleagues and I reviewed the state of the art of outpatient treatment in terms of definition, diagnosis and neurochemistry, individual and group psychotherapy, issues in men's groups, women's issues in recovery, sex therapy and addiction recovery, and the cultural context of sex and love addiction recovery. Much of the information presented in that volume is useful in the treatment of adolescent sex and love addicts. What is presented here shall build on this previous work and will clarify the modifications in treatment necessary for working with teenagers.

Psychotherapy is different from psychoeducation, which concentrates on providing clients with information in ways that filter through their defenses, and different from support groups, which are completely voluntary, independent, and primarily peer-level interactions. Psychotherapy is provided by a professional. The therapist makes his or her living by offering these services, has been trained by other professionals, usually is licensed and/or certified by a state board, and should be a member of local, state, and national organizations of professionals providing similar services. The psychotherapist is in a position of power vis-à-vis the client. The therapist is in a position (based on his or her training) to provide treatment of the client's problems. The client, in turn, agrees to cooperate with the treatment by attending sessions, following suggestions, being honest and open, and reimbursing the therapist for these services. The powerful position of the therapist in the relationship gives the therapist the role of authority figure and is similar to the role of parent.

In the context of this powerful, authoritative, parental relationship, interactions take place that resemble the interactions between the client and other authority figures in his or her life—especially parents. Therapists refer to this dynamic as "transference";—that is, the client transfers feelings for parental figures onto the therapist. For example, a client who has not had good parenting might project thoughts of omnipotence onto the therapist (i.e., the therapist can do no wrong) or perhaps thoughts of worthlessness (i.e., the therapist can never do anything right). To some degree, the therapist does evoke these feelings and there is a basis in reality for them; but there is also some distortion. Figuring out what is real and what is from the past is the job of psychotherapy. When the past is clarified, then it can be let go. When it is not understood, it can be reenacted and continue to contribute to the ongoing pain of the client.

Adolescents—by nature of their stage in development—usually struggle a great deal with issues that have to do with depending on and letting go of authority figures. Consequently, psychotherapy with teenagers is more complicated around the issues of transference than therapy with people who have already become more independent or therapy with children. Parental involvement in the adolescent's therapy is essential to some degree, and this changes the dynamics of the various treatments. Just as adolescence is the period between childhood and adulthood, between dependence on parents and independence, the role of the therapist with adolescents is to walk that fine line between being a parental figure who provides nurturing, support, and discipline and one who encourages independence and responsibility.

Individual Psychotherapy

Some sex and love addicts cannot tolerate individual therapy because it is too close, too intimate, too challenging, and too threatening to them. They have been damaged in intimate (parental) relationships and are afraid to engage in individual work. Other sex and love addicts are too frightened of groups. They feel too ashamed, too vulnerable, too anxious, and too insecure to risk sharing in front of a group of people—especially peers. They prefer the trust and security available in individual psychotherapy. These attitudes are present with adolescent sex and love addicts and must be respected initially if the person is to enter treatment.

Adolescents are in a developmental phase where they should be asserting their independence from parents and discovering their identity. Individual psychotherapy provides a safe, nurturing, structured environment designed to encourage the person's growth and independence. This environment resembles the caring that should be present in a healthy home. Home should be the place where we can "let our hair down," where we can "be ourselves," where we can come back to when all else fails. The homes that adolescent sex and love addicts grew up in were far from this model of health. Even if not obviously so, their homes were not safe, nurturing, or supportive. The adolescent addicts did not experience unconditional love and acceptance. When these adolescents come to individual psychotherapy, they come expecting the same sort of shaming, hostile, critical, damaging relationship. For them, the beginning phase of treatment will surely involve testing and evaluating the therapist in terms of how effectively the therapist can handle the parental role.

In order to pass the test, the individual therapist needs to be both nurturing and disciplining, both mothering and fathering, both loving and limit setting. Some adolescents will need limits first before they can trust the caring; others will need to know that the therapist cares about them before they will be able to accept suggestions for limits and boundaries. Bob (case 8) had to know that we would not allow him to act out in seductive ways, before he would trust us enough to open up. Jane (case 12) dumped her feelings and history quickly and was surprised, and eventually pleased, when we set firm limits on her acting out with relationships in the hospital. Their different needs came from what they did not get. Bob only knew discipline, and longed for unconditional love. He wanted to find out if we would still care for him even when we had to discipline him. Jane had never had good limits and needed structure and expectations to help her learn how to control herself.

Because there is so much shame, embarrassment, and guilt associated with sexual and relational acting out, individual therapists need to guard against reenacting this dynamic with clients. Nonmoralistic, nonjudgmental attitudes are essential, as are objectivity and freedom from professional codependence. Continued acting out is one way that the client can discover if the therapist will shame, abandon, reject, attack, or hurt them. This dynamic is more powerful in the one-to-one relationship. Therapists can care too much, can have unconscious biases, and can make mistakes. Ongoing supervision is one way to protect both the therapist and the client from these sorts of pitfalls in individual treatment.

Group Psychotherapy

Group treatment is a particularly effective intervention with teenagers because peer relationships are so vital to this stage of development. In a group setting, adolescent sex and love addicts can discover that they are not alone, that others have similar problems, and that they can help each other get better. Often adolescents can hear things from other adolescents that they cannot hear from adults. Using this normal developmental phenomenon in a psychotherapeutic context can be quite powerful in ways that individual treatment can never be. For example, in individual sessions with teenagers, I would not discuss my personal problems even when I wanted to help the young person see that he or she was not the only person who had problems such as these. In a group, everyone except the leader is expected to share their problems. The result of such sharing is that isolation is broken down and group members experience a sense of universality—that everyone has problems.

Group psychotherapy is different from Twelve Step meetings in some important ways. First, in a group there is a set membership, and the same people are expected at each session. At Sex and Love Addicts Anonymous (SLAA) meetings, no one takes attendance; people may come regularly and they may not. Second, the group has a professional leader who is paid to be there, while in SLAA, the leadership is shared by members of the fellowship who are peers and no one gets paid for his or her services. Third, in group therapy, members are expected to interact with each other and to give each other feedback about what is said. In SLAA, there is no "cross-talk"; that is, other members of the group are not allowed to comment on, react to, or otherwise exchange views about what one person shares. Fourth, in group therapy there is the expectation that all group members will try to help other members of the group; whereas in SLAA, each person is expected to help himself or herself, and helping others is an individual decision—not an expectation of membership. Fifth, there is a different level and type of commitment required of group membership than there is of attendance at SLAA meetings. Sixth, in an adolescent group, the members would be around the same age; while at an SLAA meeting, members could be anywhere from fourteen to eighty. Finally, group therapy is designed to be therapeutic, and Twelve Step meetings are designed to provide a self-help opportunity and a support group for people suffering from the same affliction.

Group and individual therapy can complement each other and reenforce what happens in each setting. For example, when a teenager shares with the group an important aspect of his or her sex and love addiction, the therapist can ask the person to share it with his or her individual therapist. Or, when a teenager shares something individually, the individual therapist can ask the client to share it with his or her group. Al (case 3) first shared his involvement in pornographic movies in individual sessions. He was encouraged to share this with his group because he felt that he would never be accepted by his peers if they knew this about him. When he was able to tell them and they continued to care about him, he felt relieved and was able to see that his secret had kept him isolated and full of shame and self-hatred. Once it was out in the open, he no longer had to have this barrier between him and other people (especially his peers). Harold (case 16) was able to tell his group about his sexual acting out, but he was afraid to share this in his individual sessions because he expected the harsh judgments he would have received at home. Al was more comfortable with adults and needed to learn to be closer with peers. Harold trusted only peers and needed to learn that some adults could be trustworthy too.

Family Therapy

Some contact with family members or guardians is necessary when working with adolescents. Family therapy can be a potent part of an overall treatment plan, or it can be the main focus of the treatment. Usually, this depends on the training and orientation of the therapist. Since I have not been trained as a family therapist, I tend to use family therapy to augment individual and group work. Others, who have been trained in family therapy (e.g., Earle, Crow, and Osborn, 1989), integrate family therapy into the treatment more than I normally do.

Clearly, the adolescent is in the process of establishing his or her independence from the family. When an addiction occurs during this phase of development, it can push the adolescent into acting with pseudo-independence or it can make the teenager more childlike and dependent on the family. Jill (case 13) refused to follow any of her parents' rules about dating or any of their suggestions about appropriate partners. She was not going to be told what to do by them despite their anger, threats, and insults—for example, her mother calling her a "whore." Yet, when push came to shove, Jill always went back to her mother and apologized with childlike mannerisms and an infantile tone of voice. Her parents dumped her into treatment, wanting us to "fix" her without much from them. Then, when the parents were not satisfied with the results, they snatched her out of treatment for "one last try" at home. Family therapy was a major part of their aftercare therapy plan.

For some teenagers, family therapy is necessary for any type of positive outcome to occur. For others, they are not ready for family therapy and need to work independently for a while before there can be any effective family interventions. The family environment has been a major contributor to these adolescents' personalities and to their problems. Some teenagers need an objective, trained adult present to help guide the family's interactions into healthier patterns of communication and support. For example, if the parents are overly involved at first and then become rejecting, critical, and abandoning when problems arise, the adolescent needs help in finding some middle ground. Sam's (case 10) mother was like that. She had a "special" relationship with him, but could not stand it when he acted like his father whom she had divorced. Sam's mother needed more support from other adults so that she would not be so dependent on him, and he needed stronger limits when he acted "like a gorilla" and threatened people to get his way.

Family therapy can be instrumental in breaking typical family patterns such as the "don't talk, don't trust, don't feel" rule in most addictive families. Secrecy, distrust, and disconnection from feelings are symptoms of active addiction and need to be changed if the addict is to recover. The individual needs to make these changes on his or her own; but, if the family can be working on the same things—being honest, developing trust through openness and sharing, and creating a safe environment for having and communicating feelings—it will make it easier for the recovering person and will reenforce his or her efforts to change. Recovering sex and love addicts find open, honest, caring people in SLAA meetings. If they can find this same support in their families as well, it provides even more impetus for their successful growth and recovery.

Psychopharmacological Therapy

Psychiatric medication can be helpful to the recovering sex and love addict and a significant adjunct to the psychotherapy process. Having a sex and love addiction is stressful. If there is also a history of childhood trauma and neglect, the person may have lived most of his or her life with high levels of stress. Having an addiction is like "being on a roller coaster." In fact, sex and love addicts become quite attached to this pattern of highs and lows and find it difficult to let go. The neurochemical result is that their brains have been flooded with stimulating, sedating, and fantasy-inducing chemicals at various times in the addiction cycle. Their brains have adapted to this wide range of chemicals and take a while to change as recovery starts (e.g., the withdrawal syndrome and cravings to act out). Some recovering people need psychopharmacological assistance before they can modulate their brain chemicals on their own.

The typical medications used in treatment are antidepressants. Anti-anxiety medicines are short acting and tend to reenforce the "quick fix" mentality of addicts. Also, many recovering sex and love addicts are chemically dependent, so anti-anxiety medications are contra-indicated for them. Antidepressants take ten days to three weeks or more to become effective because a therapeutic blood level needs to be established. Because their action begins so long after the time of ingestion, they are not drugs of abuse, or "street drugs." Some antidepressants have anti-anxiety effects as well, so they can be used to treat people who exhibit both depression and anxiety. Many sex and love addicts have trouble sleeping and can benefit from the sedating effects of some antidepressants.

In an inpatient setting with adult sex and love addicts, approximately 80 percent are given a trial of one or more antidepressants. With adolescents, medications are usually prescribed more cautiously. In an inpatient setting with adolescent sex and love addicts, roughly 33 percent were on antidepressant medications. On an outpatient basis, the percentage of adults and adolescents who are given medication is lower. Typically, those patients who require inpatient care have more acute and severe symptoms and are more likely to be dangerous to themselves or others. Outpatients tend to be in less distress and are less likely to need pharmacological help. This may be due in part to their level of awareness of their need for treatment and their commitment to help themselves before things get worse. If they can use the help that is available on an outpatient basis, then their denial and other defenses are less severe and their coping skills are better.

Bibliotherapy

Reading recovery literature is good therapy. Bibliotherapy is, of course, limited to clients who can read, probably at a sixth-grade-level minimum. The bibliotherapy approach allows clients to learn about the disorder without being personally on the spot as they are in individual, group, or family therapy. When clients read about sex and love addiction, their defenses are down and they are engaging their intellectual abilities, rather than their emotional self. Often, in reading assignments, sex and love addicts find stories similar to their own. I have heard from clients that they thought I must have followed them around when I was writing my book *Sex and Love: Addiction Treatment and Recovery* (Griffin-Shelley, 1991), because it sounded so much like their own lives. The identification with the people presented in the literature makes it easier for them to accept the diagnosis of sex and love addiction.

Adolescents are terribly sensitive to the issues of fitting in and belonging. One of their major sources of resistance to seeing themselves as sex and love addicted is that they do not know any other teenagers who identify themselves as sex and love addicts. And unfortunately, in the literature to date, they have not been finding stories of other adolescent sex and love addicts. Some adult sex and love addicts indicate that they were actively addicted as adolescents, but none of them found recovery as a teenager. This book is an effort to change that. Hopefully, adolescent sex and love addicts will be able to relate to some of the case examples in this volume.

Generally, the books that so far seem to work the best for an adolescent population are my own (Griffin-Shelley, 1991), the Augustine Fellowship's *Sex and Love Addicts Anonymous* (1986), and Robin Norwood's *Women Who Love Too Much* (1985), which we used primarily for girls who were "male dependent" or love addicted. Carnes's *Out of the Shadows* (1983) has also been useful. Bibliotherapy can be helpful in the initial stages for making the diagnosis. A client can be helped to self-diagnosis with proper reading assignments. Clients can be asked to do a combined reading and written assignment in which they respond in writing to what they have read. Reading can further their understanding of the recovery process and teach them things like what a bottom line is, how to find and use a sponsor, what progression and tolerance mean, or how to know when they are relapse prone. Many recovering people make it a habit to read. They often have a morning ritual that involves reading a daily meditation book like *Answers in the Heart: Daily Meditations for Men and Women Recovering from Sex Addiction* (Anonymous, 1989), and then follow this with a period of meditation on the passage they read. This allows them to recommit to recovery each day and to keep their priorities clear in their mind as they go about the business of the day.

Written Assignments

Written work can also have important therapeutic value. Again, this intervention can only be used with literate clients who can write to some degree. Initially, I ask adolescents who have primarily acted out sexually to complete Carnes's "Sexual Addiction Inventory" (1988). Adolescent romance junkies or love addicts are asked to write a history of their relationships, along with completing a brief love addiction inventory (Norwood, 1985). In addition to these assignments focused on their addictions, they are also asked to write a life history. Some clients express themselves more openly, honestly, and clearly in written form than they can when talking to the therapist or to peers.

Other written assignments take the form of list making, essays, letter writing, step work, and journaling. Clients might be asked to make a list of the consequences of their addiction, examples of powerlessness, or ways that they have tried to control their relational or sexual acting out. Typically, more limited clients are asked to write lists, while clients with a higher level of communication skills are directed to write an essay on these topics. A daily secret list (given to the primary therapist) was often used with clients who were rather guarded, quiet, and not opening up in either individual or group sessions. Other essays could be on topics like "honesty is the key to sobriety—how this applies to me" or "how my obsession with relationships is interfering with my treatment." Usually the subject of the essay is some therapeutic issue that the person is struggling with at the time. For example, he or she might be ambivalent about recovery and will be told to write a dialogue between the side of himself or herself that wants to get sober and the side that wants to continue the addiction.

Another written assignment is letter writing. Teenagers might be encouraged to write a letter to their Higher Power, to a potential sponsor, or to someone whom they hurt in their active addiction. They might be asked to write a "goodbye letter" to their addiction, or a letter to their inner child. In our program, they were often assigned a letter to one or both of their parents. Sometimes, the content of the letter to their parents was the truth about their sex and love addiction. The letter might actually be read in a family session if this seemed to be the most helpful way for the client to communicate his or her struggle to the parents.

Most clients were assigned written step work based on Carnes's *A Gentle Path through the Twelve Steps* (1989b). The first three steps were the main focus of this work, especially in the initial stages of treatment. The Augustine Fellowship sponsors an "AWOL" (A Way Of Life) program that includes written work on each step. Step work can be shared with sponsors, therapy groups, and other recovering people, as appropriate. Doing a "first step" in group therapy can be an important initial effort in openness, self-disclosure, and trust in others.

Journaling is quite beneficial to many clients in recovery from sex and love addiction and from trauma. While whole books have been written about this method, suffice it to say here that clients are encouraged to journal about their thoughts and feelings as a way of expressing themselves. Journaling is an important expressive tool because it can be used when it is not possible to talk to people. For example, it is not always possible to get a therapist, sponsor, or trusted friend on the phone or in person. In situations like this, writing in the journal can help the client relieve the pressure to act out. Journals may or may not be shared with therapists. Indeed, maintaining a journal without always having to show it to the therapist is an indication of growing independence on the part of a recovering client.

Evocative Psychotherapies

Evocative psychotherapies such as psychodrama, gestalt, art, movement, and recreation therapies can play a significant role in the recovery process, although they are used primarily in inpatient and residential settings. These are powerful techniques that can open clients up in a way that makes them vulnerable to acting out (as a way to cope with the pain that has surfaced), and therefore must be used with skill and caution.

Psychodrama puts into action the inner conflicts and pain that the sex and love addict experiences. In a psychodramatic session, the therapist might have a sex and love addicted client act out a scene where they say goodbye to their addictive lover. Other members of the group will then play roles such as the lover, the client's superego, the client's alter ego, family members, friends, and others. Old scripts can be dramatically demonstrated, and new scripts can be written that provide the person with new ways of coping with difficult, very emotionally charged situations. Often, clients will report that the psychodrama sessions clarified their current dilemmas, provided an opportunity to express feelings, allowed them to reexperience childhood memories, and were a chance to gain some closure on family-of-origin issues.

The adolescents in our program tended to find this type of therapy extremely threatening and were eager to find excuses not to attend. When they were able to let their guard down, however, they were surprised at the benefits they experienced. A sensitive, engaging therapist was a major asset to involving the young people in this therapy process that was potentially so revealing.

Gestalt therapy is similar to psychodrama, but other group members do not play roles. Typically, a gestalt therapist would use an empty chair to represent the addictive lover who was being told the relationship was over. The client would then switch back and forth between the chairs, playing both parts. Most teenagers found this even more frightening than the psychodramatic work. The idea of talking to a chair "freaked them out." Often, they became too self-conscious to be able to engage in the therapeutic experience.

Art therapy can be like having projective tests done on a frequent basis. Since most troubled adolescents are not much better than younger children in putting their feelings into words, their art work often reveals their hidden thoughts and feelings. For instance, one of our regular art projects was to draw a group mural of the one thing that the clients would want with them if they were all stranded on a desert island. Some drug-addicted teens wanted to bring their drugs with them. Sex and love addicted teenagers tended to draw relationships and sexual partners. The project usually revealed a good deal about the group dynamics as well as individual issues. For example, if an adolescent started drawing a wall around his or her part of the island, this would suggest that the adolescent in question was isolating himself or herself from the group.

Art therapy did not seem to be as difficult for our adolescents as the psychodrama and gestalt therapy were, although they often got hung up about "not being an artist." There may have been more psychological room in this type of therapy, allowing them not to take the art work as seriously, or to avoid being overly revealing. In any case, sex and love addicted teenagers did not have any more problems with art therapy than their chemically dependent peers.

Movement therapy involves an individual and/or group response to music and topics suggested by the group leader. Adult sex and love addicts found this form of therapy much more threatening than any of the other therapists, and often found excuses for not going to the groups. Adolescents had an even more fearful response, probably because of their shame and problems with body image, sexuality, and physical presence.

Recreation therapy uses social games and athletic activities to build self-esteem and to enhance interactional skills. While adult sex and love addicts enjoyed this form of therapy for the most part, the adolescents seemed to like it more. They looked forward to the recreational activities, although they did not always want to focus on the therapeutic aspects of the experience. Often, the recreational therapists felt frustrated and unappreciated because the teenagers did not listen to their interpretations about interactional patterns and issues of support, cooperation, and consideration of others in the group dynamics.

Levels of Intervention

There are a variety of settings in which treatment can take place. The most restrictive are inpatient psychiatric hospitals and long-term residential treatment. The next level includes halfway houses and group homes. Partial hospitals or day programs provide a high level of programming without requiring that the client stay overnight. Intensive outpatient programs and traditional outpatient therapy are the least restrictive and least intense. There are some programs around the country that specialize in the treatment of juvenile sex offenders, and more programs that address issues of childhood sexual trauma. There are no programs to date that specialize in treating adolescent sex and love addicts. Some adult programs have had teenage clients as part of their programs, but nothing yet exists exclusively for teenagers who are sexually compulsive or relationally dependent.

Short-term inpatient care can provide a number of benefits in a relatively brief amount of time. Inpatient programs offer comprehensive medical and psychiatric evaluations and tests, psychological testing, daily psychotherapy, medication trials observed by skilled nursing staff, and control over acting-out behaviors like violence, drug use, and avoidance. An outpatient therapist relies mainly on what the client shares and how he or she acts during the sessions. There may be some input from family or school, but most of the observations are restricted to the therapy sessions themselves. In a hospital or residential setting, the staff can observe how the adolescent eats, sleeps, uses free time, socializes with peers, and interacts with a wide variety of adults throughout the day and evening. Transference reactions become obvious more quickly due to the high level of interaction with the teenager.

Substance abuse programs are the logical choice for housing the programs or special tracks for teenagers with sex and love problems who would benefit from an addictions approach. The clients presented in this volume were treated on a general psychiatric unit that had a treatment team that specialized in addictions issues. Much of the sex and love addiction work was limited to individual sessions, bibliotherapy, and written assignments, so the clients did not benefit from group therapies or psychoeducation that would have addressed this problem with the unit as a whole. The general lack of training among professionals in addictions work has inhibited the growth of services for sex and love addicted clients in these settings.

Adolescent clients are usually not referred to long-term treatment or halfway house programs until they have failed a couple of times after short-term inpatient care. There are fewer facilities and limited resources for adolescent programs. Most of the programs are geared around treating substance abuse; mental health issues are only dealt with indirectly. Sexual and relational acting out is most frequently dealt with as a violation of the rules (i.e., legalistically) and a "bad" thing (i.e., moralistically) in these programs. Infrequently is it seen as a therapeutic issue and rarely as a possible addiction.

Adolescent sex and love addicts tend to try to hide their problems in these settings. Unfortunately, their untreated addiction makes them much more prone to relapse after discharge from the program. Many teenage sex and love addicts need long-term programs—as do their adult counterparts—because they do not yet have the ego development and the coping skills to live without acting out. Hopefully, as our understanding of this problem grows, so will the treatment resources for adolescents and the sensitivity of existing programs to these issues.

Most treatment in the future will be in partial hospitalization and intensive outpatient programs and in traditional outpatient individual, group, and family therapy. Partial hospital programs that offer school or are integrated with schools can provide daily structure and support for the teenager who is having trouble controlling himself or herself and cannot function in a regular school setting. These programs can offer psychoeducation, group psychotherapy, and Twelve Step meetings every day. They usually do not include intensive individual psychotherapy, and family work is often held only once a week. Medications can be better supervised, although the staff does not always include nurses or psychiatrists on more than a consulting basis. The overall level of staff training and experience in day programs and intensive outpatient therapies tends to be at the Master's level and below. These programs can offer evocative therapies such as psychodrama or art therapy, which are often unavailable in traditional outpatient therapy.

Again, there are no specialized programs for sex and love addicts. There are day programs for adult sex offenders and abuse victims, but most adolescent programs are geared toward general psychiatry or substance abuse. These programs could incorporate specialty tracks or staff with specialized training to address the needs of adolescent sex and love addicts.

Traditional outpatient therapists who work with teenagers individually, in groups, and/or in families can and should broaden their expertise and include issues of sexual acting out and relationship dependency in their assessment and treatment of adolescents. They can encourage the adolescent to use Twelve Step support groups, bibliotherapy, and other psychoeducational activities to examine these issues in his or her life.

TWELVE STEP SUPPORT GROUPS

For more than fifty years, fellowships of addicted people have formed to provide mutual support in the recovery process. Most such fellowships are modeled on the Twelve Step program of Alcoholics Anonymous (AA). They are entirely voluntary and function solely to aid others, using a self-help approach. AA was formed when medical treatment for alcoholism was unavailable. (It was only in 1957 that the American Medical Association recognized alcoholism as a disease.) Religious groups at the time were trying to help alcoholics by encouraging conversion experiences and participation in religious groups. Then the founders of AA discovered that reaching out to other suffering alcoholics helped them stay sober themselves, and thus the program was formed. Today, AA is an international organization that serves millions of alcoholics.

Many other similar fellowships have been formed along the way, including Narcotics Anonymous, Overeaters Anonymous, Gamblers Anonymous, and others. Sex and Love Addicts Anonymous was founded in Boston in 1977. Its recovery program is outlined in the *Twelve Steps*:

1. We admitted we were powerless over sex and love addiction—that our lives had become unmanageable.
2. Came to believe that a Power greater than ourselves could restore us to sanity.
3. Made a decision to turn our will and our lives over to the care of God *as we understood Him.*
4. Made a searching and fearless moral inventory of ourselves.
5. Admitted to God, to ourselves, and to another human being the exact nature of our wrongs.
6. Were entirely ready to have God remove all these defects of character.
7. Humbly asked Him to remove our shortcomings.
8. Made a list of all persons we had harmed, and became willing to make amends to them all.

9. Made direct amends to such people wherever possible, except when to do so would injure them or others.

10. Continued to take personal inventory and when we were wrong promptly admitted it.

11. Sought through prayer and meditation to improve our conscious contact with God *as we understood Him*, praying only for knowledge of His will for us and the power to carry that out.

12. Having had a spiritual awakening as the result of these steps, we tried to carry this message to sex and love addicts and to practice these principles in all our affairs.

Twelve Step support group meetings, sponsors, literature, and common sayings such as "Let go, let God" are all efforts to provide addicted people with the opportunity to work the program described in these steps.

When addicts are having trouble staying sober, people in Twelve Step groups will try to help by identifying aspects of the program that the person has not completed. For instance, continued relapses might provoke a sponsor to say, "You have never really admitted powerlessness and have never really done the first step." The person would then be encouraged to start his or her recovery program over and sincerely try to "work" the first step. He or she might do this by writing down for the sponsor a number of examples of powerlessness.

Twelve Step fellowships function amazingly well as all-volunteer organizations. Their meetings start on time, are there every week, and rarely go out of existence. In many ways, they operate better than many large corporations or governmental organizations. Part of the reason they work so well is that they are governed by *Twelve Traditions*:

1. Our common welfare should come first; personal recovery depends on SLAA unity.

2. For our group purpose there is but one ultimate authority—a loving God as He may express Himself in our group conscience. Our leaders are but trusted servants; they do not govern.

3. The only requirement for SLAA membership is a desire to stop sex and love addiction.

4. Each group should be autonomous except in matters affecting other groups or SLAA as a whole.

5. Each group has but one primary purpose—to carry its message to the sex and love addict who still suffers.

6. An SLAA group ought never endorse, finance, or lend the SLAA name to any related facility or outside enterprise, lest problems of money, property, and prestige divert us from our primary purpose.

7. Every SLAA group ought to be fully self-supporting, declining outside contributions.

8. Sex and Love Addicts Anonymous should remain forever nonprofessional, but our service centers may employ special workers.

9. SLAA, as such, ought never be organized; but we may create service boards or committees directly responsible to those they serve.

10. Sex and Love Addicts Anonymous has no opinion on outside issues; hence the SLAA name ought never be drawn into public controversy.

11. Our public relations policy is based on attraction rather than promotion; we need always maintain personal anonymity at the level of press, radio, and films.

12. Anonymity is the spiritual foundation of all our traditions, ever reminding us to place principles before personalities.

The presence of these traditions promotes unity, commonness of purpose, and guides against pitfalls such as money and personalities. The philosophy is based on group conscience as the final arbitrator of disputes. There is one clear purpose. Membership requirements are simple: the desire to stop a sex and love addiction. Autonomy and anonymity are essential. There are clear guidelines about being nonprofessional. Individuals may choose to "break their anonymity" with public disclosure, but theirs is an individual decision that goes against the tradition.

In any given area, local groups band together and form an "intergroup" that assists with maintaining meeting lists, possibly operating a telephone hot line that sex and love addicts can call to get support and direction, and coordinating with the national Fellowship-wide Services organization. SLAA meetings have a variety of formats. One common format is that of a "speakers meetings," where a recovering person tells his or her recovery story. There are also "beginners meetings," which are designed for people just joining the fellowship. There are "topic meetings," where the chairperson suggests a topic such as "anger" and people focus their sharing around how anger has been part of their addiction and recovery. There are "discussion meetings," where people are free to share without a particular speaker or topic. There are "step" and "tradition" meetings, where a particular step or tradition is read and then the sharing is organized around each recovering person's experience with that step or tradition. Some meetings are restricted to men or to women. Some are limited to gays and/or lesbians. Some focus on being an incest survivor. Some are identified as "AIDS/HIV" meetings. All SLAA meetings are closed to outsiders, so someone (e.g., a therapist) who does not think they might have a sex and love addiction should not attend. AA has meetings that are open to people who are not alcoholics, but SLAA does not open its meetings. Anyone wanting to find out what a Twelve Step meeting is like should attend an open AA meeting.

Therapy and Twelve Step Programs

Self-help support groups are different from psychotherapy, as explained earlier in the chapter. This volume supports the integration of both modalities in the recovery from sex and love addiction. Psychotherapy is the forum for working on family-of-origin issues. Support groups provide a place to work on the unresolved issues of adolescence: independence, identity, and peer relationships.

In terms of independence, it is the recovering person's own decision whether or not to attend Twelve Step meetings. While I encourage using support groups, attendance is not a requirement for counseling or psychotherapy. If the person attends SLAA meetings, this fact is obvious to me because experiences in the meetings and with other recovering people become a part of his or her therapy discussions. If a person does not—or feels that he or she cannot—attend meetings, uncovering the reasons why he or she cannot make use of this form of support becomes a part of the therapy process. Often, the resistance to support is connected to shame, feelings of unworthiness, fears of being rejected, and anxiety about becoming dependent on others.

Adolescents are at the point where they are choosing their friends. A therapist who insists on SLAA attendance is in danger of being like a parent who is trying to choose the child's friends. On the other hand, the battle about attendance at meetings can be an opportunity to examine transference issues. But all in all, adolescents need to begin to take charge of their lives and to experience the consequences of their mistakes. If they choose not to attend meetings and then they relapse, their avoidance of healthy supports can be a focus of therapy. This will probably lead to issues of neglect and abuse.

Identity development is crucial to the teenage years. Sex and love addicts have a core identity of badness, worthlessness, and unlovability. Twelve Step involvement will affirm their basic goodness, their essential worth, and provide experiences of unconditional love. They can begin by taking on the identity of being a recovering sex and love addict. Often, this needs to be who they are, especially in the initial stages, and can be the foundation for building a healthy sense of self. Being a recovering person is being someone who is proactive, who is dealing positively with a serious problem, who is learning to be responsible and to think before acting, and who is honest and open to new ideas and directions. This positive identity will slowly come to replace the adolescent's prior negative identity.

Peer relationships are a major part of adolescent development. Healthy peers learn how to be in relationships that are equal and mutual. In the family, a child will always be to some degree a child or a sibling. With peers, a person has the opportunity to be an equal of someone else despite their respective chronological ages or other facts of biology. In order to maintain friendships with peers, there needs to be mutuality—a give-and-take between people. Persons who are all give or all take will find that they lose friends. Friends want mutual and equal relationships. True intimacy requires the lifelong commitment of family, but it also needs equality and mutuality to sustain the closeness over time. Sex and love addicted adolescents are stuck in painful dynamics created by their families. As a result, these teenagers want to jump over peer relationships, straight into intimacy. Or, they are terrified of closeness and cannot bond as equals with anyone. They need the experience of equality and mutuality that is provided in Twelve Step fellowships (and is not available in individual therapy), in order to mature to the point where they can be partners in truly intimate relationships.

Difficulties in Support Group Attendance

While the use of Twelve Step programs is an important part of recovery for most sex and love addicts, adolescents seem to have more difficulty attending self-help groups than do their adult counterparts. This appears to be true for the chemical dependency fellowships of AA or Narcotics Anonymous, as well as for Sex and Love Addicts Anonymous. Teenagers, being the youngest people in these meetings, often feel out of place, especially if there are no other adolescents there. A fourteen year old might find that the person closest to him or her in age is eighteen or twenty-one. A four-year gap might not be much for a thirty or thirty-four year old; but in adolescence, even a couple of years makes a big difference.

Some teenagers in AA and NA solve this problem by attending young people's meetings. They find the places where people around their age go, and those are the meetings that they frequent. In SLAA, so far, there do not seem to be any young people's meetings. Since adolescents are not yet seen as being addicted to sex and love (e.g., there are no treatment programs for adolescent sex and love addicts, as there are for teenage alcohol and drug addicts), teenagers are less likely to self-identify or to be referred to support groups by treatment professionals. The few teenagers who do attempt to go to SLAA meetings usually feel alone, isolated, and anxious. They have trouble relating to the stories they hear; often, what the older people share does not seem relevant to their situation. The easiest way to cope with their discomfort at these meetings is to stop attending.

In addition to the internal resistance of adolescents toward attending meetings that involve mostly adults, the adolescents' parents often hinder the use of support groups. Parents have trouble seeing their adolescent as a sex and love addict. And when they do, they feel the shame of having sexual and relational problems in the family. Their denial and shame contribute to their not pushing the teenage son or daughter to go to SLAA meetings. Parents most often sabotage attendance by failing to provide transportation for the young person. This and other types of resistance may be an unconscious avoidance of acknowledging a child with a sex and love addiction because of the parents' own acting out with sex and love. Saying that a son's use of pornography is addictive might point a finger at the son's father whose stash of pornography was the original stimulus for the son's masturbatory compulsion. Focusing on the child's sexual and relational problems highlights the parental relationship and possible sexual and relational difficulties there. Parents' shame, guilt, embarrassment, and inadequacy are all factors in their difficulties with supporting the adolescents' attendance at Twelve Step meetings and therapy.

There are resistances within the fellowship of Sex and Love Addicts Anonymous, as well. There is indeed a desire to "carry the message." However, when the recipient of the message is an adolescent, there can be problems for the fellowship's sex and love addicts who act out with children or adolescents. Some would prefer not to have teenagers in the meetings because they find the young people to be triggers for their obsessions. On the other hand, other sex and love addicts struggle with the issue of being attracted to members of the fellowship, so adolescents should not be excluded because of some members' problems. Still, there may be a subtle lack of support for young people who try to attend meetings.

When a recovering sex and love addict and I tried to organize an institutional meeting for adolescents, there were some concerns at the intergroup level. We had hoped to have our program's own institutional meeting—that is, a meeting in an institution (a hospital, jail, or treatment center) that is supported by other established SLAA meetings, which commit to sending speakers every week— but we could not get the support of the intergroup. When we continued on our own, we found that parents did not support attendance at the meetings and that the adolescents themselves were often not able to come because their sex and love acting out on the unit had resulted in consequences such as a loss of the privilege to go to this off-unit meeting. So, these three factors—the fears of SLAA members; the lack of cooperation by parents; and the resistance of the adolescents themselves—combined to derail our attempts to establish an SLAA meeting just for adolescents.

For adolescent sex and love addicts, recovery must involve psychoeducation, psychotherapy, and Twelve Step support groups. At this time, there is a need to improve all three of these areas before many adolescent sex and love addicts can be expected to recover. This chapter's description of the types of psychoeducational, psychotherapeutic, and support group interventions available should provide an initial basis for treatment, with room for improvement. Integrating Twelve Step recovery with psychotherapeutic interventions will provide the adolescent with more and varied support systems that should improve the odds for successful recovery from sex and love addiction. Professionals need to understand this affliction, respect the adolescents' efforts toward recovery, and refer them to Sex and Love Addicts Anonymous or the other Twelve Step programs for sex addicts.

5

Conclusion

The idea that adolescents can be addicted to sex and love is new and untested. Even the existence of sex and love as addictions is questioned by some, but there appears to be increasing support for the concept that people can become addicted to experiences as well as to things. The addicting qualities of running, exercise, food, money, religion, and work are being increasingly recognized by lay people and professionals alike. Those who work with sex and love addicts have proposed diagnostic criteria for the next edition of the American Psychiatric Association's *Diagnostic and Statistical Manual.* The National Council on Sexual Addiction/Compulsivity is working to educate the public and professionals about sexual addiction/compulsivity. Professional conferences on the national, regional, and local levels have highlighted sex and love addiction treatment and recovery. The published literature is increasing and becoming more specific to particular issues and populations. All of this points to the gradual acceptance of an addictions model for the treatment of compulsive and obsessive sexual and relational behaviors.

As treatment of sex and love addiction becomes more refined, specific populations are being examined in terms of how they should be treated with this model. This volume has presented general information defining and describing sex and love addiction, and it has focused on identifying this problem in adolescents. A major part of this work has been the presentation of examples of adolescent sex and love addicts in the diagnostic discussion (Chapters 1 and 2) and in more depth in examining the case studies in Chapter 3. The thirty-two case examples were followed in Chapter 4 by a description of the treatment tools and technology appropriate for use with adolescent sex and love addicts.

Since the addictions approach is a new one for sexual and relational acting out, the state of the art of treatment and recovery is in its initial stages. The model has grown out of our experiences with chemical dependency. Adolescent chemical-dependency treatment is relatively new and has expanded greatly since the mid-1980s. A similar development may take place in sex and love addiction treatment for adolescents in the mid-1990s and beyond.

DIAGNOSIS

In order for treatment to advance, there are a number of needs that will have to be addressed in the coming years. One of the most important of these needs is that of improved diagnostic specificity. Psychiatric professionals must codify and agree on the diagnosis of sex and love addiction so that accurate research can be done, useful treatment strategies identified, and a common basis of discussion established for both lay people and professionals concerned with these behaviors.

In the 1960s and the 1970s, sexuality became a legitimate area for discussion, research, and treatment. In fact, the public has identified this era as a "sexual revolution." Most of the focus in this change was on Victorian and Puritanical ideas that fostered sexual inhibition, shame, and secrecy. As a more scientific approach to sex was undertaken, the discussion focused on issues of inhibited sexual desire, difficulties with performing sexually—such as premature orgasm and impotence in men, and nonorgasmic responses in women—and sex education. In the 1980s and 1990s, the focus has shifted. Sex therapists report that the improved access to education and to popular literature on sexual subjects has reduced the number of people seeking help for problems related to sexual desire or performance. Now, the concern seems to be on sexual abuse and its aftereffects. One of the effects of sexual trauma is compulsive sexual acting out; another is relationship dependency. The relationship between sexual trauma and sexual addiction is becoming clearer. Childhood trauma and neglect are also now seen as being linked to relationship problems, including excessive dependency or love addiction. This latter connection is not as clearly defined as the one between sexual trauma and sexual acting out; but relationship problems exist for trauma victims, and they often take the form of over-dependency.

If researchers are finding that higher levels of sexual trauma exist in the mid-1990s than we thought even in the mid-1980s, it is likely that there are more sexually addicted and/or sexually anorexic people than have been esti-mated to date. The same is being postulated for childhood trauma and neglect, so there are probably more relationally dependent, love-addicted people than we previously thought. The growth of Sex and Love Addicts Anonymous suggests that there is a significant need being met by this type of fellowship. If adults exist who need specialized treatment and Twelve Step support groups, then it is also likely that there are adolescents who need sex and love addiction treatment. In fact, the recovering sex and love addicted adults indicate that their sexual and relational acting out started in childhood and adolescence. The case studies in this book reveal examples of what could be considered "full-blown" sex and love addiction in teenagers. While not all cases are as this extreme as these are, the relatively low level of damage in less extreme cases should argue for more preventive intervention, rather than ignoring the problem until it gets totally out of hand. In any case, treatment of adolescent sex and love addicts needs to be undertaken because teenagers are suffering and we have the tools and technology to help them.

TRAINING

Professionals treating sexual trauma and childhood neglect and abuse are often unaware of—or tend to discount—sexual and relational dependency in their clients, perhaps because the professionals think that, if the underlying issues are resolved, then the acting-out behaviors will cease. Chemical dependency and other addictions specialists also often look the other way when they encounter sex and love addiction in their clients. They may assume that these problems will go away when the drugs and alcohol are out of the picture. In fact, many sexual and relational dependency problems predate chemical dependency in the person's history. Professionals need better training about how to deal with sex and love addiction when they become aware of it in their clients, and the professionals also need to consider it a possibility even in adolescents.

RESEARCH

To support the diagnosis and treatment of adolescent sex and love addiction, research is needed. At this stage, the field is wide open for researchers. Studies are needed to define an accurate diagnosis and to evaluate current treatment methods. Researchers could do follow-up studies of existing programs, assessments of personality factors and how they impact on the person's response to treatment, or studies of pharmacological interventions and their effect on sex and love addicts. More information is needed about the etiology of sex and love addiction. Combining sex and love as a concept could be studied. Follow-up studies could compare the responses of adults and adolescents to treatment for sex and love addiction. Studies could focus on the trauma histories of clients and examine how these experiences get reenacted in compulsive behaviors. The concept of repetition compulsion has existed for years, but little has been done to validate its existence scientifically. Here is an opportunity. Studying the histories of recovery is another area of research that Dr. Patrick Carnes (1991) has initiated, and that could use more work. What works and what does not?

What works with whom and why? These are all open questions that suffering sex and love addicts should have the answers to in order to escape this devastating disease. Research will provide objectivity, concrete facts, and clearer directions for the efforts of recovering people and the professionals concerned with these problems.

Adolescent sex and love addicts need trained, compassionate professionals who have the support of accurate diagnoses and research to inform their clinical practice. They need other recovering sex and love addicts who have walked the road before them and can provide their wisdom, hope, and experience. They need an informed public that will view their difficulties as a treatable disorder, rather than as based in moral failings or self-indulgence. I hope that my presentation of their stories and the surrounding information about sex and love addiction treatment and recovery will assist them in the process of salvaging their lives and reducing their suffering.

Bibliography

American Psychiatric Association. 1987. *Diagnostic and Statistical Manual of Mental Disorders*, third edition, revised. Washington, DC: American Psychiatric Association.

Anonymous. 1987. *Hope and Recovery: The Twelve Step Guide for Healing Compulsive Sexual Behavior.* Minneapolis, MN.: CompCare Publishers.

Anonymous. 1989. *Answers in the Heart: Daily Meditations for Men and Women Recovering from Sex Addiction.* Center City, MN: Hazelden Educational Materials.

Anonymous. 1989. *What Everyone Needs to Know about Sex Addiction.* Minneapolis, MN: CompCare Publishers.

Arterburn, Stephen. 1991. *Addicted to Love: Recovering from Unhealthy Dependencies in Romance, Relationships, and Sex.* Ann Arbor, MI: Servant Publications.

Augustine Fellowship of Sex and Love Addicts Anonymous. 1986. *Sex and Love Addicts Anonymous.* Boston: Augustine Fellowship SLAA Fellowship-wide Services.

Beattie, Melody. 1987. *Codependent No More.* New York: Harper and Row.

Bireda, Martha R. 1991. *Love Addiction: A Guide to Emotional Independence.* Oakland, CA: New Harbinger Publications.

Booth, Father Leo. 1991. *When God Becomes a Drug: Breaking the Chains of Religious Addiction and Abuse.* Los Angeles, CA: Jeremy P. Tarcher.

Carnes, Patrick. 1983. *Out of the Shadows: Understanding Sexual Addiction.* Minneapolis, MN: CompCare Publications.

Carnes, Patrick. 1988. "Sexual Addiction Inventory." Golden Valley, MN: Institute for Behavioral Medicine.

Carnes, Patrick. 1989a. *Contrary to Love: Helping the Sexual Addict.* Minneapolis, MN: CompCare Publications.

Carnes, Patrick. 1989b. *A Gentle Path through the Twelve Steps.* Minneapolis, MN: CompCare Publications.

Carnes, Patrick. 1991. *Don't Call It Love: Recovery from Sexual Addiction.* New York: Harper and Row.

Covington, Stephanie, and Beckett, Llana. 1988. *Leaving the Enchanted Forest: The Path from Relationship Addiction to Intimacy*. New York: Harper and Row.

Earle, Ralph, Crow, Gregory, and Osborn, Kevin. 1989. *Lonely All the Time: Recognizing, Understanding, and Overcoming Sex Addiction for Addicts and Co-dependents*. New York: Pocket Books.

Erikson, Erik. 1963. *Childhood and Society*, second edition. New York: W. W. Norton.

Forward, Susan. 1986. *Men Who Hate Women and the Women Who Love Them*. New York: Bantam Books.

Forward, Susan. 1991. *Obsessive Love: When Passion Holds You Prisoner*. New York: Bantam Books.

Griffin-Shelley, Eric. 1990. *Maintaining Sobriety with Bibliotherapy*. Center City, MN: Hazelden Educational Materials.

Griffin-Shelley, Eric. 1991. *Sex and Love: Addiction Treatment and Recovery*. New York: Praeger Publishers.

Griffin-Shelley, Eric (ed.). 1993. *Outpatient Treatment of Sex and Love Addiction*. New York: Praeger Publishers.

Griffin-Shelley, Eric, Sandler, Kenneth, and Cameron, Rebecca Park. 1991. A follow-up study of dually diagnosed (chemically dependent) adolescents. *Journal of Adolescent Chemical Dependency*, 2(1), 1–11.

Griffin-Shelley, Eric, Sandler, Kenneth, and Lees, Cynthia. 1990. Sex-role perceptions in chemically dependent subjects: adults versus adolescents. *International Journal of the Addictions*, 25 (12), 1383–1391.

Griffin-Shelley, Eric, Sandler, Kenneth, and Lees, Cynthia. 1992. Multiple addictions among dually diagnosed adolescents. *Journal of Adolescent Chemical Dependency*, 2(2), 35–44.

Halpern, Howard. 1982. *How to Break Your Addiction to a Person*. New York: McGraw-Hill Publishers.

Herman, Judith Lewis. 1992. *Trauma and Recovery: The Aftermath of Violence—From Domestic Abuse to Political Terror*. New York: Basic Books.

Hunter, Mic. 1988. *What Is Sex Addiction?* Center City, MN: Hazelden Educational Materials.

Hunter, Mic, and Jem (a recovering codependent). 1989. *The First Step for People in Relationships with Sex Addicts*. Minneapolis, MN: CompCare Publications.

Kasl, Charlotte Davis. 1989. *Women, Sex, and Addiction: A Search for Love and Power*. New York: Ticknor and Fields.

May, Gerald G. 1988. *Addiction and Grace: Love and Spirituality in the Healing of Addictions*. New York: HarperCollins.

Milkman, Harvey, and Sunderwirth, Stanley. 1987. *Craving for Ecstasy: The Consciousness and Chemistry of Escape*. Lexington, MA: Lexington Books.

Norwood, Robin. 1985. *Women Who Love Too Much: When You Keep Wishing and Hoping He'll Change*. New York: Pocket Books.

Peele, Stanton, and Brodsky, Archie. 1975. *Love and Addiction*. New York: Signet.

Pope, Kenneth S., Sonne, Janet L., and Holroyd, Jean. 1993. *Sexual Feelings in Psychotherapy: Explorations for Therapists and Therapists-in-Training*. Washington, DC: American Psychological Association.

Robinson, Barbara L., and Robinson, Rick L. 1991. *If My Dad's a Sexaholic, What Does That Make Me?* Minneapolis, MN: CompCare Publications.

Schaeffer, Brenda. 1987. *Is It Love or Is It Addiction?* Center City, MN.: Hazelden Educational Materials.

Schneider, Jennifer P. 1988. *Back from Betrayal*. San Francisco, CA: Harper and Row.

Schneider, Jennifer, and Schneider, Burt. 1989. *Rebuilding Trust*. Center City, MN: Hazelden Educational Materials.

Schneider, Jennifer P., and Schneider, Burt. 1991. *Sex, Lies, and Forgiveness: Couples Speaking out on Healing from Sex Addiction.* New York: HarperCollins.
Sexaholics Anonymous. 1985. "Sexual Addiction Inventory." SA Literature.
Woititz, Janet G. 1985. *Struggle for Intimacy.* Deerfield Beach, FL: Health Communications.
Whitfield, Charles. 1987. *Healing the Child Within.* Pompano Beach, FL: Health Communications.

Index

About the Author

ERIC GRIFFIN-SHELLEY is the Director of Addiction Services, The Sanctuary, Northwestern Institute. Dr. Griffin-Shelley is the author of *Sex and Love: Addiction Treatment and Recovery* (Praeger, 1991), and *Outpatient Treatment of Sex and Love Addiction* (Praeger, 1993).